Transcendent
LOVE

Transcendent LOVE

DOSTOEVSKY
and the Search for a
GLOBAL ETHIC

LEONARD G. FRIESEN

University of Notre Dame Press
Notre Dame, Indiana

University of Notre Dame Press
Notre Dame, Indiana 46556
undpress.nd.edu

Published in the United States of America

Library of Congress Cataloging-in-Publication Data
Names: Friesen, Leonard G., author.
Title: Transcendent love : Dostoevsky and the search for a global ethic /
  Leonard G. Friesen.
Other titles: Dostoevsky and the search for a global ethic
Description: Notre Dame, Indiana : University of Notre Dame Press, 2016. |
  Includes bibliographical references and index.
Identifiers: LCCN 2016004190 (print) | LCCN 2016012848 (ebook) | ISBN
  9780268028978 (hardback) | ISBN 0268028974 (cloth) | ISBN 9780268079857
  (epub) | ISBN 0268079854 (epub) | ISBN 9780268079819 (pdf) | ISBN
  0268079811 (pdf)
Subjects: LCSH: Dostoyevsky, Fyodor, 1821–1881— Criticism and interpretation.
  | Dostoyevsky, Fyodor, 1821–1881—Ethics. | Ethics in literature. |
  Religion in literature. | Jesus Christ—In literature. | BISAC: RELIGION /
  Christianity / Literature & the Arts. | PHILOSOPHY / Ethics & Moral
  Philosophy.
Classification: LCC PG3328. Z6 F75 2016 (print) | LCC PG3328. Z6 (ebook) | DDC
  891.73/3—dc23
LC record available at http://lccn.loc.gov/2016004190

∞ *This paper meets the requirements of*
ANSI/NISO Z39.48-1992 (Permanence of Paper).

For
Anna Ruth,
Isaac Paul,
and
Laura Katarina

CONTENTS

Preface   ix

Abbreviations   xiii

CHAPTER 1

Why Dostoevsky? Why Now?
Why Here?   1

CHAPTER 2

Orphans' Lament:
Seeking the Ethical in a Suicidal Age   35

CHAPTER 3

To Bow at the Crossroads:
The Joy of an Unreasonable Ethic   75

CHAPTER 4

In Search of a Universal Reconciliation:
Two Speeches, One Vision, and
"The Means to Save the World"   127

Conclusion: Dostoevsky's "Ridiculous" Ethic,
for His Time and Ours   171

Notes   189

Bibliography   211

Index   219

This book-length essay seeks to make three contributions to the multi-disciplinary field of globalization and ethics. First, it is a study of Fyodor Mikhailovich Dostoevsky. I suggest that this great Russian writer has much to offer when it comes to the search for a global ethic, an ethic that he believed was necessarily grounded in an active, extravagant, and transcendent love. Second, I investigate Dostoevsky's response to those who claimed that contemporary European trends—most evident in the emergent secularization of society—provided a more viable foundation for a global ethic than one grounded in the One whom he called simply "the Russian Christ." Third, I attempt to do this while still capturing a sense of Dostoevsky's depth and sheer loveliness, especially as this study is also intended for comparative ethicists and nonspecialists who may not be familiar with his work. Dostoevsky, after all, believed that the ethical life was sublimely beautiful, even as it recklessly embraced suffering and unreasonably forgave others.

I thank Mr. Ken Styles, who first introduced Dostoevsky to me when he assigned *Crime and Punishment* to our literature class at Beamsville District Secondary School in the early 1970s. He assured us that this was a famous novel, and we believed him—though we did not know why—even after we had finished reading it. Several years later I encountered a Dostoevsky novel in a third-year undergraduate course in Russian culture taught by Professor J. W. Dyck at the University of Waterloo. It was *The Brothers Karamazov*, in English translation, and I can still recall my first encounter with the phantasmagoria of the Grand Inquisitor's legend.

I set Dostoevsky aside almost immediately after the course ended. In a way it could not have been otherwise, for I subsequently entered graduate studies and thereafter began a career as a Russian historian when social history was the rage. I followed suit and was not drawn to Dostoevsky despite the fact that I lived in his city (St. Petersburg, then known as

Leningrad) for a year and traveled there often in the years that followed. Only recently have I retraced his steps, sought out his last home, and stood at his graveside. Only recently have I marveled at the city and its people through his eyes.

I found myself returning to Dostoevsky thanks in part to a medical diagnosis in 1997 that reoriented my life. Existential matters took on a greater urgency for me, though such a reorientation may have happened naturally as I entered into, and then departed from, the period known as "middle age." Somehow along the way I began to read Dostoevsky's writings, in almost all instances for the first time. I was surprised when other Russianists told me that they were also largely unfamiliar with Dostoevsky's works. On one occasion scholars at Ural State University in Ekaterinburg, Russia, urged me to spend a term there so that their own students could learn something about the writer whom all revered but few bothered to read. My reawakened interest in Dostoevsky coincided with an opportunity I received from my university to found an interdisciplinary program on global issues. My own reading gradually shifted to global ethics, a field from which I soon realized the Russian voice was absent, as was Dostoevsky's in particular. It was with that realization that the seeds for this volume were sown.

I owe a great debt to those who traveled with me over the past several years and who made significant contributions to this book. Thank you to Peter Erb for wise counsel at the start of this journey and for encouraging me to take on a different kind of writing project at this point in my career. Thank you to Boris Khersonsky, who first urged me to write this particular book, just to get it out of my system. He was right. Wayne Dowler and Matthew Kudelka thoughtfully and critically engaged with this manuscript along the way, and it is all the better for their efforts. The Department of History at Wilfrid Laurier University has been a most congenial setting for me to teach and conduct research; I am very fortunate. Weekly lunches with George, David, and fellow colleagues have been especially memorable. Beyond the university I owe a word of gratitude to Ardith and Marvin (†2008) Frey, who lived out the core truths of this study at a time when I was merely beginning to discern them.

I am delighted to have this work published by the University of Notre Dame Press, which has long been a leading voice for thoughtful reflection in the humanities. I am honored to be included with authors as distinguished as Alasdair MacIntyre and Vigen Guroian, and I hope that my contribution will be seen as worthy of the path that others have blazed. I thank Charles Van Hof for his initial interest in this work and his willingness to move it forward. Stephen Little has been as thorough, demanding, and supportive an editor as one could hope for; I thank him and the many others at the press who helped prepare *Transcendent Love* for publication. Thank you also to the press's two external readers, whose observations and suggestions significantly improved the final shape of this study.

No fellow traveler has meant more to me in my entire adult life than Mary. Over more than thirty-eight years of marriage she has taught me a great deal about love and ethical engagement. Mary also knows more than anyone how much Dostoevsky became a part of my life during these past years, for his writings were always close at hand and forever scattered around our home. There was one exception to this, and it occurred in May and June of 2008, when I promised Mary not to take anything written by Dostoevsky along as we wandered about the Italian peninsula. Yet even this did not stop us, on one particular day in Florence, from setting out to locate the very apartment where Dostoevsky lived in 1867 and 1868 as he finished work on *The Idiot*. The impact of Dostoevsky's writings on me was such by then that he was never truly absent from my mind or heart. Through all of this and more, Mary's role in my life cannot be overstated, nor can my debt to her.

I dedicate this study to our three dear children, who have brought deep joy to our lives. I hope that this study will be part of the plethora of conversations and ruminations that will engage them in the years to come. I have written it in the hope that they and their generation will always seek out deep ethical truths, even if they find themselves part of a larger culture that seems dangerously fixated on nothing in particular, existentially and ethically speaking. Why not choose instead to engage Dostoevsky's depiction of the ethical life as sublimely beautiful, transformatively forgiving, and transcendently lovely?

So it is that I dedicate this book to Anna, Isaac, and Laura, and to a love that transcends, eternally.

Isthmus Bay
November 2015

ABBREVIATIONS

ADT   *The Adolescent*

BK   *The Brothers Karamazov*

CP   *Crime and Punishment*

DEAD   *Notes from a Dead House*

DEM   *Demons*

IDT   *The Idiot*

PSS *Pol'noe sobranie sochineniĭ v tridtsati tomakh F.M. Dostoevskago*

UND   *Notes from Underground*

WD   *A Writer's Diary (Diary of a Writer)*

WIN   *Winter Notes on Summer Impressions*

CHAPTER I

Why Dostoevsky?
Why Now? Why Here?

This study gives Fyodor Mikhailovich Dostoevsky a voice in the ongoing discussion about what it means to be ethical. I argue that this great nineteenth-century Russian writer has much to contribute to that conversation in our time even though he died in 1881, and even though his cultural milieu seems vastly different from our own. How is that possible? This chapter lays the foundation required to answer that question.

We will look at a fragment from one of Dostoevsky's great novels to examine how he engaged with ethical issues in his time and how those same issues continue to be relevant. Then we review how today's moral philosophers suggest we respond to the various ethical conundrums we face, from whether violence can be justified for noble ends to whether we are obligated to care for the stranger in our midst. Until recently, scholars maintained that the Western philosophical tradition offered sufficient guidance for us to determine the ethical life, and I explore how that argument has been made. After that I discuss how scholars have begun to challenge the West's assumption that its own traditions are sufficient to develop a comprehensive moral philosophy. I also identify several other ethical traditions that have recently attracted scholarly attention—in particular, those of the Crow of the North American plains, medieval Islamic ethicists, and twentieth-century ethicists Simone Weil and Emmanuel Levinas. I contend that the Russian ethical voice—Dostoevsky's voice in particular— deserves careful consideration in this increasingly globalized discussion of moral philosophy and the ethical life.

But before all that, and before we can begin to hear his voice, we need to know who Dostoevsky was. So we begin with his birth in Moscow in 1821 and his education at St. Petersburg's elite engineering academy. Dostoevsky was never drawn to engineering, but he was to writing, and he enjoyed spectacular early success with it. But he soon shifted his focus, immersing himself in revolutionary activities against the tsar. He was arrested for that involvement in 1849 and sentenced to death by firing squad. His life was spared at the last moment and his sentence commuted to a prison term in Siberia. He wrote his greatest works in the two decades that followed his return from exile, and I will introduce each in its turn. Scholars have rarely agreed on how to "read" Dostoevsky's novels, much less on his deepest convictions about modernity and the ethical life. I will introduce that broader debate and discuss how I arrived at my own position. Put another way, I will be taking sides in this vibrant debate, so it is best that I make my position clear at the outset. In this chapter's penultimate section I outline four ways in which Dostoevsky's ethical critique of the West was based on his intimate knowledge of it. Only with that solid background will we be ready to enter the heart of this study. This chapter concludes with anticipatory comments on the remainder of this monograph.

A Son's Murderous Outrage:
An Ethical Dilemma

In *The Brothers Karamazov*, Mitya loathes his father to the point of wishing him dead, and understandably so. As the eldest of Fyodor Pavlovich Karamazov's three sons (more likely four, if the claims concerning the bastard son proved true), Mitya was conceived within a hate-filled marriage only to be relegated by his father to an orphan-like existence. Left to his own devices while his father lived a life of a debauchery, Mitya survived thanks to the goodwill shown to him by Grigorii and Martya, Fyodor's faithful servants. Mitya grew up in a house "full of eternal scenes" and frequent arguments that ended in physical assaults. Fyodor, who entered the marriage full of empty bravado, had shamelessly laid claim to all of Adelaida's considerable wealth after their dramatic elopement (Adelaida's parents had opposed any union between their daughter and the reprobate Fyodor). Fyodor seized everything and left her with mere kopecks. Eventually, Adelaida

abandoned both child and husband for a lover and new life in St. Petersburg, where, soon after, she died. Three-year-old Mitya found himself
tossed between members of Adelaida's extended family.

With this background, it is perhaps no surprise that Mitya becomes a
man of superficial desires, a sensualist without moorings, much like his father. Indeed, father and son soon find themselves pursuing the same
woman, Grushenka, and this pathetic melodrama only fuels the hostility
between them. No less important, Mitya is convinced that his father is refusing to give him the inheritance due to him from his late mother's estate.
Mitya desperately needs that money in order to woo Grushenka.

He can hardly be expected to endure such outrages indefinitely, or to
repay a lifetime of neglect and abandonment with anything but hostility.
In fact, Mitya has been musing for months about murdering his father.
Many witnesses have heard him wonder aloud "why such a man should
even be alive." And he has already physically assaulted his father in a public setting. Now, in the chapter titled "In the Dark," he suddenly believes
that his father has succeeded in claiming Grushenka's affections. This,
for Mitya, is the final outrage. So he rushes madly to his father—his
"tormenter"—who has destroyed his life so utterly. Surely the son now
has murder on his mind, for he arrives at his father's estate under cover of
darkness, carrying a pestle, which he has just seized from an acquaintance.
What other purpose could it possibly serve than to strike his father dead?

Mitya later confesses that he felt a "sudden, vengeful, and furious
anger" at Fyodor Pavlovich in that dark moment as he gazed up at his father through the bedroom window. Suddenly his father, not sensing that
he was in imminent danger, leaned out the window and into the darkness,
within easy striking distance of his concealed son. In that moment the son
reached for the pestle in his pocket and brought it out. The reader knows
that Mitya must decide instantly: will he murder his father, the person who
had essentially orphaned him so long ago?

Just moments later, Mitya faces another decision. He runs from his
father's estate, utterly certain that he has just killed a man he has known all
his life. What to do next? He knows the answer to that, or at least thinks he
does. With his world now in shambles, he reclaims a gun he had recently
pawned to an acquaintance. With the loaded gun firmly in hand, and certain his own life is ruined, he sets out for one more night of wild partying,
after which he intends to end his own life. But will he?

Just this one fragment from *The Brothers Karamazov* suggests how many layers of ethical decision making are found within its pages. Does Mitya have the right to murder his father? If not murder, does he have the right to at least ignore him, or discard him in his old age? Does he in fact owe his father anything? Is it unethical for father and son to woo the same woman? And what about the ethics of self-inflicted wounds? Does Mitya have the right to take his own life, and if he does, are rights the same as ethics? How might we go about answering these questions?

We, like Mitya, are awash in ethical choices. We may not directly confront the question of murder, though all of us have accepted some level of force in exchange for personal protection (our nations are defended by armies, our cities by police and the courts). Looking further afield, what ethical choices are involved in the so-called War on Terror? Who gets to make those choices? Who decides whether violence can ever be justified, and if so, when?

We might also look beyond the violence done to others and consider instead the violence we do to our world. The earth is warming, its glaciers melting, its lakes evaporating. What are our ethical choices concerning that? What are our obligations to the world itself? And what about the ethics of consumption, especially in a world of gross inequality where, paradoxically, those least in control already bear the greatest burden of climate change? At the dawn of the twenty-first century, people in the developing world are facing their own war against drought, floods, disease, and starvation.

According to a recent UN development report, the average American uses about 575 liters of water a day, compared to less than 10 for a citizen of Mozambique. And Mozambique is hardly unique — one-fifth of the world's people lack access to clean water, and half the people in developing countries lack adequate sanitation.[1] This may be unfortunate, but is it an *ethical* issue? Should we be concerned about who is responsible for drought and poor sanitation in places such as Mozambique? When does watering my lawn become an ethical decision? Do countries own water, and should companies be able to buy water rights in distant lands at the expense of the local people?

Leaving aside wars on terror and environmental ethics, what does it mean to be ethical in our more immediate and quotidian existence? What does ethics entail in terms of our own daily choices as individuals? Do I have rights and ethical obligations when it comes to my children, or my parents or neighbors, or the stranger who approaches me on a city street asking for spare change? A problem confronts us when we set out to live ethical lives, one that concerns which questions are ethical ones and how we are to go about answering them. How are we to determine ethical content?

Ethical Formation, Modernity, and the West

According to contemporary introductions to moral philosophy, the answer to this question ultimately depends on individual ethical predilections, which in all of us have been shaped by the Western philosophical tradition. Torbjörn Tännsjö's *Understanding Ethics* is perhaps the best introduction to this field, though by no means the only good one.[2] Tännsjö offers principles for determining what it means to live the moral life. Several such principles stand out in his study and in a more recent one by Kimberly Hutchings. These include the following:

1. One need look no further than Western traditions in order to determine what is ethically normative for individuals in our world (and ethics are, first and last, an individual matter). In Tännsjö's telling, this story begins with Aristotle and then fast-forwards to one German, one Norwegian, two American, and three English philosophers.[3] Hutchings's introduction to global ethics is also largely derived from the Western philosophical tradition.[4] Much like Tännsjö, Hutchings follows a thread that includes Aristotle, Bentham, Mill, Hobbes, Rawls, Kant, and Habermas. Although Hutchings does allow for alternative approaches, she emphasizes that these are also grounded firmly in Western philosophical thought.[5]

2. Such a sampling is not narrow. Tännsjö maintains that his aforementioned philosophers, who account for all seven moral theories considered in his overview, are sufficient for us to develop our own moral theory in our time: "Are there other theories that we should have discussed as well? Although it may seem rash to say so, I think not! The ones selected for consideration are, as far as it is possible to tell today, the most plausible candidates for a true or reasonable moral theory."[6]

3. Faced with the certainty that only selected Western theories need be considered in the search for a normative and global ethic, Tännsjö also stresses that each individual is required to develop her or his own ethical code. True, we must all seek to "eliminate inconsistent arguments," but this task is a highly solitary one—which is not surprising, given the centrality of the individual in Western philosophical streams. So we each must "choose between the different theories. . . . We have to make up our own minds."[7]

4. If the task of seeking out individualized and normative ethical systems seems daunting, Tännsjö offers at least some comfort with the assurance that no single ethical system is superior to any other. In this sense, he writes, "truth may be thought to be relative." So if we cannot make the correct ethical choice in an absolute way, we can at least try to make the most reasonable choice, though even here he urges the reader to always be open to new approaches and new possibilities. Tännsjö does not think it possible for any one ethical system to be absolutely right; indeed, he dismisses that notion absolutely. He also dismisses any contention that religion and morality are linked, and he objects to the "rather pompous terms" by which various religions assert the absoluteness of their claims.[8] (It is unclear whether he appreciates the irony of his own position.) Hutchings agrees with Tännsjö. She states that religions "do not provide us with shortcuts to answering the *why, what, who,* and *how* questions of Global Ethics, although they do certainly provide one way into those questions." The way in question here is provided by Christianity, which Hutchings argues has played a pivotal role in shaping the Western philosophical tradition.[9] She sees no need to explore any religiously based ethic, Christian or otherwise, though she does acknowledge the role Christianity played in birthing Western secularism.

5. Tännsjö ends his introduction to normative ethics by encouraging individuals to think creatively within and between the various ethical theories identified in his overview (something that is easily done if none are absolutely correct). He wonders why we do not develop an ethic that will allow us to say and do the following: "Why not in general maximize the sum total of welfare, but allow that, when the cost is too high for an agent, the agent pays some special attention to his or her own interests? . . . Why not say that even though it is wrong to kill

an innocent human being in order to save lives, if more than twenty-five innocent lives can be saved, it might be right to do so?"[10]

Lest he be seen as prescriptive, Tännsjö tells us it is up to the individual to think through "combinations of the sort mentioned." Even then, he invokes yet another British moral philosopher, C. W. Ross, to remind the reader that even if murder might appear to be wrong all the time, we should always be open to the fact that it might be the proper thing for us to do if "a particular situation" arises.[11] So, one imagines, it might be wrong for the Mityas of this world to murder their fathers most of the time, but not always. In the end, it seems, Mitya will need to decide for himself. But how can he decide for himself what to do, especially in that very moment, in the darkness of a night that mirrors the darkness of his own heart? For, as I have noted, Mitya has clearly lost his moorings.

The rejection of certain and fixed moorings in favor of multiple ethical options is the logical endpoint of Western philosophical thought, according to critics as diverse as Zygmunt Bauman, Michael Gillespie, and Charles Taylor.[12] Alasdair MacIntyre's summation of the contemporary moral opportunity or predicament this presents is worth citing at length:

All this of course does not entail that the traditional moral vocabulary cannot still be used. It does entail that we cannot expect to find in our society a single set of moral concepts, a shared interpretation of the vocabulary. Conceptual conflict is endemic in our situation, because of the depth of our moral conflicts. Each of us therefore has to choose both with whom we wish to be morally bound and by what ends, rules, and virtues we wish to be guided. These two choices are inextricably linked. In choosing to regard this end or that virtue highly, I make certain moral relationships with some other people, and other moral relationships with others impossible. Speaking from within my own moral vocabulary, I shall find myself bound by the criteria embodied in it. These criteria will be shared with those who speak the same moral language. And I must adopt some moral vocabulary if I am to have any social relationships. For without rules, without the cultivation of virtues, I cannot share ends with anyone else. I am doomed to social solipsism. Yet I must choose for myself with whom I am to be morally bound. I must choose between alternative forms of social and moral practice.[13]

Thus MacIntyre, albeit with markedly less enthusiasm, appears to accept Tännsjö's assessment of our age as one in which each individual must choose the moral code that is right for her or him among myriad possibilities that are all equally valid. That challenge of ethical discernment is especially difficult because many no longer feel themselves to be part of larger communities of support and counsel as they work these matters out. For Russian scholar Marina Kostalevsky, the problem is that we have abandoned the idea of unity altogether and in its place celebrate diversity without moral unity—a celebration that barely conceals our manifest moral fragmentation.[14]

So there is reason to believe we are in a quandary about what it means to be ethical in our time. It is as if something within us still longs to know what is absolutely the right thing to do and then to do it. Also, many of us find ourselves deeply divided as individuals. We want clarity on what it means to be ethical, but only if it allows us to keep our options open. Perhaps the greatest gift bequeathed to us by modernity is that we rarely want to do as we are told. At the same time, it is hardly satisfactory to be told that each individual "I" has a host of ethical options available, all of which are more or less right for me, à la Tännsjö. Indeed, I can hardly judge others for the choices they make when we all agree that an absolute standard for making such an ethical call does not exist. So if Western ethical traditions have not entirely succeeded in meeting this pressing human need to determine what is ethical, perhaps it is time to look elsewhere, if only for the sake of comparison.

A Time of New Ethical Possibilities and Comparative Engagements

The ethical speculations set out so far in this chapter all presume that the intellectual events in western Europe over the past half-millennium have been universal. But what if this is not the case, or not necessarily? In *Provincializing Europe*, Dipesh Chakrabarty reminds his readers that many of the key ideas associated with political modernity (including contemporary understandings of social justice, human rights, and the individual), while they may have a universal ring to them, emerged within the narrow confines of "European thought and history."[15] So it is not at all surprising that studies on comparative ethics by Tännsjö, Hutchings, and countless others have relied overwhelmingly on (western) European intellectual traditions to the near-total neglect of all others.

But times may be changing. Immanuel Wallerstein has argued that we are living in an era that marks the end of "European universalism"— a time when even the assumptions of "the last and most powerful of the European universalisms—scientific universalism—is no longer unquestioned in its authority."[16] For Chakrabarty, the trick will not be disregarding the great advances of European civilization over the past five hundred years so much as starting the process by which that particular civilization engages with other worldviews that are no less worthy of our attention.

This study attempts to make its own modest contribution to that process, with a particular focus on what it means for us to be ethically engaged in our time. Fortunately, other options *are* available for our consideration, many of which resonate with the one explored here. We have Jonathan Lear's recent examination of ethics in a time of devastation through the reminiscences of Plenty Coups, the last great chief of the Crow people of the North American plains. Through his wide-ranging reflections on Plenty Coups's oral history of his people "after the buffalo went away," Lear suggests that the ethics of survival are relevant for all (and not merely for the Crow) at a time when our existence is threatened by multiple crises, from the War on Terror to global warming.[17] Similarly, Michael Cook has recently directed our gaze toward Islamic understandings of the ethical. In ways that point to this present study, Cook sets out an Islamic worldview that espouses an ethic of obligations over an ethic of rights. In it, the collective is no less important than the individual, and we are commanded to respond to injustice with our whole being, including the hand, the tongue, and the heart.[18]

Richard Bell's investigation of Simone Weil's ethical stance is especially relevant to this study, for it focuses on her understanding of ethics as rooted mainly in love and compassion. Weil (1909–1943), whose life was woven from agnostic, Jewish, communist, and Catholic threads, was always suspicious of the universalizing Western cultural tradition, with its focus on rights and individual autonomy. Such an approach, she warned, risked producing little more than "moral mediocrity." She wrote at a time when her beloved France was crumbling under the onslaught of Nazi Germany and her fellow Jews were being rounded up for the death camps. She responded to the greatest horrors of her age by pleading for us to embrace God's all-encompassing love and goodness, unilaterally if need be, compassionately engaging our enemies lest we merely replace one people's suffering with another's.[19]

Reading Bell, one is reminded of Levinas, for whom the "Other" always comes first, another challenge to the West's ethic of individualism. Contrary to a rights-based ethic, Levinas maintains that the Other always exists before we do, to such a degree that we do not really exist apart from our relationship with that Other. That truth having been grasped, our obligation to the Other always comes before whatever rights we may think we have as individuals. Catherine Chalier contends that, for Levinas, justice can never be achieved through universal principles or a legal code—it can only happen when we open up our hearts to the Other. Indeed, laws and codes can be counterproductive if they permit us to imagine that our personal moral obligations come second to the state's responsibility (or someone else's) to uphold them.[20]

This is where Levinas becomes especially interesting for this study. Near the end of his life, an interviewer asked him to identify some of his intellectual roots. He responded with a long list of influences that combined Lithuanian cultural markers and his own Jewish identity with an intellectual upbringing that gave pride of place to the great Russian authors of the nineteenth century, including Dostoevsky. This is not surprising, given how often he referred to the Russian literary canon. It also suggests that the notion that obligations precede rights has an Otherness about it, especially if we combine this with a rather different understanding of human suffering—one that we may have to embrace for the sake of the Other.[21]

Clearly, even a brief perusal of one limited segment of the ethical global village reveals a wide range of moral constructs. Together they call into question the assumption, derived from Western philosophical thought, that ethics are an individual matter for which there is no absolutely right or wrong choice. And it is at this point that we approach the core of the present study.

So Why Dostoevsky?
Why Here? Why Now?

Why Dostoevsky? Why now? I hope this book will answer those questions, but I ask for your patience. The challenge is considerable, given the magnitude and complexity of Dostoevsky's personality and legacy. It is no small irony that he often began his own writings, including *The Brothers Karamazov*, with this same sort of request. In that spirit, we will get to that book as quickly as possible.

Dostoevsky's Russia is of intrinsic value in the search for an ethic for our time. Russia has always been a global borderland between East and West. It emerged out of a Mediterranean culture, albeit an overwhelmingly Eastern (Greek) variant, with Western (Roman) influences taking hold only in the late eighteenth and early nineteenth centuries. It was Christianized along with the Latin lands, but through the Greeks and Orthodoxy, not the Romans and Catholicism. Russia is part of Europe, but it extends so far to the east that most of its territory is actually in Asia. Russia endured the Mongol invasion; the West did not. It was profoundly shaped by a conservative religious reaction in the late seventeenth century, in sharp contrast to the more liberal reformation of western Europe in the early sixteenth century.

Russia did find itself caught up in the Western project, largely because of the ambitions of Peter the Great (who reigned from 1682 to 1725). But this "capture" was incomplete and was carried out in a manner that created a vast gulf between the multitude of commune-based peasants and the Westernized nobles of the major urban centers. Throughout the nineteenth century some Russians called for the aggressive Westernization of the entire population; meanwhile, others in the emerging intelligentsia sought to safeguard the empire's Russianness against Western-style cultural forms. The Russian Empire emerged from the Napoleonic Wars as the greatest of landed empires; then a humiliating defeat in the Crimean War helped instill a strong commitment to industrial development and modernization. To achieve those ends, the serfs were emancipated in 1861 (more or less, depending on which historian one consults), and soon after, so were the peasants who lived on state lands. These sweeping social reforms catalyzed the empire's industrialization before 1900. But that burst of industrialization and urbanization was of a different nature than what the West experienced. There were other substantial differences, including of course the fact that Lenin was Russian, as were the multiple Russian revolutions associated with 1905 and 1917.

There is reason to see Russia as similar to the West and reason to see it as distinct. What more fascinating place of comparative ethical inquiry in a global context can there be?

Fyodor Mikhailovich Dostoevsky

Who actually was this man, and why might he be of particular interest as we search for a global ethic? It is worth taking time to answer this question, all the more so because I mean for this study to be accessible to non-specialists (of Russia, or of Dostoevsky) who work in the fields of comparative ethics and cultural studies. Dostoevsky was born on October 30, 1821, in Moscow, to a father (Mikhail) who was a physician in the Mariinsky Hospital for the Poor and a mother (Marya) who came from a long-established merchant family. It is a mark of Russia's otherness that this date was from the Julian calendar then in use within the empire (by the Gregorian calendar, he was born on November 11, 1821).

Dostoevsky's childhood environs exposed him to Moscow's impoverished underbelly, for the Mariinsky Hospital was on the edge of the city, alongside a prison and an orphanage. But not all of his childhood and youth was spent in this urban setting: his father acquired a noble estate around 150 kilometers from the city. A year after that purchase, the family also acquired the adjoining estate village, a setting that would figure prominently in Dostoevsky's poignant short story "The Peasant Marey."

Fyodor was diagnosed with epilepsy at the age of nine, and that condition figures prominently in several of his major novels, including *The Idiot* (whose hero is epileptic) and *The Brothers Karamazov* (in which Smerdyakov is the sufferer). Dostoevsky's world was tragically and permanently altered when he was fifteen: his mother died of cholera, and he and his brother were dispatched to an elite engineering academy in St. Petersburg. It cannot be coincidental that some of the characters in his novels, especially Arkady in *The Adolescent* and Alyosha in *The Brothers Karamazov*, have achingly beautiful and vivid childhood memories of loving mothers long deceased and tender embraces long past, or that so many of his characters (including, of course, Mitya) long for closer ties with their fathers.

In 1843 Dostoevsky graduated as a civil engineer with the rank of lieutenant. Just two years later, in 1845, when he was only twenty-four, he made his literary mark with the publication of *Poor Folk*. Vissarion Grigoryevich Belinsky, the renowned literary critic, heaped praise on that book, rocketing its author to fame. The reception of Dostoevsky's next book was much more subdued, however, and some suggested that his career had ended before it had truly begun. By this time, however, Dostoevsky had other irons in the fire. In the late 1840s he had become involved in the Petrashevtsky circle, one of many revolutionary groups then forming in St. Petersburg in response to the repressive regime of Nicholas I. Dostoevsky was arrested in April 1849 along with other members of that circle. Neither his life, nor world literature, nor modern philosophical inquiry would be the same again.

Dostoevsky and his alleged co-conspirators were imprisoned on the direct orders of Nicholas I. These had been issued in the wake of the revolutions of 1848 that had so unsettled western Europe—and terrified tsarist Russia. After months imprisoned in the Peter and Paul Fortress, Dostoevsky and more than two dozen others were condemned to death by firing squad. The sentence was to be carried out on December 22, 1849, with the tsar's approval.

His sentence was commuted at the last possible moment to exile in Siberia, though not before the staging of a mock execution that left him psychologically transformed. "We shall be with Christ": these words, attributed to Dostoevsky in conversation with the self-proclaimed atheist Nikolai Speshnev as both awaited death in the freezing cold of that St. Petersburg December, capture something of this young writer's trauma at the time. But what exactly did he mean by those particular words at that particular moment? Joseph Frank, Dostoevsky's extraordinary biographer, contends that he was expressing terror as much as faith: terror because he, unlike Speshnev, was convinced that something profound awaited him after death. Even at that point, he did not accept that life could end in the abyss of nothingness. But if "something" was to be instead of "nothing," of what relation was he to what he was to become within moments?[22] He spent the rest of his life trying to answer that question and express what its answer required of his readers.

En route to exile in the east, he stopped in the town of Tobolsk, the gateway to Siberia. It was there, in the shadow of the city fortress, that the wives of Decembrist revolutionaries presented Dostoevsky and his co-conspirators with copies of the New Testament.[23] He later wrote that it was the only book he was permitted to take with him into exile. He read it through repeatedly as he served four years in penal confinement near Omsk, followed by five years of required service in a regiment in nearby Semipalatinsk. When a new tsar came to the throne, he was granted permission to leave Siberia.

Dostoevsky now turned to literature for his livelihood, and as one might expect, his post-exile writing was strongly shaped by his Siberian experiences. He soon founded several literary journals with his brother Mikhail, including *Time* (*Vremya*), followed by *Epoch* (*Epokha*). Neither journal succeeded from a literary or financial point of view. Then, in 1873, after his brother died, Fyodor's fortunes changed when he founded the monthly magazine *Diary of a Writer* (*Dnevnik pisatelia*). With a few interruptions, he published it in regular installments until his death. *Diary of a Writer* contains a wealth of material, from monthly observations on Russia, (western) Europe, and international relations (including his often disparaging reflections on the Ottoman Empire) to some of his most moving short stories. It was in *Diary* that he presented readers with "Vlas," about a peasant who undertakes the most outrageous acts of sacrilege on a whim, only to be crushed in the attempt, and "Bobok," about a cemetery where a passerby hears the entombed dead endlessly repeating the word *bobok* in haunting whispers.

Diary of a Writer is a vital resource for us in understanding Dostoevsky, though he unquestionably left his greatest mark with a series of novels that began with *Notes from a Dead House* (1860), the fictional prison memoir of Alexander Petrovich Goryanchikov, a gentleman who served ten years' hard labor in a Siberian prison for the murder of his wife. *Notes from a Dead House* includes character portraits, philosophical reflections, and accounts of events ranging from the convicts' Christmas service to an otherworldly bathhouse scene. The work was an immediate sensation and relaunched Dostoevsky's literary career.

His next major work was *Notes from Underground* (1864), which features a sardonic, modern antihero who begins, "I am a sick man. . . . I am a wicked man." Dostoevsky wrote this work in two parts that together form a fictional memoir very different from *Notes from a Dead House*. In the first part, the Underground Man makes the case for man's essential irrationality. That is the heart of his "sickness." Our protagonist rages against the scientific rationalists of his day, refusing to believe that humankind will ever create a just society based on sound principles. The second part is a prolonged confession, during which the Underground Man describes the pivotal events in his life that shaped his cynicism about the human condition. This work has endured in importance. One reviewer called it "the beginning of the modernist movement in literature," without which the works of Nietzsche, Freud, Kafka, and "half of Woody Allen's work" would have been all the poorer.[24]

Greater novels followed, starting with *Crime and Punishment* (1864), a torturous tale of murder and responsibility. It opens with a student named Raskolnikov plotting and then carrying out the murder of an elderly pawnbroker. Thereafter, Raskolnikov evades the legal consequences while wrestling with whatever moral responsibility he may carry for her murder, as well as the murder of her sister, who happened to be in her apartment at the time. The question is not whether he murdered them both, for his responsibility is clear. Rather, the issue is whether murder is legitimate if it leads to a greater good and whether "supermen" have the obligation to break society's laws in order to advance society.

Raskolnikov is one of the great characters in Russian literature. In *The Idiot*, Dostoevsky created yet another one. Published as a serial (as were many of Dostoevsky's novels) in 1868 and 1869, this novel is about Prince Myshkin, who returns to Russia after a long stay in Europe. Myshkin finds himself torn between two women in St. Petersburg—a bipartite split that is emblematic of the entire work. *The Idiot* has been hailed as Dostoevsky's most autobiographical novel, given the prince's epilepsy and his reflections on beauty, Christ, and mortality, and also given its depiction of what convicts experience when they know their execution is imminent.

The Idiot focuses on one man and shows little interest in place. By contrast, Dostoevsky's next novel, *Demons* (1872), shows a sharp eye for time and place. He wrote it after revolutionaries inspired by the nihilist Sergei Nechaev murdered the student Ivan Ivanovich Ivanov in 1869. The conspirators acted after wrongly surmising that Ivanov had abandoned their cause and turned police informer. St. Petersburgers were shocked by the cold-bloodedness of the crime, and the incident immediately attracted

Dostoevsky's attention. He used the novel to link the nihilist revolutionaries of the 1860s to their liberal "fathers" of the 1840s. *Demons* is his most political novel. In it he eviscerates a generation he deems demonic, yet the same work contains passages of rich humor and others of transcendent beauty.

Next came *The Adolescent* (1875), a coming-of-age story that hearkens back to the first-person perspective of *Notes from Underground*, but with a much more hopeful tone. It is among Dostoevsky's least appreciated works: Edward Wasiolek has called it "a failure," and other scholars have overlooked it in their discussions of Dostoevsky's accomplishments.[25] Yet this novel, which follows young Arkady Dolgoruky's search for paternal love amid deep familial fragmentation, contains some of Dostoevsky's most unforgettable characters. In particular, the respected peasant Makar (Arkady's ostensible father) and the flighty Versilov (Arkady's actual father) are important types for Dostoevsky. They represent the worldviews that Dostoevsky saw everywhere in Russia—the pious peasant and the Europeanized noble—and that could not have been more starkly opposed to each other. Richard Pevear observes that the promise of youth has been vanquished in *Notes from Underground*, whereas all is still possible in *The Adolescent*.[26]

Dostoevsky took two years to write his next novel and last major work, *The Brothers Karamazov*. This extraordinary novel focuses on the murder of the brutish and generally despised family patriarch Fyodor Karamazov, whom we met at the start of this chapter, and its consequences. The eldest son, Mitya, is charged with the murder and later convicted of it, yet nothing is as it seems in this novel of endless counterpoints and sudden, dramatic twists. On its publication in 1880 it was greeted with wild acclaim, in part because Dostoevsky had included an almost bewildering range of dynamic character types and literary styles, from the outlandish legend "The Grand Inquisitor" to the pietistic "Talks and Homilies of the Elder Zosima." Critics to this day consider *The Brothers Karamazov* one of the monumental literary works of our age.

This brief overview hardly does justice to the depth or range of Dostoevsky's writing, which goes to the heart of the dilemma before us. What can one say about any of these works that will allow even a portion of their essence, their profound beauty, to come through? In a sense, this book will have succeeded if its readers turn next to Dostoevsky's own words, in any translation.

Dostoevsky intended *The Brothers Karamazov* to be the first book in a trilogy, The Life of a Great Sinner.[27] He did not live to complete that project: soon after suffering an internal hemorrhage, he died on January 27, 1881, having taken confession and communion the evening before.

Tens of thousands of Russians attended his funeral four days later. Almost seventy associations and societies joined his funeral procession, including the entire Imperial Opera Company and fifteen separate choirs. The varied tributes included a delegation of female students who carried the shackles that Dostoevsky had worn into Siberian exile decades earlier.[28]

But *why* did so many care? The Russian philosopher Nikolas Alexandrovich Berdyaev famously described Dostoevsky as by himself sufficient justification for the existence of the Russian people on this earth.[29] Berdyaev believed this to be so because Dostoevsky had proven to be the most Russian of all writers; yet at the same time he had transcended his Russianness to achieve universal significance.[30] In other words, Dostoevsky had been able to present a Russian understanding of universal truths, including Russian understandings of Spirit, Humankind, Freedom, Evil, and Love. Berdyaev argued that Dostoevsky's enduring attraction to Western readers lay precisely in his ability to present this Russian vision of the universal.

More than three-quarters of a century have passed since this exiled Russian philosopher made his bold declaration of Dostoevsky's worth, yet his words still ring true. The many scholars who continue to investigate Dostoevsky's life and work are evidence of his enduring appeal. Kostalevsky comes close to echoing Berdyaev's sentiments, concluding that Dostoevsky was remarkable because he possessed the art of integral vision—a system that allowed for "a unity inclusive of plurality" as opposed to "a unity exclusive of it."[31] Unfortunately, the vast community of Dostoevsky scholars has not yet sufficiently engaged the community of non-Russian ethicists in our time. As a consequence, the Russian voice has generally not been heard in that broader discussion, and neither has Dostoevsky's in particular.

This study attempts to give Dostoevsky that voice. It is my conviction that he has something substantive to offer both specialists and nonspecialists. This book complements recent works by Rowan Williams and Bruce K. Ward that have had a similar intent.[32] The chapters that follow are geared toward ethicists as well as students of globalization, though the focus will necessarily be on Dostoevsky's life and times.

I do not want to make the sourcing so specialized that it will discourage readers from following the tracks laid down for them. But if most of my citations are in English translation, what guarantees are there that they will be true to a writer who wrote exclusively in Russian? It is a fair question, given that most of those who turn from this book to Dostoevsky will not have Russian language skills. Yet a grasp of Russian is not always essential for Dostoevsky's ethical worldview to be heard in the West, especially given the number of high-quality translations now available. So I will occasionally refer to the original texts, especially where I am inclined to present an alternative translation from those currently available. This approach will enable those who are not Russian specialists to follow my citations back to Dostoevsky's own words. As often as I can, I will cite his works in translation; in that regard I prefer the translations by Richard Pevear and Larissa Volokhonsky. Very occasionally I will cite and translate works that are unavailable in English.

A word of clarification regarding the Russian word for "people" that Dostoevsky tended to use: *narod*. How best to translate it into English? This is an especially vital issue in chapter 4, where the word appears often. The best translation of *narod* may not in fact be "people," for which another Russian word exists: *liudi*. *Narod* carries associations with a deeply rooted Russian identity, much like what is communicated by the German word *Volk*. It points to a collectivity of profound national significance — certainly, it did so for Dostoevsky and for his time. *Narod* was most closely associated with the peasants, the ones he repeatedly linked to Russia's Orthodox heart, though it was not necessarily limited to them. It did *not* refer simply to a collection of random individuals in one place, which *people* often suggests in English. It was not always clear who was encompassed (or not) by *narod*, and both Derek Offord and Elise Kimerling Wirtschafter have demonstrated that ambiguity.[33] I will be translating *narod* as "People" (rather than "people") so as to be consistent with Gary Saul Morson and other scholars who have done the same.

Dostoevsky's readership grew steadily with each of his publications, and we now have the opportunity to join that circle, even though we live fourteen decades and often more than half a world away from him. His words continue to echo if we but open our ears, and our hearts.

Dostoevsky was a serious and committed craftsman; each of his many works was complete in and of itself. I will not discuss his unpublished correspondence or his notebooks unless something in them clarifies a point I draw from his published works. I have tried to model my approach after that of Peter Erb, who writes, "Respect for the novel, and the novelist, is manifested first in offering full *attention to*, that is *waiting on* the words in the text (as Simone Weil suggests), allowing it to speak for itself in its world and the world to which it alludes, and reflecting on its manifest reality in the same way as one reflects on human and natural reality generally, rather than forcing from it the necessary answers from preconceived questions."[34]

This captures well my own attitude. It is also consistent with Rowan Williams's suggestion that to rely unduly on Dostoevsky's notebooks would be to deny him the opportunity to work out in his final prose the problems he first pondered in draft form.[35] So I will allow Dostoevsky to speak largely as he chose. I wish thereby to make his oeuvre available to those who struggle with ethical issues and approaches in our time—those who may have become restless from a sense that something vital is missing in the broader ethical debate or in their own understanding of it.

Finally, this ethical encounter with Dostoevsky will reinforce Alice Crary's suggestion that fiction contributes to "a wider conception of rationality" because it moves the reader from a set of abstract propositions to an active engagement with "our larger visions of the world."[36] Anton Leist and Peter Singer suggest that this literary and ethical engagement challenges those who have relied exclusively on Western philosophical traditions; it invites us to consider a shift from "foundational projects" to an encounter with the "more practical problems of the world." Leist and Singer conclude that "ethics, and applied ethics especially, is helped by the literary imagination, if it confronts the conflicting forces visible in different philosophical positions as well as in our everyday culture."[37] Though their work focuses on the South African writer J. M. Coetzee, they could have been writing about Dostoevsky.

But Which Dostoevsky?

One caveat remains, albeit a significant one. Translations aside, how will the reader know that I have accurately represented the Dostoevskian view of the ethical? It is all the more difficult to answer this question given that Dostoevsky deliberately communicated almost all of his ideas within the

relatively ambiguous medium of fiction, rather than the more certain strictures of nonfiction. It is no wonder he has been assessed in wildly different
ways over time. Was he the defender of Orthodoxy or its subtlest critic?
Was he the father of existentialism, which would make Sartre his heir? Or
was he a coldhearted and anti-Semitic Russian chauvinist whose ethical
musings are forever tainted and who is best forgotten in our time? Was he
truly a Christian, or simply a deist who was fascinated by Christ but alienated from the church?[38]

The distinguished Russian semiotician Mikhail Bakhtin perhaps came
closest to the truth when he concluded that Dostoevsky was the master
of the polyphonic novel.[39] By this reckoning, Dostoevsky's genius lay in
his ability to present various and contradictory ideal types in literary form
without resolution. This would explain the wildly different conclusions
that scholars have reached regarding Dostoevsky's literary intent. Bakhtin
argues that one needs to find the truth of Dostoevsky within the dialectic;
even if he is right, absolute certainty as to Dostoevsky's intent will always
remain elusive. So it is quite possible that we may best capture the writer's
heart by listening to the myriad voices he presents rather than any particular one. That said, our understanding of that polyphonic approach has
changed dramatically over the past several years. Did Bakhtin adopt a polyphonic interpretation because he could not resolve Dostoevsky's ultimate
moral indeterminacy, as was long maintained, or was his polyphonic discourse a barely concealed attempt to portray a trinitarian (and therefore
profoundly Christian) tri-unity at a time when Bakhtin himself was working under a Soviet regime that was hostile to religion?[40] So it is that even
the study of those who study Dostoevsky can become multilayered, and
simple conclusions found wanting.

There is much to be said for the view that Dostoevsky's prose will
never be pinned down, that we will never grasp his ultimate intent. Scholars
have long disagreed on almost all aspects of Dostoevsky's worldview. How
is it possible to know the mind of any writer with certainty, especially one
who emerged from the nonlinear, almost mystical traditions of nineteenth-
century Russian Orthodoxy? Bakhtin was correct to declare that Dostoevsky never intended his novels to be narrowly ideological. Rather, they always unfolded dialogically among a wide range of actors. Bakhtin's greatest
insight, though, may have been that many of Dostoevsky's actors were

"unfinalizable," internally dialogic within their own persons. Even more boldly, he proposed that Dostoevsky himself entered into a dialogic relationship with his fictional creations, who became strangely independent of him. By this reckoning, Dostoevsky was their conversation partner more than their creator:

> In Dostoevsky's subsequent works, the characters no longer carry on a *literary* polemic with finalizing secondhand definitions of man (although the author himself sometimes does this for them, in a very subtle ironic-parodic form), but they all do furious battle with such definitions of their personality in the mouths of other people. They all acutely sense their own inner unfinalizability, their capacity to outgrow, as it were, from within and to render *untrue* any externalizing and finalizing definition of them. As long as a person is alive he lives by the fact that he is not yet finalized, that he has not yet uttered his ultimate word.[41]

So we can conclude that no single character created by Dostoevsky was ever complete; all were constantly engaged, ever in formation, ever in dialogue, both with others around them and with themselves. Only the bravest or most foolish of commentators on Dostoevsky will disagree with this. But if that is the case, what can we conclude with any certainty regarding Dostoevsky's intentions or moral voice?

The only possible answer here is "very little indeed," especially if one considers that Dostoevsky may have deliberately obscured his views to evade tsarist censors. Edith Clowes has demonstrated how Russian literary trends were a necessarily ambiguous vehicle for philosophical discourse in the first half of the nineteenth century, when Russian philosophical inquiry was still in its infancy, especially given the Russian state's stringent restrictions on such after the Decembrist revolt of 1825.[42] State surveillance agents would have been especially sensitive to the literary outpourings of convicted criminals—a term that applied to Dostoevsky for much of his literary career.

Yet there may have been more profound reasons for Dostoevsky's decision to write in a heavily layered manner. For one thing, almost all of his writings rail against inevitable outcomes and easily grasped equations. Already in *Notes from Underground* he had formulated this as humankind's deep aversion to living within the constraints of mathematical certainty. Such an existence was, for him, the tyranny of two times two equals four,[43] the tyranny associated with laws of nature deemed unassailable and with the idea that humans were compelled to see themselves within similarly rigid systems. Why, he wrote, cannot two times two sometimes be made to equal five?[44] Such a writer, one imagines, did not want to be pigeonholed, and I hesitate to present his ideas in this study as if they were so many ordered principles.

It is clear that, for Dostoevsky, reality was as complex as it was dynamic—a view no doubt instilled in him by Orthodoxy. Thus, his dislike of much of Western art related directly to its artistic representation. True, there were noted exceptions, including the *Sistine Madonna*. But exceptions aside, he generally believed that Western art veiled much more than it revealed because of its stifling empiricism. In an 1873 entry in *Diary of a Writer*, he criticized the superficial reality of Nikolai Ge's *The Last Supper*, which had clearly been painted in the Western style. Such a painting might be considered accurate in terms of three-dimensional realism, but Ge had failed to grasp the divine nature of Christ. The mathematically precise realism of his human-looking Christ masked more than it revealed.[45] Yet another painting in the Western style, Holbein's *Dead Christ*, convincingly portrayed only the humanity of Christ immediately after His death through crucifixion (as opposed to what Dostoevsky took to be Christ's divinity, which eternally coexisted with His humanity).[46]

Dostoevsky was drawn to active, worshipful engagement with Russian icons, and almost all of his works make strong references to them.[47] Early in *The Brothers Karamazov*, Alyosha—Mitya's brother and the novel's purported hero—recalls a beautiful childhood memory of being lifted up by his mother to a Mother of God icon. That icon was in the corner of Alyosha's childhood home, as was the Russian manner, and placed before it was a lit oil lamp. In the novel, devotion to that icon is linked directly to Alyosha's love for all the people he meets later in his life.[48] At their heart, then, icons were, for Dostoevsky, the antithesis of "two times two equals four" in that they require contemplation and prayer in order to be even partly grasped; they are never simplistic and precise portrayals, for if they were, it would profoundly distort the truth they are capable of revealing. Icons are sacred for the Orthodox Church—they are essential gateways to the divine. Thus, icons can portray Mary, the virgin Mother of God, with a Christ who even in infancy is already the mature and ageless ruler of the universe. They mark the intersection of the human and the divine in a manner that Dostoevsky finds impossible in the Western styles of Holbein and Ge. Indeed, icons can be said to embody the "unfinalizability" that Bakhtin repeatedly observes in Dostoevsky's writings.

I suggest that Dostoevsky's entire body of work can be read contemplatively, almost iconographically, and in a manner that eschews simplistic conclusions on complex themes.[49] I also suggest that such a reading will allow us to discern Dostoevsky's deeply felt positions. I agree with Morson that much more can be gleaned from the *Diary* than has been previously assumed, especially if we view the entire corpus together.[50] That publication allowed Dostoevsky to comment directly on the events of his day. It served—as Jacques Catteau aptly put it—as "the launching pad from which the imaginary fiction of the writer soars in search of the ends and the beginnings."[51] Even though Dostoevsky's fiction followed the *Diary* and was often woven into it, the writer's intent was never in question.

This does not negate Geoffrey Kabat's powerful insight—supported by Laura Engelstein—that Dostoevsky works dialectically between ideological (as in journalistic) and imaginative (as in fictional) modes of thinking, with the latter deservedly predominant in any assessment of the writer's final word on any matter.[52] For example, a reading of his journalistic record makes it clear that he was completely—one could even say violently—supportive of his empire in the Balkan wars of his day, while in his fiction one encounters repeated calls for nonviolence and Christlike suffering. Robert L. Jackson argues along these same lines when he suggests that "Akulka's Husband"—a story in which the steadfastly innocent and defenseless Akulka is given up to a paschal slaughter at the hands of her own husband—is Dostoevsky's final word on violence. As Jackson puts it, Akulka "embodies in her life the principle of love and self-sacrifice that Dostoevsky placed above all other values."[53] If it is the case, then, that Dostoevsky utilized his fiction to work through the issues of his day, we need to exercise the utmost caution when reading and interpreting his canon in its entirety.

Yet I have concluded that it *is* possible to discern the core of Dostoevsky's impassioned critique of the West's ethical project, as well as to deduce his cure for the damage it had already done Russian society. I agree with James P. Scanlan's assessment, which is that Dostoevsky philosophized in a dialogical manner but was ultimately monological in substance.[54] Of course, most scholars have come to this position, even as they disagree on what that monological word actually is. The best way to make sense of this may be to accept A. Boyce Gibson's summary statement: "Of books on Dostoevsky there is no end. The only excuse for another is that everyone sees him differently. He is the sort of writer whom everyone *will* see differently. He is as far as possible from the well-organized one-piece writer with an assured direction and intention. He is, more than most, an [*sic*] universal writer, but his comprehensiveness is not orderly or systematic."[55]

With almost every new contribution, scholars half-apologize for having written yet another study on Dostoevsky. Putting my own cards on the table—an idiom that goes to the heart of one of Dostoevsky's greatest vices—I have been most drawn to those scholars who understand Dostoevsky as a profoundly Russian and Orthodox writer. That places me in the company of Berdyaev, Vladimir Soloviev, and many of the above-named authors, including Jackson. But I hasten to add that Dostoevsky was Orthodox in the sense explicated by Williams. I have also concluded that Dostoevsky can best be grasped if we consider him to be, above all, an Orthodox believer.[56] His works do not systematically explore the formal world of Russian Orthodoxy; even so, his entire worldview was profoundly shaped by that religious tradition. So we will need to come to grips with Orthodox understandings of the ethical if we are to understand Dostoevsky's own convictions.

Dostoevsky was not a "mere" Slavophile, as has been argued. I am reluctant to go the distance with those who view him as far removed from that powerful ideology of Russian preeminence and exclusivity, but I do agree with Wayne Dowler's strong insight that Dostoevsky was determined to bridge the gap between the People (Russia's famed *narod*, the peasantry) and the empire's Europeanized elite.[57] Why else would he repeatedly raise up the former, albeit occasionally in despair, while writing almost exclusively for the latter?

Taking all things into account, I believe we can obtain a monological understanding of Dostoevsky's ethical worldview if we follow the countless clues he lays out for us. For example, he begins *Demons* with this passage from Luke 8:32–36:

Now there on the hillside a large herd of swine was feeding; and the demons begged Jesus to let them enter these. So he gave them permission. Then the demons came out of the man and entered the swine, and the herd rushed down the steep bank into the lake and was drowned.

When the swineherds saw what had happened, they ran off and told it in the city and in the country. Then people came out to see what had happened, and when they came to Jesus, they found the man from whom the demons had gone sitting at the feet of Jesus, clothed and in his right mind. And they were afraid. Those who had seen it told them how the one who had been possessed by demons had been healed. (NRSV)

Though Dostoevsky also incorporates an epigraph from Pushkin for this novel, it is consistent with the Lucan account just quoted. It is difficult to imagine any uncertainty about Dostoevsky's intent when one reads the entire novel through the lens he provides at the outset. In Luke's account, Jesus comes across a man possessed. The Son of God asks the demon to name itself, and it replies, "Legion," a technical term referring to an entire division of five thousand troops in the Roman army. A strange request follows—that is, if it is not already strange enough to have Christ confront a man possessed by a legion of demons—for the demons themselves beg to be returned to the "abyss." The request suggests that the demons know that Christ has authority over them. It is here that Dostoevsky picks up the story in his epigraph. Contemporary readers would have understood Dostoevsky's intent for what it was: the man possessed in Luke's account is a barely veiled allusion to Russia. And the legion of demons? The Lucan account anticipates that the solution to Russia's momentary crisis did exist for Dostoevsky; it was to be found in the One Dostoevsky repeatedly called "the Russian Christ." Put another way, the hope for the future lay solely in the Christ who had been preserved by Orthodox Russia. As Victor Terras has observed, any ambiguities contained in *Demons* cannot negate its "explicitly stated dominant idea: a revolt against God, religion, and the existing social order leads to death and destruction."[58]

Dostoevsky provides a similar clue to his authorial intent at the start of *The Brothers Karamazov* when he includes a passage from John 12:24: "Very truly, I tell you, unless a grain of wheat falls into the earth and dies, it remains just a single grain; but if it dies, it bears much fruit" (NRSV). This saying, spoken by Christ and found in the Gospel that was unquestionably closest to Dostoevsky's heart,[59] alerts the reader at the outset that the author will not be impartial to the Ivans and the Smerdyakovs of this world, even as he will not be to Father Zosima or to his beloved Alyosha; this, even though Dostoevsky will allow all to speak in their own voices, even relentlessly so. We will return to this passage in chapter 4, but at this point I want to underline how a careful reading of it influences our reading of the whole. And none of this negates the reality that Dostoevsky's own literary output—including *Demons* and *The Brothers Karamazov*—was sufficiently multivocal to allow for a rich and dialectical engagement of thesis and antithesis.[60] If readers want to debate my findings, I will be more than pleased, as it will mean that Dostoevsky has entered the debate on the search for a universal ethic where he seems most needed.

Dostoevsky and the West

We must attend to one more bit of business here, that of Dostoevsky's knowledge of the West. How can we say that he knew what he was talking about when it came to the West, ethically or otherwise? As so much of my argument touches on his competence in this area, it behooves us to consider how he was both an insider and an outsider to the West, as well as to examine the process of modernization under way in the middle decades of the nineteenth century.

There are four ways in which Dostoevsky did in fact encounter the West closely enough to comment thoughtfully about it. First, he spent significant portions of his life in western Europe. He once wrote that even as a child he had dreamed of traveling to Europe, which he called (perhaps ironically?) the "land of holy wonders." But instead he had seemingly been fated to be marooned forever on the distant Siberian steppe. His dreams were not realized until June 1862, a few months after he returned from exile to St. Petersburg, when he was granted permission to consult with specialists abroad about his epilepsy. Leaving his wife, Marya (Masha), and stepson back home, he traveled for ten weeks that summer, from Germany to Belgium, France, Britain, Switzerland, and Italy. En route he saw firsthand the grandest monuments the West had to offer in Florence and Paris, though he was no less dumbstruck by London's squalor and splendor. It was in that great capital on the Thames that he observed the famed Crystal Palace, the self-styled temple to the most recent technological achievements, which the British had constructed in 1851. This celebration of the Industrial Revolution was more than 500 meters long and reached a height of almost 40 meters. Dostoevsky considered this palace to be the embodiment of the West, and he referred to it as such almost immediately in *Notes from Underground.* He described much of his sojourn to Europe in *Winter Notes on Summer Impressions,* published shortly after his return to Russia in 1863. By then his prose had transformed this vaunted "holy land of wonders" into another metaphorical location to which we shall return: Baal.

Dostoevsky returned to Europe (Paris, Wiesbaden, and Baden-Baden) from August to October of 1863 and again in 1867, less than five years after the first journey and four after his second. He intended this third odyssey to last three months.[61] As it turned out, he did not return to St. Petersburg until the spring of 1871. Though the time between his second and third European odysseys seems short, Dostoevsky's own world had changed overwhelmingly. His first wife, Marya, died in 1864; he was rebuffed in a subsequent marriage attempt; then in 1867 he married again. By all indications, Anna Grigorievna, his second wife, was the love of his life and remained so until his death. That was already enough in terms of significant events, and yet there was more, for his beloved brother and business partner Mikhail died suddenly in 1864, leaving Fyodor overwhelmed with debts from their unsuccessful literary ventures. He also assumed financial responsibility for his ne'er-do-well stepson, as well as for Mikhail's widow and her four children. Through all this, he managed to write one of the great novels of the nineteenth century, *Crime and Punishment,* along with several shorter works, including the often-overlooked *The Gambler.*

In the midst of these mounting crises, Dostoevsky needed respite from his creditors, and to that end he and his bride left for Berlin in April 1867. Their travels took them from the Prussian capital to Dresden, Baden-Baden, Geneva, Vevey, Florence, and back finally to Dresden for the final twenty months, with various stops, detours, and returns along the way. *The Idiot* was written during this period, and it is not surprising that it features the railroad, to which we will return, as well as a certain dislocation from Russia, especially when we contrast it with *Crime and Punishment*'s fixation on Peter's city on the Neva in all its magnificence and degradation.

So Dostoevsky had more than a passing knowledge of the West from his own travels. He was always a keen observer of life on the street, in the railroad carriage, and in the apartment house. Nor was that all: sadly, he threw himself into Europe's gambling halls, to his own ruination and despite the anguish it caused his young bride. Fyodor experienced great joys and sorrows in Europe as well: his first daughter, Sofya, was born in Geneva in March 1868, and it was there that she died barely two months later of cold and an inflammation of the lungs. Dostoevsky's anguish at the loss of his firstborn and of an infant son, Alexei, in 1878, later received profoundly compassionate literary treatment, when Father Zosima goes out to comfort a young mother who is worn and wasted beyond her years because she cannot get over the recent death of her infant son.[62]

Dostoevsky's second manner of engagement with the West merges easily with the first: he had long engaged with his counterparts in the various European cultural movements. He was enthusiastic about a number of western European authors, including Charles Dickens (*Nicholas Nickleby*, *The Old Curiosity Shop*, and *The Pickwick Papers* at least) and Victor Hugo (*Les Misérables* and *The Last Day of a Man Condemned to Death*).[63] His novels are packed with references to Dante, Shakespeare, Goethe, Cervantes, Dumas *père*, and Voltaire, as well as to many writers within the Russian literary tradition. He dedicated an entire issue of the *Diary* (June 1876, 1.1) to the French writer George Sand, who died that same year.[64] Travis Kroeker and Bruce Ward suggest that Dostoevsky based *The Idiot* on Cervantes' famed *Don Quixote* and Dickens's *Pickwick Papers*.[65]

Dostoevsky was similarly fascinated by Western art, as was most dramatically evident when he visited the Basel museum in August 1867. There he sought out the Holbein painting of Christ mentioned earlier in this chapter. (Pevear has stressed that Dostoevsky simply refers to this painting as *The Dead Christ*.)[66] Dostoevsky had read about this painting after it was mentioned by Nikolai Karamzin, the famous Russian historian of the early nineteenth century. He now stopped with his beloved wife to see it for himself. She wrote in her memoir some forty years later,

On the way to Geneva we stopped for a day in Basel, with the purpose of seeing a painting in the museum there that my husband had heard about from someone. This painting, from the brush of Hans Holbein, portrays Jesus Christ, who has suffered inhuman torture, has been taken down from the cross and given over to corruption. His swollen face is covered with bloody wounds, and he looks terrible. The painting made an overwhelming impression on my husband, and he stood before it as if dumbstruck. . . . When I returned some fifteen or twenty minutes later, I found my husband still standing in front of the painting as if riveted to it. There was in his agitated face that expression as of fright which I had seen more than once in the first moments of an epileptic fit. I quietly took him under the arm, and sat him down on a bench, expecting a fit to come at any moment. Fortunately that did not happen.[67]

In one way *The Idiot* can be read as a long reflection on Holbein's painting, for Dostoevsky feared that a work like it could on its own lead viewers to atheism. Not surprisingly, two of his major characters have long encounters with a copy of this painting that hangs in a St. Petersburg flat.[68] The first of these characters is Prince Myshkin (the supposed idiot), who sees it hanging in Rogozhin's flat. Myshkin, who is noteworthy for his extraordinary and transparent sensitivity, tries to flee the house. Rogozhin stops him and interrogates the prince about whether he believes in God's existence. Myshkin replies that a person "could even lose his faith from that painting"[69] and goes on to reflect on three distinct encounters he has had with peasants for whom the cross (and, presumably, faith) is central, even though they may carry out unspeakable crimes simultaneously.

The second character to encounter the painting is Ippolit, who is dying young from consumption. At one point he gathers together Myshkin (a sort of confessor throughout the novel) and his friends to give them what he calls "A Necessary Explanation." He tells them how he sought to live a rich and generous life of good deeds despite the certainty of his imminent death. Then one day he saw Rogozhin's copy of Holbein's painting. Like Myshkin before him, Ippolit is transfixed and transformed by his encounter with the painting, but unlike Myshkin, he is unable to escape its grasp. Ippolit leaves Rogozhin's home no longer interested in good deeds, convinced that the laws of nature cannot be overcome, and determined to kill himself immediately after the reading of his "Necessary Explanation." He sees no other escape from the tyranny of the absurd existence starkly portrayed in Holbein's painting. For our purposes here, it is enough to conclude that Dostoevsky repeatedly encountered the West at an aesthetic level, one that left him fully engaged with the leading artistic and cultural trends of his day.

Dostoevsky's two other encounters with European developments did not require him to leave his beloved Russia. Given their prevalence within the empire, European ideas shaped virtually every day of Dostoevsky's life. This was not a recent trend: Europeans (especially Italians, English, and Germans) had played a vital role in the development of the Muscovite state even before Peter the Great's reign in the early eighteenth century. This was evident in everything from Russia's politics and armed forces to the architecture of Moscow's most sacred churches. Interactions with European ideas had accelerated after Napoleon's defeat in 1815 as returning Russian armies brought with them the intellectual ferment then washing over western Europe. The Decembrist uprising of 1825 that followed Nicholas I's accession to the throne was only one consequence of this. Salons in cities across the empire attracted an emerging intelligentsia who actively debated Russia's place in the new Europe. Did Europe represent the way forward for the empire, or was its path to be avoided at all costs? Dostoevsky's involvement in the revolutionary Petrashevtsky circle suggests how fully he embraced intellectual debates in his own land. His literary outpouring after he returned from exile is best understood as a prolonged and impassioned engagement with Western ideas, which continued to attract many Russian intellectuals. One remarkable episode in his broader engagement with European thought serves as the heart of my penultimate chapter. It is enough to say now that the West's influence on Dostoevsky was such that he often referred to himself and his peers as both Russians and Europeans. In that sense alone, the West was never for him a distant land, never at great remove. The only question in his mind seemed to be which of these two identities would win in the end, and what the consequences would be.

This relates directly to the final means by which Dostoevsky encountered the West—through St. Petersburg itself. Dostoevsky returned to this great city after his Siberian exile in December 1859, and it is ironic how at home this most Russian of writers felt in this most non-Russian of cities. Peter the Great had founded it in 1703 to be the Russian "window on the West." In that spirit, Peter's city was centered from the beginning on the Admiralty spire, the symbol of its secular and therefore Western stamp. (Moscow, by contrast, rippled out from the Kremlin churches.) In keeping with this nonreligious focal point, Peter refused to appoint a new patriarch for the Russian Orthodox Church when the old one died; thus, in Dostoevsky's time the church was administered by a bureaucratically appointed synod. There were of course Orthodox churches in St. Petersburg; the principal one, St. Isaac's Cathedral, was completed in 1858, just before Dostoevsky's return from exile. Yet it was a Frenchman, the famed neoclassicist architect Auguste de Montferrand, who designed it, and he did so along Western lines. Its single golden cupola alluded to St. Paul's in London and St. Peter's in Rome rather than to any of the empire's countless Orthodox churches.

Dostoevsky knew Peter's city intimately, as is especially clear in *Crime and Punishment*. Raskolnikov's wanderings in that remarkable novel take him from the Anichkov Bridge, with its epic statuary, to the Haymarket, to the avenues of Vasilievsky Island and back again. On that island we meet new immigrants to the city, some of whom are mesmerized by the city's extraordinary imperial grandeur, while others fall prey to its many cesspools.[70] The city's main promenade, Nevsky Prospect, is central to the Underground Man's machinations in Dostoevsky's famed depiction of the antihero.[71] Dostoevsky had encapsulated the West in London's Crystal Palace, but he could have done so without leaving his own post-exilic city, the Russian Empire's capital.

What Happens Next

We are now ready to build on the foundation laid in this chapter. In chapter 2 I set out why Dostoevsky deemed Western, modern understandings of ethics to be profoundly hopeless. These are harsh words, but as *The Brothers Karamazov* makes clear, Dostoevsky found it impossible to imagine a contemporary morality without a belief in immortality, for without the latter, all would be permitted. All? It seems so by his reckoning, for without immortality no law of nature would be able to compel humankind to love; and without that, "nothing will be immoral any longer, everything would be permitted, even anthropophagy."[72] In the circumstances, it is not surprising that Dostoevsky more than once referred to Europe as a beautiful graveyard. I will examine how he arrived at this assessment and what he feared most about Russia's nineteenth-century transformation into a European society. For that purpose, I will focus on two of Dostoevsky's apparent obsessions: orphans and suicide. Yet he did not scorn those who had abandoned a firm and fixed belief in an Orthodox and triune God. In chapter 2 I pay careful attention to Dostoevsky's treatment of Versilov in

The Adolescent, to Stepan Trofimovich in *Demons*, and to Dostoevsky's own reflections on the death of George Sand.

Chapter 3 makes a positive statement about Dostoevsky's ethical worldview. For him, ethics was a matter of moral obligations and was rarely about rights. In his world, shame was to be sought out, as was forgiveness. Power was to be lamented, but not the willing embrace of suffering and powerlessness. Perhaps most surprising of all, given the oppositions found in the previous sentences, Dostoevsky believed that such a world would be matchlessly beautiful even in the attempt—as beautiful as the last rays of a setting sun. Such an ethical world would be one of joy, of mystery, and of transcendence, even as it confounded our own understanding of what it means to be ethical. And this entire ethical worldview was captured in the Orthodox Christ, whom Dostoevsky and others of his era referred to as the God-man, or the divine-man. We will try to understand this through an engagement with Orthodox understandings of ethics.

Chapter 4 begins where the previous one leaves off, with Dosto-evsky's depiction of Christ as the key to the ethical life. This claim created an enormous problem for those in Dostoevsky's time who maintained that sectarian Christian beliefs could not possibly become the basis for a universal ethic. It reminds us why Tännsjö, as noted earlier, sets aside ethi-cal frameworks that are too closely linked to religious claims of absolute truth in our time. This chapter interrogates Dostoevsky's own critique of this perspective, for his time and in his own words. To that end, it focuses on two phenomena that marked the zenith of Dostoevsky's life and work. The first occurred on June 8, 1880, less than a year before his death, when at the unveiling of a monument to Alexander Pushkin he gave a speech in which he argued that the poet's greatness had been his ability to see in Russia a moral position that would one day unite all peoples. That moral unity resided in no less a place than—in Frank's words—"the suffering and humiliated Christ."[73] I will consider at length Dostoevsky's speech and the critical reaction to it (in particular that of the well-known liberal A. D. Gradovsky), as well as Dostoevsky's own sharp response. But I will also parallel these nonliterary declarations with an examination of how Dostoevsky engaged the same issue in his masterpiece, *The Brothers Kara-mazov*, the publication of which marked the second literary high point of Dostoevsky's final months. He wrote that novel at a time when great pub-lic events were being held to commemorate Pushkin, which helps explain why Dostoevsky was the subject of such immense public adulation in the last year of his life. Through the Pushkin speech and the Karamazov novel we will explore Dostoevsky's declaration that all attempts to create a contemporary ethic were doomed to failure if they were not grounded on "the Russian Christ."

In the conclusion to this book I return to some of the questions about ethical engagement raised in this chapter. But we are still a long way from that, so it is best to get started.

CHAPTER 2

Orphans' Lament

Seeking the Ethical in a Suicidal Age

We seem to be listening in on the most intimate of soliloquies, for it concerns a husband's ruminations as he gazes upon his wife. She is a young beauty, only sixteen years of age, and is laid out before him on two card tables pushed together in their modest St. Petersburg apartment. We never learn her name, or his; it is as if they could be any of us. Someone will bring a white coffin to place her in tomorrow, for she is, most horrible thought, dead, the victim of a suicidal leap only moments before from their apartment window to the street below. Her husband now tries to put the pieces together, and we, like the most reluctant of voyeurs, realize quickly that he will spare us nothing in retelling all that has led up to this.[1]

At forty-one he had been more than double her age, and he was already financially secure. These two factors gave him a definite power advantage over her, and both knew it. She, by contrast, was destitute, not to mention orphaned and without any means of support. That is how she ended up at his pawnshop in the first place, trading her paltry household possessions in exchange for funds sufficient to purchase an advertisement: "So-and-so, a governess: willing to travel, give lessons in private homes, etc., etc." Yet she had received no offers, so eventually her advertisement in *The Voice* changed to "Willing to work without salary, for board alone."[2] Even then nothing came her way, so he knew that she had few options left, especially after she had pawned her most cherished possession: an old family icon of Mary, the Mother of God, with the Christ-child, encased in a silver gilded frame. The pawnbroker offered her a reasonable payment as

35

compensation and set it with his other icons, before which an icon lamp was burning. What exactly did that lit lamp signify? Was he some sort of believer? We are not certain, though his soliloquy leaves little room for optimism. Surely he wanted above all to dominate this most vulnerable adolescent and thereby avenge those who in the past had accused him of cowardliness. Here, with this pretty little thing at his beck and call, he would show them. In his own words, "And the main thing was that I regarded her then as *my own* and had no doubt about my power over her."[3] He made her an offer of marriage, knowing she could hardly refuse. For this orphaned adolescent was bound to take anything to free herself from her two merciless aunts, who had decided in that very moment to sell her off to a storekeeper, the one who had previously beaten two of his wives to death. The storekeeper now wanted a third wife, and she would do just fine.

What madness this all was. In the end, she chose the avenger of past humiliations over the murderer of past wives. She even innocently hoped she could bring enough love into their marriage to transform his heart. She was young! Yet he would have none of it from the start: she, who had wanted freedom from tyrannical aunts, now found her new life in the bonds of a new lord and master. When she attempted to assert her own will by concealing a transaction she had made without his approval in the pawnshop, he responded with self-satisfied and glacial coldness: "Then, without raising my voice at all, I stated calmly that the money was mine, that I had the right to regard life through *my* eyes, and that when I brought her into my house I had hidden nothing from her."[4]

Assorted other silences, woundings, and humiliations followed. One day she had had enough, and as he awakened from sleep he saw her pointing a loaded revolver at his forehead. Even here she relented, and thereafter the most curious circumstance began to unfold. On the one hand, he found himself curiously drawn to her, even sympathetically so. Was it because he had finally vanquished her? But had he really? She, on the other hand, as if sapped of her will, as if that act of defiance killed something within her own being, began to fade away. Had she not, after all, become like him in that moment? In the end he had come to adore her in his own way; he certainly needed her. But in the end, he stepped out of their apartment for just a few minutes one day, enough time for her to grab the icon and bow before it one last time. Was she seeking forgiveness for the act she was about to undertake, or was she was praying for something holy to believe in? One supposes it hardly matters. What does matter is that she then leaped to her death several stories below, clutching the icon she had once pawned to him in desperation.

But we already know she is dead, don't we, for she's lying on two tables pushed together before our eyes. Her shoes stand ready for her feet beside her cot. What sense does he make of this great tragedy, this unspeakable horror? Does the world as a whole make sense, even if this single act of self-inflicted violence does not? Alas, we are left with an ambiguous picture at best. By the end his hard heart had softened toward her; she had become his paradise and his only hope for true happiness. Now her death rids him of this last illusion, that paradise can be found on this earth. Instead, he sees in her corpse a metaphor for the earth itself, which itself is destined for death.

As is the sun. As is everything.

And here we are, individually facing the certainty of our own meaningless deaths within the larger death cycle of a meaningless universe. None of it will have made any sense in the end, for in the end none of it will have endured. He cannot help but conclude that we are all silent prisoners to so many laws of nature, which unfold machinelike, as a pendulum. Someone once said, long ago, that we are to "love one another" in this place, but he cannot recall whose command that was.

————————

No more poignant story was ever penned by Dostoevsky. No one can read these words, even in the crude synoptic form found here, without being moved by them. If it is true that the young woman's vulnerability captures something about the vulnerability of us all, can we not conclude that her orphaned existence is also no stranger to us? And if the pawnshop owner is driven ultimately by the need to exert power within a meaningless universe, might we not be tempted in similar fashion?

Orphans factor powerfully in Dostoevsky's prose, including in this short story, titled "The Meek One" (1876), published five years before his death. Dostoevsky based it on a brief newspaper article he had read in the fall of that year and reported on in his *Diary of a Writer*, but he gives no hint that the young woman mentioned in the original article was an or-phan.[5] Dostoevsky likely added that detail, which should not surprise us, for the theme of parental abandonment pervades his published work.

Even where fathers exist, they often seem incapable of playing more than an initiatory and biological role in the lives of their offspring. Thus, in *The Brothers Karamazov*, all three brothers (or four if we include the bastard son Smerdyakov) become orphans after their father is murdered, though they had long lived an orphaned existence, given Fyodor Pavlovich's disin-clination to be a parent. Indeed, he competes with Mitya for a lover, and he constantly refers to his youngest son, Alyosha, as his friend, not his son.[6] Smerdyakov is permitted inside the home, but only as a house ser-vant to someone who is almost certainly his biological father. Smerdya-kov's mother, the infamous "Stinking Lizaveta," died shortly after his birth, and she herself had been an orphan.[7] Mitya and Ivan seem to have no memories of their long-deceased mothers. Nor are the brothers alone in this regard. Fyodor's "double,"[8] the wondrous Father Zosima, was also fa-therless at the outset of his life—he was only two years old when his fa-ther died. Kolya, with whom hope for the future resides by the end of the novel, is also fatherless from birth. Grushenka, who is wooed by both Mitya and his birth father, is an orphan.[9] In short, there is no single persona in Dostoevsky's last and arguably greatest novel who is not orphaned, be it in fact or effect.

Dostoevsky's penultimate novel, *The Adolescent*, is no different. One can argue that the entire novel amounts to Arkady Makarovich's search for his true father. His name confuses the issue, for Russian rules surrounding the patronymic suggest that Makar is his father. This makes sense, given that the peasant Makar is the lawful husband of Arkady's mother. However, Arkady's biological father, as all in the novel know—including Arkady—was Andrei Petrovich Versilov, owner of the estate where Arkady's nomi-nal father had once been enserfed. Versilov, who had been recently wid-owed when he first met Arkady's mother, had two children from his first marriage. He became attracted to Arkady's mother, Sofia Andreevna, her-self an orphan,[10] and quite literally laid claim to her. Arkady was born to that barely concealed union, as was a daughter, Lizaveta Makarovna, Ar-kady's full sister. Though Sofia Andreevna stays close to Versilov for the rest of her days, Andrei Petrovich keeps all four of the children he fathered at arm's length. At one point Versilov woos the daughter of an aging prince at the same time his biological daughter woos the prince himself, and we cannot help but wonder who would be the parent of whom, should both marriages occur. All of this unfolds while Versilov is informally committed to Arkady's mother, and while Arkady wants nothing more than to be loved by his true father. But Versilov is not easily given to fatherhood of the loving sort. In one especially poignant scene, Arkady encounters Versilov and tells his natural father how they had met once early on in Arkady's life, at a time when Versilov had just returned after a long absence in Moscow (during which he lived with yet another woman). Now, on the occasion of their first encounter in years, Versilov is coming down the stairs as Arkady is going up. He sighs when he sees his son but does not stop. Thus Arkady realizes that Versilov has no desire to father him, despite his son's longing to be embraced, to be loved. Instead, Versilov, like the patriarch in *The Brothers Karamazov*, repeatedly refers to his biological child as "my friend," never as "my son."[11]

Similar trends are evident in *Demons*,[12] in which the main characters struggle to know what it means to parent their offspring, and in *Crime and Punishment*, where the isolation of all of the main characters is depicted in the starkest terms. And well before these great works, the original Underground Man, struggling to find his place in a world he deems cold and impersonal, was introduced to the reader as an orphan.

Dostoevsky was fascinated by orphans because he believed that such was the modern condition. Something about the state of being orphaned profoundly affected modern understandings of what it meant to be ethical, at least as Dostoevsky saw it in his time.

What follows will, I hope, mirror the tragic story with which I began this chapter in yet another sense. It seems clear to me, as Leatherbarrow has concluded in his eloquent study of the demonic in Dostoevsky's fiction,[13] that Dostoevsky believed modern society was dangerously given to suicide. This was not an illogical stance for an age when all were orphans and seemingly the only ethical base available was the one that individuals willfully (one might even say "forcefully") created. In that sense, Dostoevsky suggests that we, like the husband in "The Meek One," seek to enforce our individual wills in a world that has been robbed of its magic; and like the wife, we individually struggle to live meaningful and ethical lives in an age that has left us strangely orphaned. How can it be otherwise in a universe that is—as Liza Knapp has written to great effect—"the god-forsaken and dead nature of a post-Newtonian world"?[14]

In this chapter I investigate how Dostoevsky portrayed modernity's understanding of the ethical. We can achieve a great deal of clarity if we treat "The Meek One" as my argument in miniature. In what follows we will consider in detail the elements of that argument. If this seems too intricate, let me repeat that the short story above has already distilled all I want to say about Dostoevsky's understanding of modernity and ethics.

Modernity Has Left Us Orphaned

Without God

In the Western tradition, it was Nietszche who first announced that God is dead and that with His death all other truths have fallen away.[15] As he famously wrote, "God is dead. God remains dead. And we have killed him. How shall we comfort ourselves, the murderers of all murderers?"[16]

But before Nietzsche, there stood Dostoevsky, whom the former almost certainly read while studying the nihilistic movements that infested mid-nineteenth-century Russia—movements that Dostoevsky battled with his own literary means. Much of Dostoevsky's ethical angst for contemporary Western thought was rooted in its rejection of the divine, even though the shape of that rejection was not easy to define.

Dostoevsky presents many voices who remind us that God has ceased to be relevant in the modern world. Father Paissy, who has begun to replace Father Zosima as Alyosha's mentor in *The Brothers Karamazov*, warns his young and disillusioned charge of the threat posed to notions of the sacred by the Western intellectual tradition: "'Remember, young man, unceasingly' Father Paissy began directly, without any preamble, 'that the science of this world, having united itself into a great force, has, especially in the past century, examined everything heavenly that has been bequeathed to us in sacred books, and, after hard analysis, the learned ones of this world have absolutely nothing left of what was once holy.'"[17]

Similarly, in *Demons*, we meet Liputin, a "provincial official, no longer a young man, a great liberal and known around town as an atheist."[18] Elite society is consistently intrigued with the progressive ideas associated with the death of God. For much of the novel, the lovable (or lovingly pathetic?) Stepan Trofimovich Verkhovensky is the epitome of this progressivism. We encounter him early on when he declares his belief in the divine, sort of. "I believe in God, *mais distinguons*, I believe as in a being who is conscious of himself in me. . . . So far as Christianity is concerned, for all my sincere respect for it, I am not a Christian. I am rather an ancient pagan, like the great Goethe."[19] This diluted theism is tied to the West through language, for French is the universal language[20] and culture. It is not that progressive thought necessarily rejects the existence of the divine so much as that it reduces such a being to irrelevance.

In *The Idiot*, it is the educated who are drawn to atheism, whereas the peasant remains a believer.[21] Those who espouse openly nihilist views are courted in elite society,[22] even if their atheism is incomplete. In one conversation in *Demons*, a general is asked whether he believes in God. He replies that at times, in the terror that comes with the middle of the night, he occasionally crosses himself in front of an icon. But such feelings tend to disappear with the return of daylight (or, we might say, "enlightenment").[23] So it is that atheism can be flexible in presentation and Christ a prop to be called upon in times of distress. Even the highly progressive Stepan Trofimovich sometimes allows an icon lamp to be lit "for effect,"[24] but not in a way that sustains his life. We keep the image of God, or Christ, alive, as in Holbein's so-called *Death of Christ*—but even when alive, it is almost always powerless.

This presentation of an essentially absent God who may or may not exist is strikingly portrayed in *The Brothers Karamazov* in the famous chapter "The Grand Inquisitor." Just prior to the telling of this legend, we meet Mitya's two half-brothers sitting in a tavern: Alyosha is the youngest and seemingly will become a monk; with him is his older brother Ivan, who most certainly will not. Their conversation quickly turns to "the universal questions": Does life have purpose? What of love? Does one have responsibilities for one's brother? Where does suffering come from? And the greatest question, which seems to contain all of the above: is there a God?[25]

Alyosha is eager for this brotherly encounter, for he heard Ivan declare recently in response to their father's questioning that there is no God. Now, when pressed by his younger brother in the tavern, Ivan expands on his atheism. He quotes an eighteenth-century French philosopher (whom readers will instantly recognize as Voltaire) that God would have to be in-vented if He did not exist. It is noteworthy that Dostoevsky has Ivan speak these words in both Russian and French. He often resorts to French quotations (especially in *Demons*) to indicate that the speaker has lost his (Russian) way and is therefore profoundly lost. In the depths of this tav-ern, Ivan now confesses that it makes no difference to him whether God created mankind or man created God.

Ivan goes so far as to declare his "acceptance" of God.[26] The key ques-tion though, is this: what kind of God will Ivan accept? We soon find our answer as he begins to recite a poem to Alyosha, one that he has memorized word for word. This leads into "The Grand Inquisitor," which concerns the return to earth of Christ in sixteenth-century Seville.[27] It is the time of the Spanish Inquisition, when the Roman Catholic Church is burning heretics at the stake and the horrors of a Catholic hell on earth are being realized. In the midst of this madness, Christ suddenly appears: "He passes silently among them with a quiet smile of infinite compassion. The sun of love shines in his heart, rays of Light, Enlightenment, and Power stream from his eyes."[28] He is arrested as soon as the Grand Inquisitor becomes aware of His presence in Seville. Most of the legend then unfolds in the prison cell where Christ has been placed pending His execution the following day.

The Grand Inquisitor enters the darkness of this cell and begins to de-nounce Christ for having misled humankind. The specifics of these charges do not concern us at the moment. At this point, what is striking is Christ's response at the end of the Inquisitor's tirade, a response made in the knowl-edge that He will again be executed the following day. He approaches the Inquisitor and silently kisses him on the lips. The Inquisitor is taken aback, but then utters to his prisoner, "Go and do not come again. . . . Do not come at all. . . . Never, never, never!"[29]

So Christ leaves, in a manner that has been fiercely debated over the decades. Does Christ leave triumphant (for He is not executed, but simply departs) or vanquished (for He is never heard from again)? The key for me is that it is Ivan who recounts this legend, for he has already rejected God, or at least is ambivalent as to His existence. Whatever else may be un-known, Ivan is certain that God is powerless in the world. In making this conclusion, I place considerable weight on a reading of this text through Ivan's eyes. Through that portal, we recognize how both Christ and the Grand Inquisitor, who has no belief whatsoever in immortality,[30] are Ivan's creations in this poem and are made in his image. The Christ presented by Dostoevsky through Ivan's eyes is in many ways a thoroughly humanized Christ; He is able to disappear into the crowd. He is not heard from again, and as we read this passage we cannot help but recall a similarly Western portrayal of a humanized Christ in Holbein's painting.

It is as if the entire Western tradition and all progressive thinking have brought Dostoevsky's readers to this point, at least as Dostoevsky understands it. Perhaps there is a God, perhaps there is not, but it really does not matter. Either way, Russian moderns of the mid-nineteenth century were on their own.

It is in this sense that Dostoevsky deemed all moderns to be orphans, as he powerfully declares in Versilov's confession to Arkady in *The Adolescent*. Versilov, we recall, spends the vast majority of the novel refusing to acknowledge that Arkady is his son and in need of a father's love. At one point near the end of the novel, Versilov describes a time he visited the Dresden art gallery, where he came upon Claude Lorrain's *Acis and Galatea*. Lorrain, one of France's great landscape painters, depicted the mythic love of Acis and Galatea against an idyllic setting of gently sloping mountains, coastal forests, and a calm, expansive sea. A mood of deep serenity pervades this painting, which Dostoevsky had himself gazed upon during his visits to Dresden. It is widely thought that in this painting Lorrain was capturing the first great day of European civilization; yet Versilov tells Arkady that he saw it rather as a depiction of Europe's *last* day. We have here a European death knell, not a wondrous birthing.[31]

Why is this so? Versilov, who for much of the novel has struggled to believe in anything beyond his own whims, contends that Europe took its first "executive step" toward its destruction, its "last day," when it proclaimed atheism—a belief that continues to cast a powerful spell on Versilov. Arkady, who is spellbound by Versilov's telling, asks what this all means. Versilov responds, "I imagine to myself, my dear, . . . that the battle is over and the fighting has subsided. After the curses, the mudslinging and the whistling, a calm has come, and people are left *alone*, as they wished: the great former idea has left them; the great source of strength that had nourished and warmed them till then is departing, like that majestic, inviting sun in Claude Lorrain's painting, but it already seemed like the last day of mankind. And people suddenly realized that they remained quite alone, and at once felt a great orphancy."[32]

Liza Knapp has powerfully linked the departing sun in this vignette with Versilov's recognition that such a world will ultimately and inescapably be given up to death, for in Dostoevsky's telling, all we have without God is a universe ruled by inertia. In a universe governed by Newton's laws of thermodynamics, there is no escaping the scientific certainty that the sun that sets today (as captured by Lorrain) will one day cease to exist. As will all life. As will all hope.[33]

So it is that moderns are left on their own, for just as the father, Fyodor Karamazov, has been killed off by one (or perhaps all?) of his sons, so might that murder in Dostoevsky's last novel act as a metaphor for a larger killing off in which all moderns have participated. How, then, are we to respond to the willful rejection of this "great former idea"? Versilov, following the quotation just cited, hopes that an era of profound and mutual love will follow. But as Versilov's literary creator, Dostoevsky will have none of it.

Without Horizon

Nietzsche writes in *The Gay Science* that modernity's elimination of the divine has wiped away the horizon. With the loss of the eternal, with the final setting of the sun in Lorrain's painting as recounted by Versilov, our gaze is forced to shift to this place, to now. When we have lost any meaningful belief in that which we cannot see, we are compelled more than ever to focus on what we *can* see. We end up assuming that all that we have is right here, and right now. Eventually our ethical gaze will be similarly constrained.

Dostoevsky, writing decades earlier, seems to have anticipated Nietzsche. For example, at one point in *The Brothers Karamazov* the father, Fyodor, muses that most people today have become unbelievers out of carelessness and assorted other pursuits that are deemed more important. Regarding the latter, he says, "we're too beset by business," especially as our days have only twenty-four hours. Soon after, Fyodor goes even further when he suggests that all deists should be done away with, for they hold up progress.[34]

Arkady, the protagonist and narrator in *The Adolescent*, is obsessed with material progress. He wants to become extraordinarily wealthy, and to achieve that end he wants power. In order to obtain power he wants to be left alone, even as, ironically, he longs to know Versilov as true father and to be known by Versilov as true son. In this one moment we sense Dostoevsky's ability to work at several layers simultaneously. Arkady realizes that his future earthly success depends on having the kind of individual freedom that comes only from money and power.[35] His companion Lambert reinforces this point for Arkady, who at the time is still seeking a father's love. Arkady concludes that "if Lambert is right about anything, it's that nowadays all this foolishness is simply not required, and that the main thing in our age is the man himself, and then his money."[36]

The Idiot is no less fixated on Western notions of progress, starting with the novel's very first scene, which takes place on the train from Warsaw to St. Petersburg. On this journey the prince encounters several Russians, including Lukyan Timofeevich Lebedev, who will soon equate the spread of the railroad network with the biblically anticipated apocalypse. Railroads are part of the great march of progress; they are also symbols of a world that has gone mad on money, and both are linked to the Europeanization, or modernization, of Russia.[37]

There is a thread here that is consistently visible in the fabric of Dostoevsky's written work, one whose origins go back at least to his published reflections on his first European journey. As noted earlier, Dostoevsky warned his readers about ominous trends in *Winter Notes on Summer Impressions*. London especially—that great symbol of the West and progress— was a city of madness:

> A city bustling day and night, as immense as the sea; the screeching and howling of machines; the railroads built over the houses (and soon under the houses); that boldness of enterprise; that seeming disorder which in essence is bourgeois order in the highest degree; that polluted Thames; that air saturated with coal dust; those magnificent public gardens and parks; those dreadful sections of the city like Whitechapel with its half-naked, savage, and hungry population. A city with its millions and its worldwide trade, the Crystal Palace, the International Exposition. . . . You look at these hundreds of thousands, these millions of people humbly streaming here from all over the face of the earth . . . and you feel that here something final has been accomplished, accomplished and brought to an end.[38]

And what *was* that end? Dostoevsky believed that the inescapable end was the worship of Baal, a reference to the Old Testament Canaanite god that sought in vain to do battle with the One True Hebrew God. Joseph Frank suggests that this linkage of London's pantheon of progress with the "false god of the flesh" allowed Dostoevsky to paint a picture of the city's enthrallment to "modern materialism" in colors even darker than Dickens had dared to use. For Frank, "the Crystal Palace thus became for Dostoevsky an image of the unholy spirit of modernity that brooded malevolently over London, and in his imagination this spirit takes on the form of the monstrous Beast whose coming was prophesied in the Apocalypse."[39] In this one example we can see how the physical and metaphysical—the Crystal Palace and Baal—intersect in Dostoevsky's world. To deny one would leave us at the pitiless mercy of the other. That, at least, is his succinct conclusion in March 1876, when he writes that there is everywhere in Europe "a passionate desire to live and a loss of a higher purpose for living."[40]

Ends over Means

A materialist modern worldview will always privilege ends over means. Knapp concludes that this must be so because the universe of the husband in "The Meek One" is governed solely by inertia, whereby the ultimate act is death.[41] In such a world, all that matters is the degree to which "he" will be able to impose his will on "her." In the same way, it is no accident for Dostoevsky that ten thousand people could be dying from the effects of coal dust in England, and all the while a fortunate and wealthy few enjoy their afternoon promenade in a London park. The first part is tied directly and essentially to the second.

Dostoevsky repeatedly asserted throughout his writings that all ends are possible once the divine is removed from the picture. In his novels, almost all Europeanized progressives do not hesitate to proceed accordingly once they have jettisoned their metaphysical foundations. Raskolnikov, for example, in *Crime and Punishment*, is initially obsessed with the notion that rights matter above all else, including the right to cast others aside or even kill them if such acts would advance a good cause. If leaders in the West, such as Napoleon for supreme example, are lionized for blazing their own trail, why can the same not apply to Raskolnikov? If Napoleon can authorize the killing of a few in order to make the world a better place for others, why can Raskolnikov not do the same? Would Napoleon not have had a similar impulse if he had been a common Russian instead of the ruler of France? If there is any danger in this novel, it is that Raskolnikov's brutal murders may loom so large that they obscure relatively similar undertakings by almost every other character. For this two-time ax murderer is not alone in the modern belief that ends justify means: Svidrigailov is content to abandon his wife for a new love; Luzhin is prepared to marry Dunya (Raskolnikov's sister) as a measure of his own greatness; and Dunya is prepared to enter into a loveless marriage if it will help her finance her brother's education.

All of this is really a reflection of "The Meek One."[42] Semyon Zakharovich Marmeladov accepts that his daughter needs to sell herself as a prostitute, for he is unprepared to take responsibility for his family's well-being. Luzhin reflects, "Science says: Love yourself before all, because everything in the world is based on self-interest. . . . It follows that by acquiring solely and exclusively for myself, I am thereby precisely acquiring for everyone, as it were."[43] Or not, one imagines, but either way our primary goal needs to be progress, and by whatever means necessary. As Rowan Williams sees it, the removal of God from the equation, in Dostoevsky's reckoning, is not the same as removing one particular item from a long list. Rather, it has the effect of throwing off the last constraint against violence, for "we are no longer able to see violence against others as somehow blasphemous, an offense against an eternal order."[44] Indeed, violence becomes but one more means of suasion available to moderns, and if they know what is best for them they will learn how to use it to their advantage.

Orphans Struggle with the Ethical

To risk understatement, Dostoevsky was clearly troubled by modernity because it left moderns orphaned and obsessed with what is material. Once the physical world has been deemed a physical thing to be manipulated, it is a rather straightforward next step to regard those who people it in a similar manner. This posed enormous problems for those who sought out the ethical life within the modernist worldview.

Life in Fragments

We touched on this perspective in chapter 1, so it is perhaps enough here to show how Dostoevsky compellingly presents the modern person as profoundly fragmented. The name Raskolnikov has the term *raskol'* at its root. This term is most commonly associated with the formal division of the Russian Orthodox Church in the second half of the seventeenth century that produced the Old Believers, but it can also refer more generically to a division. This does not seem to be coincidental, for Raskolnikov is clearly torn between an old morality (not to kill) and his new idea (ends justify means, and murder can sometimes be justified). Dostoevsky reminds us repeatedly that Raskolnikov has only fragmented thoughts and that his life seems out of control. In a sense, his desire to be left alone after the murder reflects his strong sense of isolation.[45] It is not that his crime drives him to a life of isolated individualism, writes Vyacheslav Ivanov in his telling study on Dostoevsky and the tragic life. Rather, Raskolnikov's willful "incarceration within himself" finds final expression in his murderous crime. The two are connected in sequence, but not in the way that most readers would imagine. The individual fragmentation comes first; only then is his double murder possible.[46]

Similarly, regarding "The Meek One," Robert Jackson focuses on the husband's profound inability to make sense of anything in his universe. It has simply become too incoherent for him, too fragmented, and the loss of a sense of his moral universe follows quickly. Dostoevsky's decision to compose this entire short story as an "interior monologue" points to the utter isolation and individual fragmentation with which the husband speaks. He is literally on his own and talking only to himself.[47]

The narrator of *Demons* struggles to understand why Europeanized Russians with the best of intentions have been so willingly deceived by young revolutionaries. He blames the youthful instigators for their own violence, but he is no less troubled by their intellectual parents, the liberals of the previous generation. We are told that their liberalism had more to do with inattention than with malice. They deemed their actions to be merely frivolous, not realizing that they had murderous consequences. Lacking an understanding of cause and effect, they regarded everything as the result of mere chance. In the narrator's words, "a certain disorderliness of mind became fashionable." He later laments that people long ago lost the thread as all continuities were hidden from view.[48]

Arkady, in *The Adolescent*, repeatedly describes his own state as highly fragmented. This is mirrored in his strong sense of isolation from others. At one point early on he writes, "My soul was very troubled, and there was nothing whole in it; but some sensations stood out definitely, though no one of them drew me fully to itself, owing to their abundance."[49] His biological father, Versilov, fares no better; we are told that all of Russia's influential society turned away from him. His legitimate children distance themselves and live as if on their own. Even his conversations with Arkady, who has so desperately sought to end his own isolation through a union with his birth father, reflect a broader fragmentation. Arkady writes, "All my conversations with [Versilov] always bore some sort of ambiguity in them."[50] The essence of the ambiguous conversation, of course, is that its overall intent remains unclear. We may understand the pieces, but we cannot make sense of the whole.

In *Diary of a Writer*, Dostoevsky often speaks directly to his readers on this theme as he bemoans modernity's tendency to mark everything as transitory and unstable. In March 1876, in perhaps his most impassioned lamentation on this failing, he writes,

> I keep thinking that we have begun the epoch of universal "dissociation." All are disassociating themselves, isolating themselves from everyone else, everyone wants to invent something of his own, something new and unheard of. . . . Granted, a great many people don't undertake anything and never will, yet they still have torn themselves away and stand apart, looking at the torn place and waiting idly for something to happen. Everyone in Russia is waiting for something to happen. Meanwhile, there is scarcely anything about which we can agree morally; everything has been or is being broken up, not even into clusters but into single fragments.[51]

One can argue that all of Dostoevsky's novels are obsessed with the crisis of fragmentation, a crisis that in his telling clearly has Western origins and threatens to overwhelm Russia. We see it in "Bobok," his short story about a man who falls asleep in a graveyard and wakes up hearing the isolated dead talking in their coffins, each one of them utterly alone.[52] We see the same in Dostoevsky's often-overlooked opening to *The Brothers Karamazov*. Here the author speaks bewilderingly, albeit tenderly, about the great senselessness of the present time, when there are so many particulars. It is a time in which many find themselves blown about by every trend. But there is almost no sense of the whole, "no general sense in the general senselessness."[53]

Ethics Means Little without Good and Evil

The young Nikolai Vsevolodovich Stavrogin undertakes several actions early on in *Demons* that are deemed mad, if not outright outrageous, by the cultured—as in Europeanized—society all around him. In one of these, Stavrogin finds himself at wit's end with an elderly and distinguished member of society, Pavel Pavlovich Gaganov, who tends to respond to every outrage by declaring, "No, sir, they won't lead me around by the nose!" In one scene, having heard that utterance one time too many, Stavrogin does just that, seizing the elderly gentlemen by the nose and leading him forcibly around in the midst of an especially prestigious gathering. In the scene immediately following, another aged member of elite society, Ivan Osipovich, demands an explanation from Stavrogin for his treatment of Pavel Pavlovich. Ivan Osipovich is hard of hearing, so Stavrogin invites him to lean forward. He does, and Stavrogin promptly bites him on the ear and holds his jaw clenched for a full minute.[54]

Stavrogin conducts a barely concealed affair with the wife of one of his closest acquaintances, without regret. He impregnates the wife of another acquaintance. And once, while inebriated, he proposes marriage to a witless and tragic woman for no other reason than he is dared to do so.[55]

Does Dostoevsky want us to see any of these actions as ethical? Are all of them? Actually, Stavrogin doubts that any of these are matters of ethical importance, at least at the start of the novel. In fact, he doubts whether morality exists beyond mere and meaningless aesthetics and past practices, all of which deserve to be held up to modern scrutiny. As a self-proclaimed atheist,[56] he has come to accept that he alone trumps what was once deemed sacrosanct. His new god is reason, it is science, and neither reason nor science can separate good from evil. This may be a harsh reality, but in Dostoevsky's telling it is one that will sweep over all of Russia if it abandons Orthodoxy.[57] In this sense, Stavrogin is the heir to the more moderate liberals of the so-called 1840s generation in Russia: liberals who would have included the suddenly offended Pavel Pavlovich (with the bruised nose) and Ivan Osipovich (with the tooth-marked ear). In the circumstances, it is not surprising that the offending Stavrogin has lived so long in Europe by the time the novel opens — so removed from his Russian homeland that he barely recalls his native language. That, for Dostoevsky, means something great indeed.

So it is that ethics is dispatched in Dostoevsky's portrayal of Stavrogin. No wonder, then, that Stavrogin does not distinguish between sublime and base beauty.[58] Nor does he discriminate good from bad. All of this follows from his inability to distinguish morally between his seduction of a minor (in a chapter that censors forbade Dostoevsky to publish in the initial run of *Demons*), his unconcealed affair with a colleague's wife, and his deliberate engagement and subsequent marriage to a physically and mentally fragile woman. After all, in the words of one young student who arrives at one of the youthful gatherings, "There's no such thing as moral or immoral!"[59]

Nor is he alone in this novel. We see no less in Alexei Nilych Kirillov (his patronymic itself suggests that he comes "from nothing"), who confesses complete indifference to almost everything, including life itself. For if nothing is absolutely bad, then all must be good, or one day may be so, including if someone dies of hunger, or offends a young girl, or kills someone else because he offended someone. For Kirillov these things are all eerily good, if such a thing as goodness even exists. His typical response to anything asked of him is, "It makes no difference."[60]

In *Notes from Underground*, the prostitute Liza asks the protagonist if his life is on a good path. It is impossible for this thoroughly modern antihero to answer, for he has lost the ability to distinguish good from bad.[61] Long ago he confessed that he viewed civilization as capable only of cultivating sensations that are neither good nor bad. No wonder he spends much of the novel plotting over what we might consider trivialities, including the "re-bumping" of a gentleman of superior social standing who accidentally brushed against him on Nevsky Prospect one day. (Knapp views this incident as the embodiment of social Darwinist survival of the fittest.[62]) He also cannot ethically distinguish between his desire for tea and the wish that peace come to the whole world. If anything, he attributes more importance to the former. Jackson concludes that the real tragedy for Dostoevsky's Underground Man is not his own pathetic life, but rather "the universal tragedy of man's alienation in a blind meaningless universe. The universe is his prison, his underground."[63]

The same indifference to good and evil lurks on almost every page of *Crime and Punishment*. This indifference is what allows Raskolnikov to murder and Luzhin and his comrades to disregard convention by favoring civil ceremonies over church marriages and multiple lovers over monogamous unions. One character muses that principles are the last thing one needs in a thoroughly modern city such as St. Petersburg.[64]

In *The Adolescent* Dostoevsky advances the same position, albeit in a different setting. Versilov confesses that he simply cannot determine whether the measurement of his life is good or bad. Arkady, too, concludes that there are no absolute principles, only individual cases. Seen in this light, it is possible that biting an ear, or killing someone, is wrong in one particular instance but not absolutely so for all time. That being the case, Arkady suggests, we have really not said very much.[65] Furthermore, a comrade named Kraft realizes that there are no fixed moral ideas in his time; there is only mediocrity.[66]

Let us pause briefly with Ivan Karamazov, whose Grand Inquisitor has already drawn our attention. We have noted Ivan's agonizingly reasoned indifference to God's existence. For Dostoevsky, this is a key indicator of moral indifference. In *The Brothers Karamazov*, it is Ivan who first links moral indifference to the absence of the divine, though Dostoevsky returns to this theme several times in the course of the novel. We see this connection made in one of the earlier chapters where Ivan is deep in conversation with his brothers and father, all of whom have gone to the local monastery in the hope of resolving a family dispute over inheritance. At one crucial moment in their lively discussion, they ponder where love for those around us comes from. Is it present in liberalism or in its slightly more radical face, socialism? However comforting a positive response might have been for those who first read *The Brothers Karamazov*, Dostoevsky will have none of it. Instead, Ivan repeats what he had declared several days earlier: that love for humankind is irrational, something that emerges out of the mistaken belief in immortality. Dostoevsky, through the novel's narrator, continues, "Ivan Fyodorovich added parenthetically that that is what all natural law consists of, so that were mankind's belief in its immortality to be destroyed, not only love but also any living power to continue the life of the world would at once dry up in it. Not only that, but then nothing would be immoral any longer, everything would be permitted, even anthropophagy."[67]

These words are, of course, a damning indictment of those who refuse to accept the existence of any being beyond this world. Dostoevsky presents us with at least one individual, Rakitin, who calls for a humanly constructed morality in the absence of immortality. This sardonic seminarian, who cynically befriends Alyosha, scoffs at Ivan's charge that morality and immortality are linked. The seminarian continues, "[Ivan's] whole theory is squalid. Mankind will find strength in itself to live for virtue, even without believing in immortality of the soul! Find it in the love of liberty, equality, fraternity"[68]—an allusion to the ideals and agenda of the French Revolution. Thus Rakitin embodies a voice of progress in *The Brothers Karamazov*, as does the lackey son Smerdyakov, who confesses that Russia will always be an inferior country to great and progressive France. At one point, Smerdyakov goes so far as to bemoan Napoleon's failed attempt to defeat the Russian Empire in 1812, which for him would have meant the victory of an "intelligent" nation over a "stupid" one.[69] It is clear from the depictions and fates of both Rakitin and Smerdyakov that neither spoke for Dostoevsky's own heart. In fact Smerdyakov comes as close as anyone to the embodiment of pure evil in this great novel.

Dostoevsky recalls Ivan's linking of morality and immortality at least five more times in the novel. As brother Mitya begins his own conversion, he recalls Ivan's words.[70] Smerdyakov twice taunts Ivan directly with these words as justification for his own actions.[71] The devil—yes, the devil, or at least Ivan's version of it, we are never quite certain—reminds Ivan of these words when they meet in Ivan's room.[72] Finally, the prosecutor invokes Ivan's dictum, without proper attribution, as he struggles to explain the horrific crimes that have been committed in the Russia of his day. In all these ways and more, Dostoevsky suggests that a thoroughly modern world is one in which distinctions between good and evil have given way to a modern indifference toward, and thoughtless acceptance of, both. Are good and evil not mere prejudice, and the same in the end?

The Need for Distractions

Harvie Ferguson, in his masterful study *Melancholy and the Critique of Modernity*,[73] has probed Søren Kierkegaard's tendency toward the melancholic. He quotes the great Danish religious philosopher: "From a child I was under the sway of a prodigious melancholy, the depth of which finds its only adequate measure in the equally prodigious dexterity I possessed of hiding it under an apparent gaiety and *joie de vivre*. So far back as I can barely remember, my own joy was that nobody could discover how unhappy I felt."[74]

Ferguson suggests that Kierkegaard's melancholy was a reasonable response to the condition of modernity; it was a means by which he could respond to a universe he deemed meaningless. Thus, if moderns suddenly find themselves alone, if the horizon has suddenly been wiped away by us or our forebears, it is not surprising that some will find that realization unbearable. Some will even enter a time of deep despondency and self-absorption, even if it is ultimately fruitless.[75] That may not surprise us. What might surprise is that an influential seventeenth-century work on melancholy by Robert Burton recommended that those afflicted with melancholy mask its symptoms through a life of distraction.[76] Moderns needed to be distracted. Perhaps this was because some realized that, in the end, it made no difference what they did, ethically or otherwise. Perhaps Pascal was right when he declared that boredom was a key characteristic of modernity.

I have taken the time to introduce Burton, Pascal, and Kierkegaard through Ferguson's insightful analysis because a similar reading can apply to Dostoevsky. Many of his characters struggle with the boredom associated with melancholy, and many of these are on the lookout for distractions. Any form of entertainment will do, it seems. Anything that is new is worth trying, even if doing so drives ethical considerations deeper under the surface. Let us consider all of this more closely.

Too Bored for the Ethical Life

Boredom is a constant motif in Dostoevsky's portrayal of Europeanized Russians. It is more a permanent state of mind than a passing irritation. It afflicts those who are well satisfied materially and yet babble endlessly in order to fill the void they suddenly find in their lives. In a direct reference to the modernity associated with London's Crystal Palace, the Underground Man muses, "Of course, there's no guaranteeing (this is me speaking now) that it won't, for example, be terribly boring then (because what is there to do if everything's calculated according to some little table?), but, on the other hand, it will all be extremely reasonable. Of course, what inventions can boredom not lead to? Golden pins also get stuck in from boredom, but all that would be nothing."[77]

Writing more directly around this same time in *Winter Notes*, Dostoevsky goes further when he ponders why so many Russians go to Europe for restoration after they have found themselves somehow worn out by their own country. Paradoxically, those who were doing poorly before they left end up worse for the effort, for they find nothing in their wanderings abroad that can dispel "their meaningless melancholy and weariness." Thus the author of this "memoir"—is it Dostoevsky speaking directly to his readers?—finds himself bored on the train to Europe and in search of any distraction.[78] No wonder the prince in *The Idiot* links the appeal many Russians find in Western-style atheism with boredom as much as with satiety.[79]

Years later, in *The Brothers Karamazov*, we meet two not-so-minor characters (no character in Dostoevsky's writings is ever truly minor). Madame Khokhlakov and her daughter Lise are both bored. The mother in particular takes offense at a new newspaper, aptly called *Rumours*, that implies that many high-society women are bored. Moments later her daughter tells Alyosha that much of life is boring. She is not comforted when Alyosha replies that her prosperous lifestyle is the cause, and so is her refusal to reflect on things "that are holy."[80]

When Any Diversion Will Do

In Dostoevsky's world, those who are bored are too busy seeking diversions to care much about the ethical life. And these diversions—akin to what John Horton has provocatively called "transgressions"[81]—come in all shapes and sizes, especially now that the line between good and evil has long ceased to be relevant. How can it be otherwise when a destructive act, for instance, can be deemed equivalent to a religious pilgrimage? Who is to say it is not? Thus Fyodor Pavlovich Karamazov will not part with his funds; he will not give even a portion of them over to his own sons because he needs them all to indulge in wickedness. All may denounce him for it, but he is cynically aware that all seek similar gratification. No wonder he intends to live long and to spend all he has on earthly pleasures. Smerdyakov, his bastard son, seeks no less, equating true enlightenment with material possessions: "good clothes, clean shirt fronts, and polished boots."[82] We are told that he may well lose his boredom by whatever means are at his disposal: "perhaps suddenly, having stored up his impressions over many years, he will drop everything and wander off to Jerusalem to save his soul, or perhaps he will suddenly burn down his native village, or perhaps he will do both."[83]

Dostoevsky observed directly in the early 1860s that Europeans were passionate about living in the present, but without purpose. Ironically, most also lived in perpetual search of distractions, none of which seemed to satisfy.[84] In "Bobok," the extraordinary account of the departed who converse from the confines of their graves, all of those specters whose voices we hear wish they had lived just a bit longer, with pleasure foremost. Even now, as consciousness fades, they seek nothing more than one more grand amusement.[85] It is for good reason that Konstantin Mochulsky calls this short story "the most terrible of Dostoevsky's metaphysical visions." (How terrible does it have to be, one wonders, to achieve this notoriety in Dostoevsky's vast canon?) This is so because it makes plain that "the putrefaction of souls is more horrible than the corruption of bodies."[86] And putrefaction it is, for—as Leatherbarrow concludes in his study of the demonic in Dostoevsky's fiction—souls deprived of an afterlife have literally nothing left save for debauchery, gambling, and the all-inclusive abandonment of moral restraint.[87]

Empty talk and meaningless chatter are two other important diversions from boredom. Arkady, our by now somewhat familiar adolescent, is keenly aware that while he may manage to speak often with his biological father Versilov, it will never be about essential matters. Is it any wonder that Arkady concludes that the modern condition is one of idleness and ignorance?[88] Stepan Trofimovich Verkhovensky, the aging liberal of the 1840s generation in *Demons*, gained his fame from earlier researches about, it seems, nothing much. In a passage that is characteristic of Dostoevsky's extraordinarily subtle and humorous prose, we read a synopsis of Stepan Trofimovich's greatest work, one that is so convoluted in style and metaphoric content that it defies easy summary here.[89] Nor does it matter, for Dostoevsky found the essence of Russian liberalism to be its emptiness.

The narrator of *Demons*, who serves as a companion to Stepan Trofimo-vich, notes the following to capture a world built on nothing: "For a while there was talk of us around town that our circle was a hotbed of freethink-ing, depravity, and godlessness; and this rumor has always persisted. Yet what we had was only the most innocent, nice, perfectly Russian, jolly lib-eral chatter. 'Higher liberalism' and the 'higher liberal'—that is, a liberal without any aim—are possible only in Russia."[90]

If talk of nothing at all was an essential entry point into a life of di-versions, the same could be said about assorted sexual pleasures, even if—especially if—they involved crossing social boundaries. This is most notoriously captured in two characters of Dostoevsky's creation. The in-volvement of one of them in a single disturbing incident in *Demons* was initially banned by censors when the novel was released; the other's sordid activities were not banned from the public eye.

The tale that was not banned involved Svidrigailov, a predator of sorts in *Crime and Punishment*, whom we have already met in these pages. He de-clares to Raskolnikov that he is existentially bored; solely for that reason, he is happy to hear anything new. He overhears Raskolnikov confess to Sonya that he has murdered two people with an ax. Svidrigailov tells this anguished ax murderer that he is drawn to depravity, which is a constant in his life, "something that abides in the blood like a perpetually burning coal, eternally inflaming, which for a long time, even with age, one may not extinguish easily."[91] He admits that each person needs to seek his or her own form of sexual depravity; he then describes how he has recently become engaged to a vulnerable sixteen-year-old whose family has abso-lutely no financial means left. Here again, in Dostoevsky's challenge to the modernity of his time and place, the ends justify the means. Svidrigailov has set aside this adolescent for his own amusement; he knows that when he is bored with her, he will easily find another.[92]

The other notorious character is Nikolai Stavrogin, whose biting of ears and pulling of noses has already drawn our attention. In a chapter from *Demons* that was initially banned from publication for its searing de-tail, Stavrogin tells his confessor, Bishop Tikhon, that he was at one point so bored with his life that he wanted to kill himself "from the disease of indifference."[93] He sought a diversion, evil or not, as long as it cured him of boredom. He found his "cure" in a fourteen-year-old adolescent, whom he first subjected to unfair punishment from her mother after Stavrogin's unfounded accusation of theft. He then sexually assaulted her, though he was bored in the act—bored! Stavrogin then silently monitored her profoundly tormented life until she hanged herself in despair.[94]

Even to type this out, even to read it, is to be filled with a certain fixed revulsion. This is precisely the sinister place where Dostoevsky takes his readers as he shows how moderns risk becoming so distracted that they will fail to notice their own profound moral impoverishment. For if everything is morally up for grabs, how will we ever be able to decide with certainty what is immoral?

Three other distractions must be noted, because for Dostoevsky, they are at the core of the distracted modern life. The first involves self-loathing, as happens when Alyosha leaves Lise after suggesting to her that her boredom may be the result of an excessively prosperous life: "Lise . . . unlocked the door at once, opened it a little, put her finger into the chink, and, slamming the door, crushed it with all her might. Ten seconds later, having released her hand, she went quietly and slowly to her chair, sat straight up in it, and began looking intently at her blackened finger and the blood oozing from under the nail."[95]

The second diversion occurs through another person's tragedy. This is tragedy as voyeuristic entertainment, and it was not unknown to Dostoevsky. One day, in *Demons*, a group of young radicals, liberals, and society-types are traveling to St. Petersburg when they are told that someone has just committed suicide in a nearby hotel room. Stavrogin is among them, as is Pyotr Stepanovich, the son of Stepan Trofimovich, the 1840s liberal. They all quickly decide to take a look. They enter the room where a nineteen-year-old male has just shot himself and learn that he did so because he had madly wasted precious funds that his near-destitute family had entrusted to him. We are told that his body had already stiffened; "His white face looked as if it was made of marble." Dostoevsky, through the novel's narrator, observes, "Generally, in every misfortune of one's neighbor there is always something that gladdens the outsider's eye—and that no matter who you are."[96] We are told that the group soon left the hotel room at the police chief's bidding, but even that brief observation left them merry and laughter-filled for the remainder of the day.

The third and final diversion that Dostoevsky utilizes is that of taunting and its close relation, direct violence toward other people or other creatures. We see examples of both in *The Adolescent*. On one occasion, when he is still a child, Arkady joins a friend of sorts named Lambert (one doubts that the French appellation is accidental). One day, Lambert gets his hands on a double-barreled shotgun; later, while walking out of the town, he purchases a canary. He then lets the bird out of its cage, from which it can barely fly, but even then he has difficulty shooting it. So they tie the bird to a branch, and shoot again, this time with the rifle mere centimeters from the bird. Later that day, after they have had a bit too much to drink, Arkady and Lambert come upon a woman who is distinctly vulnerable. They humiliate her by taking away her dress, and they strike her when she protests.[97]

Later in the novel, Arkady often finds himself drawn to taunting women who promenade on the grand boulevards of St. Petersburg. In Arkady's "memoir,"

> I went to the boulevard, and here's what trick he taught me: we went around the boulevards together, and later on, the moment we spotted a woman of a decent sort walking along, but so that there was no public close by, we'd immediately start pestering her. Without saying a word to her, we'd place ourselves, he on one side, I on the other, and with the most calm air, as if not noticing her at all, would begin a most indecent conversation between ourselves. We called things by their real names with a most unperturbed air, as if it was quite proper, and went into such details, explaining various vile and swinish things, as the dirtiest imagination of the dirtiest debaucher could not have thought up.[98]

Thus is Arkady's search for a father interrupted by a range of diversions that may or may not be ethically acceptable. Does it really matter for this particular orphan-of-sorts?

The Modern Obsession with the New

It cannot surprise us by now that Dostoevsky's moderns are obsessed with the new. Svidrigailov, Fyodor Karamazov, his son Mitya, and a host of others are constantly seeking, and finding, new sexual conquests. But this obsession is not limited to sexual trysts—Mitya is enamored by every new thing.[99]

Stavrogin's circle is also obsessed with new ideas: "They got every-thing out of books, and even at the first rumor from our progressive corners in the capital were prepared to throw anything whatsoever out the window, provided they were advised to throw it out."[100] They embrace atheism likewise, for it is new, fashionable, and deemed progressive. In-deed, the mere notion of "progressiveness" leaves one favorably disposed to whatever comes next. On one level, *Crime and Punishment* can be under-stood as a prolonged reflection on the new. This includes the recent immi-grants who are making their way in St. Petersburg, for whom everything encountered is new. It is no coincidence here that Svidrigailov is keeping a thirteen-year-old girl and her mother in an apartment in the capital for some possible future enjoyment (this is distinct from the vulnerable sixteen-year-old to whom he is currently "engaged"). The impoverished mother and daughter have recently arrived in the imperial city and have nowhere else to turn, and they all know it.[101]

Raskolnikov, for his part, is prepared to murder the old pawnbroker on the principle of newness, for it is surely the right of elites in an other-wise absurd world to assert their will in this new age. By the same reason-ing, he suggests that Newton would have had the right to kill even a hun-dred people as long as it advanced his new discoveries. He suggests that all recent lawgivers, up to and including Napoleon, have really been criminals when judged by the old laws. They stood out because they were not afraid to discard the old, even the sacred, in favor of the new.[102] Luzhin, the lawyer who seeks Dunya's hand in marriage as a trophy, also favors new ideas over old ones, and the present over the past, even as Svidrigailov is inter-ested in any new principles that have come to Raskolnikov.[103]

In this way, Dostoevsky links newness to the distracted life. Moderns depend on distractions to keep their minds off certain realities, such as their orphaned state. Perhaps it is the Grand Inquisitor who knows this best. In the midst of his denunciation, he tells Christ that people want to be "happy" more than they want their freedom; they want to have their physical needs met, and that is what he is prepared to give them: "Then we shall give them quiet, humble happiness, the happiness of feeble creatures, such as they were created."[104] Though they will need to sacrifice their free-dom to the Inquisitor, it is a freedom that most have already come to find oppressive. In its place, he says, "we will make them work, but in the hours free from labor we will arrange their lives like a children's game, with children's songs, choruses, and innocent dancing. Oh, we will allow them to sin, too; they are weak and powerless, and they will love us like children for allowing them to sin. . . . Peacefully they will die, and peacefully they will expire in your name, and beyond the grave they will find only death."[105]

No passage written by Dostoevsky better captures the degree to which the distracted life must be an entertained life as well—one in which new trumps old, and then the same the next day, when a brand-new new is required. It is a world where the divine hold over us, and our imagination, has long given way, and with it any substantive distinction between good and evil. We are left with a world where all of life's choices are contingent and all decisions are grounded in mere personal preference. Nothing has absolute sway. Even those who believe in God's existence only acknowledge a god who is finite in capability. As Stewart Sutherland suggests with respect to Ivan in his telling of the Grand Inquisitor, "the invention of a Euclidian mind" means that "one *can only* think and talk in anthropomorphic terms."[106] But if that were true, how could we live at all? This is a question that can be answered in our time. And it is one that did not stymie Dostoevsky in his own.

The Trinity of Modern Ethics: Individuals, Rights, and Violence

So far I have attempted to tease out three basic points from the Dostoevskian canon. First, his repeated reference to orphans points to his concern that modernity had left his readers profoundly isolated. Their very thinking, the way they attempted to make sense of things, was deeply fragmented. Thus, as Peter Holquist has written, life for the Underground Man is but an endless collection of disjointed stories . . . that is, until death comes.[107] Second, this orphaned state made it almost impossible for Dostoevsky's modernizing readers to make absolute sense of the whole, and as a result, the notions of "ethics" and "morality" had lost their substantive meaning. Third, Dostoevsky was well aware that such meaninglessness was too discouraging for most moderns to accept; that is why they sought a host of diversions—to be occupied with this and that so that they did not have to ponder the ethical life. If he is correct, modern societies discourage all but the most elemental pondering.

That may all be true, but did Dostoevsky maintain that the ethical life for moderns had any content that could be positively stated? If so, what was it? We turn to these questions now.

Individual (and Orphaned) Self-Assertion

Dostoevsky repeatedly creates personae who state in various ways that we, here, are individually on our own, and that henceforth it is up to us to assert our will. We see this in the husband in "The Meek One" who seizes his right to compel an adolescent to marry him. Her vulnerability excites him, for it opens the door for him to dominate her and thereby assuage his past humiliations. In that alone, the husband is no different from a list that includes Luzhin and Svidrigailov in *Crime and Punishment*, both of whom are quite prepared to assert their will against vulnerable women, and Fyodor Karamazov, the patriarch who asserts his right to do absolutely anything he wishes, whether it is hosting orgies in his marital home or spending whatever funds he has acquired, by whatever means at his disposal, in whatever way he sees fit.

Or take the Underground Man, who once felt slighted when he came upon some men in a tavern playing billiards. One of them, an officer, tried to get past the Underground Man, who had unwittingly blocked his way. As the Underground Man writes, "He took me by the shoulders and silently, without warning or explanation, moved me from where I stood to another place, and then passed by as if without noticing. I could even have forgiven him a beating, but I simply could not forgive his moving me and in the end just not noticing me."[108] There is every reason to believe that the officer was unaware of what had transpired. But the Underground Man knew. Is there any wonder he had revenge on his mind? In time, he is able to assert his own will—his right to be. The revenge is carried out on Nevsky Prospect, the city's main promenade, where the powerful regularly encounter one another. The Underground Man is not one of those, of course, but the officer is. On a street where the less powerful routinely give way to the powerful, the Underground Man one day arranges it so that he is walking directly toward the officer. But this day he does not give way. Instead, and "within three steps of my enemy, I unexpectedly decided, closed my eyes, and—we bumped solidly shoulder against shoulder! I did not yield an inch and passed by on a perfectly equal footing! He did not even look back and pretended not to notice; but he only pretended, I'm sure of that."[109]

We may not personally identify with this level of seeming pettiness, though most of Dostoevsky's readers surely would have, even as they would have defended the right of an individual to assert his own will against perceived injustice. We do have rights, as declared most directly by Evgeny Pavlovich in *The Idiot*: "'I wouldn't mind adding,' Evgeny Pavlovich went on with a smile, 'that everything I've heard from your comrades, Mr. Terentyev, and everything you've just explained, and with such unquestionable talent, boils down, in my opinion, to the theory of the triumph of rights, before all, and beyond all, and even to the exclusion of all else, and perhaps even before analyzing what makes up these rights.'"[110]

That last clause points us back to observations made earlier in this chapter: for moderns in Dostoevsky's moral universe, rights even precede any particular content to those rights, at least as he imagined them. At one point Arkady, who longs only for a father's love, is assured by Versilov that this particular son does have rights.[111] Although it is unstated, we all know that Arkady may have the right to be loved; he simply has no right to expect it.

The Right of Physical Force

Dostoevsky's moderns end up legitimating the ethical use of force in two ways. First, many acknowledge that a world based on science has little else available to it beyond the use of force, for science simply cannot define good and evil. Shatov, who is murdered in the plotline that shapes the entirety of *Demons*, puts it this way: "Reason has never been able to define evil and good, or even to separate evil from good, if only approximately; on the contrary, it has always confused them, shamefully and pitifully; and science has offered the solution of the fist."[112]

Shortly after Evgeny Pavlovich makes his declaration about the primacy of individual rights in *The Idiot*, he links rights directly to the use of force. Both are cherished traditions in western Europe. He suggests, "I merely want to observe that from this case it's possible to jump over directly to the right of force, that is, to the right of the singular fist and personal wanting, as, incidentally, has happened very often in this world. Proudhon stopped at the right of force. In the American war, many of the most progressive liberals declared themselves on the side of the plantation owners, in this sense, that Negroes are Negroes, inferior to the white race, and consequently the right of force belongs to the whites."[113]

The "case" referred to above, in which he argues for the primacy of rights, is the brutal American Civil War, which ended less than five years before Dostoevsky began this novel. Evgeny Pavlovich's suggestion that progress might justify mass killing may offend, and so may his justification of slavery, but there are voices in Dostoevsky's moral universe who claim that the use of force is the epitome of modernity.[114] We will return to this theme.

If there is a single most chilling character in *Demons*, it may not be Stavrogin, whose "confession" was banned. It is more likely Erkel, who willingly takes part in the deception and murder of Shatov. What makes Erkel so horrifying is that he is described as the most reasoned of the lot. It seems he has no feelings,[115] and that, along with his non-Russian name, clearly indicates where Dostoevsky wanted to position him.

Violence can be seductive, especially when it is equated with the exercise of justice. In *The Brothers Karamazov*, just before the tale of the Grand Inquisitor, Ivan and Alyosha are "getting acquainted" in the tavern. Ivan lays out his accusation against God and explains why he cannot believe that the divine can have any real power in a world going to hell. He recounts some of the stories he has read in the newspapers (Dostoevsky often commented in *Diary of a Writer* on what he had read in the various daily newspapers). He points to horrific accounts of torture and murder, especially those in which children were the victims.

For instance, Ivan tells of a retired general who returned to his landed estate. He was told that a peasant boy had possibly hurt the paw of one of his dogs. So the general had the boy locked up for the night, then had the hounds go after him in the morning. The boy was only eight years old. His mother was forced to watch as her son was chased down and torn to pieces. Ivan then asks his monkish brother what should be done with the estate owner. Should the retired general be shot? His youngest brother responds, "Shoot him!"[116] Both brothers know, in that moment, that Alyosha has let evil into his heart in a way that the wife in "The Meek One" had not when she put down the loaded revolver. One imagines that Dostoevsky's moderns might view shooting as an ethical response, especially if carried out by the state (as in the American Civil War). By the end of the novel, both Ivan and his half-brother Smerdyakov will justify the ethic of violence,[117] and both will have spent much time as far from Dostoevsky's heart as can be imagined.

Similarly, in *Crime and Punishment*, everything about Raskolnikov, Svidrigailov, and others suggests that violence can be justified, especially if it is to advance human civilization. How could we celebrate great leaders, such as Napoleon, if we did not acknowledge that the mighty have the right to use violence against others?[118] Raskolnikov often ponders that question. Surely the celebration of Napoleon suggests that murder is ethically acceptable if it is for a good end. And beyond Napoleon, the killing of one person or even a hundred or more is morally justified if it can be shown to lead to the betterment of others in the long run—that is, to progress. We are told in the novel that all lawgivers are criminals, for the introduction of a new law always amounts to the acceptance of something previously deemed criminal.[119]

A World of Gross Inequalities

Shigalevism is not a term that has caught on in our time. Yet it did exist as a phenomenon in Dostoevsky's after Shigalev's appearance in *Demons*, in which he is a member of Stavrogin's circle. Shigalev states, "Starting from unlimited freedom, I conclude with unlimited despotism."[120] He comes to this point through a reasoned argument and concludes that one-tenth of the world's population is to be granted "complete freedom of person" as well as "unlimited rights" over the remaining nine-tenths. Though this may seem harsh, it flows from Shigalev's desire to establish a paradise on earth while rejecting comrade Lyamshin's suggestion that the vast majority simply be killed. Shigalev favors a generations-long educational regime by which the vast majority on earth "must lose their person and turn into something like a herd, and in unlimited obedience, through a series of regenerations, attain to primeval innocence, something like primeval paradise—though, by the way, they will have to work."[121]

Put another way, Shigalev envisions a world where perhaps 10 percent or so will ethically justify a planet on which they live extraordinarily well while the vast majority cannot. And this can be accomplished if the 10 percent are able to control the life circumstances of the vast majority, by armed force if necessary, having deemed themselves part of Europe's modernizing project.

One encounters a somewhat similar ratio in "The Grand Inquisitor," in which those who are with the Inquisitor are a distinct minority. They contrive to provide the vast majority with the illusions they need in order to survive, "for their own happiness."[122] The masses need a sense of miracle, mystery, and authority, and it is fascinating that Dostoevsky did not regard this tri-unity to be in the Orthodox domain. Instead, he maintained that humans would need mysteries more than ever in a godless world. Later, the Grand Inquisitor—at least in Ivan's retelling—will denounce Christ for having failed to grasp this simple truth.

A world this unbalanced would be most easily achieved, of course, if the majority agreed to surrender their individual freedoms for material security, though they would need to know who is in charge. As the Inquisitor knows, they would happily make this trade in exchange for bread alone. Of course, the question of *why* Dostoevsky's moderns would choose to give up their freedom for slavery continues to haunt. For me, Nikolas Berdyaev's explanation in the context of Dostoevsky's canon remains compelling:

> Thus does Doestoivsky [*sic*] set out the fate of man and his freedom. . . . [Modern man] lets freedom become debased into servitude and at last kill him, because he is too intoxicated by it to see anything above himself— and if there is nothing above himself, then man does not exist. And if there is no content or object in freedom, if there is no bond between human freedom and divine freedom, then freedom does not exist either. If all things are allowable to man, then freedom becomes its own slave, and the man who is his own slave is lost.[123]

The contemporary socialist theoretician Zygmunt Bauman accounts for the modern condition differently, as did Erich Fromm more famously, but they came to the same end result. In their tellings, modern individuals are ultimately so isolated, fragmented, and insecure that they will happily sacrifice their freedom in exchange for a sense of security, even if it be through one of many subsequent enslavements: political, social, and otherwise.[124]

This point was indisputable for Dostoevsky, who saw the world that resulted as necessarily one of stark contrasts between those with and those without. He had seen this with his own eyes during his travels to London and Paris. A similar 10/90 division is found in *Crime and Punishment*, in which Raskolnikov contends that the world comprises two groups: a minority who are superhumans and a majority who are louses. The latter hardly deserve to live, or at least their lives are expendable if their deaths would allow the superior minority to flourish. That is why he refuses, until almost the end of the novel, to acknowledge that it was wrong for him to murder the pawnbroker. How could it be wrong when she was a louse and he was a progressive superhuman? He makes this declaration of legitimacy at the point in the novel where his "shadow," Svidrigailov, is trying to convince Sonya that one is permitted to do a single evil deed if it will improve the lot of a hundred good people.[125]

It seems that Dostoevsky associated modernity with ethically sanctioned inequality. He spoke most directly to this in the April 1876 issue of *Diary of a Writer*, in which he caustically responded to Vasilii G. Avseenko's criticisms of him in *The Russian Messenger*. Dostoevsky had claimed that the Russian People were the inspiration for the empire's great literary tradition; Avseenko had disagreed and bore Dostoevsky's wrath as a result.[126] In his response, Dostoevsky pointed out that Avseenko was combining two contradictory positions: on the one hand, he glorified the Russian peasant as the backbone of the empire and as the foundation on which Russia's great historical mission to the world had been founded; on the other, he confessed that the People were truly backward culturally. If they could be likened to anything, it was to bloodsuckers, kulaks, or stupid and petty tyrants.[127]

So, although moderns such as Avseenko might declare their appreciation for the common folk (who were approximately 80 percent of the empire's population), it was always in generalized and distant terms. The Avseenkos of this world loathe the great unwashed masses, mainly because they have not grasped the greatness of modern culture, which all moderns maintain can be measured in terms of individual rights and material possessions. Dostoevsky would have none of this and told his readers, "To put it briefly, [Avseenko] has prostrated himself and is worshiping the gloves, carriages, perfumes, pomades, silk dresses. . . . It turns out that the critic Avseenko sees the whole point of our culture — its whole achievement, the whole culmination of the two-hundred-year period of our debauchery and our suffering — in carriages, in pomade, and particularly in the manner in which servants go out to greet their mistress; and he admires these things, without a hint of mockery."[128]

Dostoevsky here is suggesting that moderns have a great deal of difficulty not being hostile to the masses, their public professions of care and concern notwithstanding. An estate owner can live in the midst of people he physically sees[129] but cannot grasp or appreciate; similarly, scratch the surface of any modern and you will find a Shigalev.

Or so, at least, Dostoevsky will have us believe. Moderns may not like the grieving husband in "The Meek One," but we are more like him in spirit than we want to admit.

Two Responses to a Baseless Ethic

The Appeal of Suicide

The picture painted above, of orphans struggling to live an ethical life in a world they find profoundly meaningless, is hardly a pleasant one to contemplate. Europeans and Europeanized Russians might believe that a secularized society is more just, but according to Dostoevsky, they end up in the company of the grieving husband who began this chapter, along with Stavrogin, Svidrigailov, the Underground Man, the Grand Inquisitor, Smerdyakov, and many others. They might imagine that they have become somehow kinder and gentler, but Dostoevsky speaks only of their individual fascination with power and self-assertion. They might imagine that theirs is a more sophisticated, advanced, and engaged life, but Dostoevsky speaks primarily of the moderns' need for senseless and endless diversions.

And diversions alone do not suffice for the most observant of his many moderns. Instead of power, they see only powerlessness. His readers imagine themselves to be in control of their lives, but that control is of little value, given that in the end they will all be dead, never to rise again. In a profoundly meaningless world it may be that the only truly meaningful act we can undertake is to kill ourselves. That, at least, is the view of Ippolit, the young consumptive in *The Idiot*. Ippolit knows that his life will end within three weeks or so, perhaps a month. He feels powerless against the death that awaits him, and he deeply regrets he has no time left to do anything meaningful before it comes. What can he do to assert his will in the time that remains to him? He offers this answer to his own question: "Finally, there is the temptation: nature has so greatly limited my activity by her three-week sentence that suicide may be the only thing I still have time to begin and end of my own will."[130]

We have already met an even more dramatic character, Alexei Nilych Kirillov, in *Demons*. The lack of profound meaning in the world has left him overwhelmingly, tragically, and ethically indifferent, for it means that we live for no reason at all. This leaves us vulnerable to lives filled with pain, fear, and unhappiness.[131] If that is the case, then all that matters is our will, for God's will has long since ceased to exist. And the best way to exercise our will is for us to remove ourselves from an absurd world:

> If there is God, then the will is all his, and I cannot get out of his will. If not, the will is all mine, and it is my duty to proclaim self-will. . . . Because the will has become all mine. Can it be that no one on the whole planet, having ended God and believed in self-will, dares to proclaim self-will to the fullest point? . . . I want to proclaim self-will. I may be the only one, but I'll do it. . . . It is my duty to shoot myself because the fullest point of my self-will is — for me to kill myself.[132]

Who can utter such words? Who can believe such a notion? Perhaps the wife in "The Meek One" did, for she would have understood that she could exercise her power in almost no other way. Perhaps Ivan Karamazov, too, grasped the core of this as he made plans to live with wild abandonment until he reached thirty years of age. He said he would likely kill himself then. Norman N. Shneidman has pointed out that Dostoevsky describes twenty-two successful suicides in his literary outpouring, and a number of attempted or contemplated acts (including Ivan's).[133]

Dostoevsky's readers were living their lives as if there was literally no tomorrow. After all, there really is no tomorrow without a firm belief in immortality, is there? He repeatedly came to this conclusion in his *Diary*, in which his fascination with suicides was clear. Irina Paperno has shown that Dostoevsky wove "reality" and "fiction" together, with the latter allowing for a depth unavailable to the former.[134] In one such reflection, prompted by a recent suicide notice, he concludes, "Underlying this confession of a man who is going to die 'by logical suicide' is the necessity of the immediate conclusion, here and now, that without faith in one's soul and its immortality, human existence is unnatural, unthinkable, and unbearable. And it certainly seemed to me that I had clearly expressed the formula of the logical suicide, that I had found the formula. Little by little the thought of his own aimless existence and his hatred for the unresponsiveness of the stagnant life around him leads to the inevitable conviction of the utter absurdity of human existence on earth."[135]

Scholars have concluded that educated Russians in the late Imperial era were drawn to the idea that immortality was illusory. Dostoevsky believed that this same cohort was also the most inclined to adopt the ethics of indifference. This should not surprise us, given the sudden and dramatic increase in the reporting of suicides in the European press generally, and the Russian press specifically, in the 1860s, as Paperno and Susan K. Morrissey have documented. Even more to the point, Morrissey has shown that St. Petersburg, the most thoroughly modern of all Russian cities, was the epicenter of the empire's suicide epidemic.[136] Dostoevsky was not the only observer who linked suicide to mounting atheism in the empire, or who warned of a corresponding decline in "traditional forms of moral governance."[137] In the words of Father Zosima from *The Brothers Karamazov*, we may have set out in search of the fullness of life, but we have ended up fragmented into separate units, in complete isolation. A few pages later he calls this a spiritual suicide, one that could easily be avoided if we but willed it so.[138] But how, and by what alchemy, can this dreary fate be avoided?

The Craving for a Meaningful Ethic

Fortunately, not all of Dostoevsky's moderns end up at this rather hopeless cul-de-sac, and even when they do, Dostoevsky writes with moving compassion about their struggles. On the verge of his own suicide, Kirillov in *Demons* longs to believe in something beyond himself. Even Kirillov will light the lamp before his icon of the Savior.[139] In *The Brothers Karamazov*, Mitya and Ivan both seek their way back to wholeness even as oblivion beckons them.[140] In *Crime and Punishment*, even a reprehensible character like Svidrigailov desires to do the right thing, for he still believes somehow that the right thing exists. On the edge of his own suicide, Svidrigailov bows low before Raskolnikov and Razumikhin.[141] Later on, Raskolnikov, in prison, expresses his own longing to live beyond mere existence.[142]

In many ways, *The Brothers Karamazov* hinges on a scene of longed-for redemption during which the desire for good suddenly erupts in the midst of what moments before had appeared to be certain moral collapse. This happens when the previously devout Alyosha agrees to visit the seductress Grushenka after the corpse of Father Zosima begins to decompose (a scene of such high drama that the novel is almost worth reading in its entirety for this one moment). Alyosha is shattered by this "odor of corruption." He had hoped that his beloved mentor's remains would not decay, thus confirming that Zosima was equal to the blessed saints of old. Now, with each passing minute, a noticeable odor wafts from Zosima's body as the derision of the Elder's critics becomes more pronounced. An anguished Alyosha flees the scene and agrees in that moment to give himself up to Grushenka's long-expressed wish to despoil him sexually. Why not? However, when casually told of Zosima's death, Grushenka responds with an unexpected act of kindness, and all because she recalls a tale of a single onion and its miraculous ability to redeem even the hell-entrenched.[143]

Such acts of conversion were essential for Dostoevsky, who believed that his readers had a deep longing to do the right thing as well as the capacity to do so. He was determined to portray a world of manifold possibilities, even for Russia's Europeanized moderns, and for those who had long expressed only the most modest understanding of what the good was. This ethical worldview is still remarkable more than a hundred years after Dostoevsky's death, and yet curiously it is still within our grasp. I will next lay out its main characteristics, after one essential and final word of caution.

Postscript: An Unexpected Tribute and a Necessary Caution

The French novelist George Sand (Amantine-Lucile-Aurore Dupin) seemed to embody all that had gone wrong in the West by Dostoevsky's reckoning. Born in 1804, Sand lived a life that challenged a wide range of societal conventions and moral principles. For example, she rejected the institution of marriage and refused to abide by it in theory or practice. Nor did she stop there: this cigar-smoking self-proclaimed atheist was palpably hostile to the Roman Catholic Church.[144] Dostoevsky himself identified Sand in the March 1876 issue of his *Diary* as one of those French socialists who had envisioned a future utopian society that was decidedly and necessarily post-Christian. As such, Sand recalled Vissarion Belinsky, a Russian literary giant of the first half of the nineteenth century who had once taunted the much younger Dostoevsky with this conjecture: "Believe me that your

Christ, were he born in our time, would be the most undistinguished and ordinary of men; he would be utterly eclipsed by today's science and by those forces that now advance humanity."[145] Bruce Ward has shown how the utopian socialists of George Sand's ilk were at the core of that great 1840s generation that Dostoevsky so skillfully eviscerated in *Demons*. Above all, he had pummeled their desire to found a new Christianity without Christ.[146]

One might have expected Dostoevsky's response to Sand's passing to be a scathing reflection on one more Western intellectual gone bad. But the exact opposite unfolded: in the *Diary* of June 1876, he praised Sand for both her style and her substance. He admired her style, he wrote, because she had demonstrated the power of literature to communicate ideas that had been banned. Nikolaevan Russia was a highly vigilant state that blocked political tracts and assorted manifestos, but "novels were still permitted at the beginning, the middle, and even at the very end of the period."[147] Ironically, that same repressive period had witnessed the flowering of many of Imperial Russia's literary greats, including of course Dostoevsky himself. It is difficult to read his comments here as anything less than an homage to someone who had blazed the trail he later took.

Dostoevsky was no less appreciative of Sand's substantial contributions, even as he derided those who focused inordinately on her personal mores or choice of apparel. "They tried to frighten Russian ladies, in particular," he wrote, "by telling them that she wore trousers."[148] Sand's value, rather, was that she had helped lead European society away from the political struggles of the late eighteenth century that had culminated in the French Revolution. Though undertaken under the mantra of "Liberté, Égalité, Fraternité," the events of 1789 had merely replaced one overlord (the nobility) with another (the bourgeoisie). Dostoevsky had previously advanced this position in *Winter Notes*, his reflections on his first visit to France in 1862, in which he recorded his bewilderment that the French bourgeoisie could proclaim liberty for all while enslaving millions.[149]

For Dostoevsky, Sand represented no less than a spiritual awakening of sorts, a rediscovery of the poetic in life, and of moral beauty. He paid tribute to the immense impact of her principal characters, to their "sublime moral purity" and their recognition of "the acceptance of one's full responsibility" in a manner that recognized "the most sublime beauty and mercy, patience and justice." She wrote of "higher truths," Dostoevsky declared, of "universal forgiveness," and of mercy.[150]

Dostoevsky praised no writer in the pages of the *Diary* more than he did George Sand. In light of this chapter's argument, does it matter that Sand was an atheist? It did, and it did not. Dostoevsky disputed Sand's atheism at the time of her death. She was, he wrote, a deist during her final days; he even described her as "the most Christian of all her contemporaries, the French writers, although she did not formally (as a Catholic) confess Christ."[151]

What was Dostoevsky saying here? Surely, that even those who had abandoned the Christian faith continued to long for spiritual and ethical wholeness, and for moral purity. We see this sort of longing in his affectionate portrayal of Versilov's ill-fated quest for wholeness in *The Adolescent*, and in Stepan Trofimovich's equally ill-fated liberal search for wholeness in *Demons*. Dostoevsky never doubted the deep spiritual yearnings of these characters, that they were on a heartfelt search for moral purity. The generation of the 1840s had given birth to the nihilists and realists of the 1860s, and this left them all the more in need of compassionate understanding, not condemnation.[152] Even those who came of age in the 1860s—an era that Dostoevsky viewed as marked by profound moral hopelessness—continued to search for moral dignity. In *Demons*, the nihilist Kirillov, who is about to take his own life in the search for the perfect man-God, acknowledges moments in his own life when he lived in the eternal now—when time itself seemed to stop.[153] No wonder this same Kirillov, who long ago abandoned any belief in the God-man (that is, in Christ), can find a joy-filled moment in the simple bouncing of a ball and in the back-and-forth play that so captivates an eighteen-month-old infant.[154] Even in the midst of hopelessness, there remained a yearning for moral wholeness; in a deist-*cum*-atheist such as George Sand there lurked a follower of Christ, or almost.

By contrast, no institution seemed more worthy of Dostoevsky's condemnation than the Catholic Church. It is no wonder that the Grand Inquisitor represents the western (Catholic) church, not Orthodoxy. By Dostoevsky's reckoning, Catholicism had long ago abandoned the principles of humility and long-suffering that he found so wonderfully alive in Sand's fiction. In March 1876, months before his heartfelt tribute to Sand, he wrote

that Catholicism deserved to die because it had substituted an earthly king-
dom for a spiritual one. In so doing it had abandoned the Christ it claimed
to serve, even as it had rejected a stance of humility and long-suffering for
political power, for material wealth, and for earthly dominion.[155]

This perhaps odd juxtaposition and assessment of George Sand on
the one hand and the Roman Catholic Church on the other requires us to
proceed with caution when we assess Dostoevsky's view of his own Russian Orthodox Church. I concur with Wayne Dowler and with Rowan
Williams; both claim that Dostoevsky sought something else by way of a
moral future than "a triumphant reassertion of Orthodox ecclesiasticism."
That said, Malcolm Jones's conclusion that Dostoevsky was a proponent
of some sort of minimalist religion is as unsatisfying to me as it is to
Williams.[156]

All of which leads to this question: What can be said about religion and
ethics in Dostoevsky's ethical world, especially given that Christ seems to
figure so prominently at the beginning and the end of his ethical thinking?

CHAPTER 3
_____

To Bow at the Crossroads

The Joy of an Unreasonable Ethic

Near the end of *Crime and Punishment*, we see a man in St. Petersburg's famous Haymarket—in itself not unusual, for he lives nearby and often crosses this square in his wanderings. But this is no ordinary day for Rodion Romanovich Raskolnikov, who is about to give up his wanderings for a fixed and certain path. He is overwhelmed by seemingly hopeless anxiety, and all he wants is to be released from it. We watch him brace himself among a crowd of shopkeepers, prostitutes, shoppers, and bystanders.

He has stopped: What is he doing now? Suddenly he kneels in the middle of this great public square as if struck by a holy fire. He bows to the earth, an action that in the Orthodox and Russian context suggests his complete prostration. He then kisses the earth, joyfully it seems. He rises, then bows once more.[1]

Surely he is drunk, or perhaps he is some mad Christian on the oddest of pilgrimages—this is, after all, quirky and unpredictable Orthodox Russia. Raskolnikov hears those around him scoff. That is probably why he stops himself from crying out the words he intends: "I have killed!" But if he is deterred from that, he will not be from his next action: he rises and walks directly to the nearby police station. He has been there many times before, including on the day he was interrogated about the ax murder of a neighborhood pawnbroker and her sister, a murder he had brutally committed. More than once he had almost given himself away. Then, to his astonishment, someone else had confessed to the crime. Indeed, Raskolnikov had returned to the station to taunt the official who dared suspect him in the first place.

Today Raskolnikov will amaze them all. He climbs the stairs to the second-floor office. There, after a bout of wild vacillation—for he is still in turmoil, the turmoil of someone who has been soundly defeated—he utters this confession: "It was I who killed the official's old widow and her sister Lizaveta with an axe and robbed them."

As many readers will know, this great novel does not end with this dramatic scene. But before I continue, I need to mention that someone is with Raskolnikov on his final walk as a free citizen: Sonya Semyonovna Marmeladov, the prostitute. She had urged him to go to the crossroads and confess after he admitted his crime to her: "Go now, this minute, stand in the crossroads, bow down, and first kiss the earth you've defiled, then bow to the whole world, on all four sides, and say aloud to everyone: 'I have killed!' Then God will send you life again. Will you go? Will you go."[2]

But he did not turn himself in just then despite Sonya's pleas. He was not ready for that act of self-conscious humiliation. It was not because he doubted he had killed someone; rather, he refused to accept that all lives are of equal value. For him, the killing of a worthless pawnbroker had been entirely justified. That is what made Sonya's desperate plea so maddening, so unjust in his eyes.

He was with her just before his final walk, in her modest flat, where his arrival had ended her torture-filled day. She had been filled with suffering for him. She had feared he was becoming unhinged and would take his own life. Thank God that had not happened.

In the end, Raskolnikov is too worn out to resist. He gives in to Sonya's persistent appeals that he confess his crime. When he bows in the middle of the Haymarket, part of him still feels that the pawnbroker's death was morally acceptable. Who was that woman after all, that supposed victim, but someone who had preyed on the most vulnerable in society? And the blood money in her possession could have secured his future for years to come, along with the well-being of his nearly destitute mother, and of his sister, who would otherwise feel compelled to enter into a loveless marriage.

But Raskolnikov could not sustain the force of his own moral argument even after an innocent had, stunningly, confessed in his place and the police investigation had ended. His will had given out; he felt he had no choice but to confess on that fateful day. To salvage his own dignity, he wanted to do it alone, so he begged Sonya not to follow him as he left her flat that day. Why should she see his shame? Why should she watch as he consigns himself to a Siberian prison term that he probably will not survive?

He asked only, and unexpectedly, that she give him a cross to wear. She had two in her drawer, one of which had once been worn by the murdered Lizaveta. After brief deliberation, Sonya gave him the other, a simpler one of cypress wood, the type that simple folk wear. He put it on, muttering that it was all nonsense, even though he seemed to recognize in that cross a portion of the suffering he was now willing to take upon himself. Yet even that was not the end of it: at her almost voiceless urging, he crossed himself several times while still in her flat.[3]

He then set out on his own. Only minutes later he saw that she had, in fact, followed behind: "As he bowed down the second time in the Haymarket, turning to the left, he had seen Sonya standing about fifty steps away. She was hiding from him behind one of the wooden stalls in the square, which meant that she had accompanied him throughout his sorrowful procession! Raskolnikov felt and understood in that moment, once and for all, that Sonya was now with him forever and would follow him even to the ends of the earth, wherever his fate took him. His whole heart turned over inside him."[4]

Through Raskolnikov's confessions and prostrations we are able to enter into Dostoevsky's vision of the ethical life. It is a world to which all are welcome: prostitutes and profligates, priests and peasants, murderers and the mean-spirited, adolescents and the aged. Those whom we admire at the outset are there, as are those whom we most certainly do not. It is not a world we associate with the good life, for it willingly embraces suffering, even death. It is light on individual rights and heavy on obligations. If anything consoles, it is that Dostoevsky viewed such a life as infinitely beautiful and full of great joy.

He wrote more than once that all of life and the whole earth could be joy-filled, if we but realized as much. The tragedy—and that is the term most directly associated with Vyacheslav Ivanov's own ruminations on Dostoevsky—is that we fail to see that beauty. We fail to see it because, and against all reason, we do not *wish* to see it.[5] Instead, we have imposed our own will, our ego, on a preexisting and absolute moral order. But in doing so we have unwittingly courted the disaster that now unfolds all around us.[6] Raskolnikov's greatest crime was at a metaphysical level, in that he chose to violate the absolute moral order. In a sense, his brutal crime was an inevitable outcome of that violation. That, of course, is the problem, as Ivanov points out: "As soon as the Absolute has passed through the phase of being a metaphysical abstraction, and has become a mere conceptualistic phantom, the human understanding is irresistibly impelled to proclaim, as its final conclusion that all accepted values are universally relative."[7]

Thus we end up pathetically and existentially alone. Ivanov writes that we are "imprisoned in a subjectivist solitude,"[8] and in that moment, we, or more accurately "I," do battle against all, against heaven and earth. This is why St. Petersburg—the city Dostoevsky famously described as "the most abstract and intentional city on earth"[9]—provides the perfect background for Raskolnikov's epic struggle. For it is in this most humanly contrived of all cities that he makes his choice and commits his crime. It is also here that a defeated Raskolnikov seeks a way back to wholeness in the scene that began this chapter. Ivanov views Raskolnikov's kissing of the earth as a gesture of submission, one that marks the beginning of the end for the murderer's internal fragmentation and his first step toward an unimaginably vast reconciliation that will envelop all of heaven and earth. He himself did not understand at the time how this simple act of self-emptying, of public humiliation, would soon result in the greatest of all acts of human fulfillment and restoration.[10]

None of this was left to chance in Dostoevsky's world: he understood clearly that perfection had already been achieved for all of humankind in an act of divine intervention. Thus the world itself might be saved if it would only embrace the Russian Christ. No less a commentator than Mikhail Bakhtin observed long ago that Christ represented the highest ideal for Dostoevsky's "form-shaping ideology," which had been arrived at through the constant juxtaposition of diverse consciousnesses. Only Christ could serve in this manner for Dostoevsky, for He alone represented the ideal human.[11] It is the cross of Christ that Raskolnikov dons at Sonya's urging before he walks toward the public square; it is a portion of His suffering that he will now take within himself as he seeks redemption. This is how Dostoevsky constructs his moral universe: not at all through ideas or convictions, but rather relationally, through an absolutely embodied truth.[12]

My challenge in this chapter is to bring Dostoevsky's worldview to life. This will require us to engage the peculiarly Christian—via Orthodoxy—

nature of Dostoevsky's moral vision. From the chapter's opening vignette, we already sense that only Jesus Christ ever mattered for him. He wrote more than once that Russia's sole purpose on this earth may well have been to preserve the Orthodox Christ for the entire world. This is sure to offend many who regard a Christ-centered ethic as reason enough to dismiss anything Dostoevsky has to say on contemporary moral issues; indeed, many of his contemporaries felt the same. Some Dostoevskian scholars are no less troubled by his ethical worldview and have interpreted his works in a non-Christ-centered manner—one that seems puzzling at best.

Two brief comments. First, I will tackle Dostoevsky's own response to the objections to exclusively Christian ethical claims and identifications in the chapter that follows this one. Second, I will highlight Dostoevsky's Christ-centered worldview at the outset because it draws attention to a distinctive characteristic of Russian Orthodox understandings of morality. If Orthodox ethicists believe anything, it is that the ethical life is always and ultimately about Christian worship. As such, Orthodox ethics can never be grasped as a mere system of rules or virtues, and to present it as such would be to grossly distort the truth. Vigen Guroian is representative of Orthodox ethicists when he writes that "the moral life in all its conscientious attention to and striving for the good is finally taken up into the spiritual life. For the good is not simply the norm of life; it is the divine life itself. Christ is the archetypal ethical human being but as such he is also the God-man. With this knowledge comes the imperative not only to do good acts but to participate in the divine life. . . . In Orthodoxy ethics and soteriology are bound together. For example, ethics cannot be done without particular attention to sacramental and liturgical theology."[13]

Ethics in the Orthodox tradition—a tradition that is inseparable from Dostoevsky's life and thought—is about the grace-filled communion with Christ as much as it is about abstract beliefs. And this communion, writes Orthodox ethicist Joseph Woodill, is always about the process by which humans grow ever more into the "ought" of human becoming— a theme to which we will return shortly. But God is much more than a guide to the good in all of this. Quite the contrary, Orthodox Christians regard God alone as the true good and as the only telos worthy of our attention.[14] It is essential to declare at the outset that in the Orthodox understanding, this God is always and eternally trinitarian. Thus Christ is not the way to God; rather, He is God incarnate, and all the difference lies in that distinction.

True, Dostoevsky never fashioned himself explicitly as an Orthodox theologian, and there are reasons to question whether his allegiance to the structures of Orthodoxy was strong. But he was unmistakably Russian Orthodox, and his fixation on Christ flows through his vast literary output from at least the time of his Siberian exile until his death. Also, there is little reason to doubt Avril Pyman's contention that Orthodoxy became more vital to the great writer as he grew older, and all the more so after his marriage in 1867 to the "unobtrusively devout" Anna Grigorievna.[15] Moreover, we know of his pilgrimages to the Optina Pustyn monastery in 1878. Simonetta Salvestroni has skillfully linked Dostoevsky's own prose to the classics of eastern Orthodox spirituality, including the eighth-century church leader Isaac the Syrian.[16] The peculiarly Orthodox nature of Dostoevsky's ethical worldview becomes obvious when we turn to his own writings, which is where we now shift in order to fully comprehend Dostoevsky's grasp of the ethical life.

A Memory that Precedes Awareness

Dostoevsky devotes the first section in his February 1876 issue of *Diary of a Writer* to questions of love, goodness, and Russian society. He affirms at the outset that even elite Russian society longs to do good, to be honest, and thereby to identify more with the common Russian People, the famed *narod* for which no adequate English translation exists. In a theme we will return to toward the end of this chapter, he subsequently identifies the Russian peasant with values that he himself prizes: "simplicity, purity, meekness, breadth of outlook, and lack of malice."[17]

Then Dostoevsky suddenly recalls an Easter week from years before when he found himself utterly discouraged. The setting had much to do with this, for he was then in the midst of his Siberian exile. Those around him were mainly of peasant stock and therefore part of the very *narod* on whom he is reflecting in this issue. Because the day was a feast day, the authorities did not require any forced labor, so most of those around him were able to become drunk on illicit supplies of vodka. Countless disturbances followed as the convicts addressed one another with the coarsest language and uttered the worst abuses. Eventually even knives were drawn, which is striking, for these items were contraband.

It is difficult to determine whether this recollection is a "mere" fictional device to make the point at hand. In any case, Dostoevsky writes that he could take no more of it and returned to his barracks to lie down. He placed his hands behind his head and covered his face, hoping to somehow transport himself from this hateful setting. To his surprise, he succeeded: his mind went back to an incident that happened when he was nine years old. It was 1830, which means that in 1876, when he was writing his *Diary*, his mind went back first twenty-five years to when he was in Siberian confinement and then through that prism back another sixteen.

In this most distant recollection, he was back on the family estate, and it was August. Young Fyodor was wandering the fields and forests when suddenly someone broke the day's heavy silence with a shout: "There's a wolf!" Terrified, Fyodor looked for safety and found it in the peasant Marey, who was plowing a nearby field. He ran to Marey and begged him for protection from the wolf. Marey stopped his plowing and assured the terrified youth there was no wolf. He then urged Fyodor to make the sign of the cross on his own person,[18] but the boy was too petrified to move. So, we read, Marey "quietly stretched out a thick, earth-soiled finger with a black nail and gently touched it on to [Fyodor's] trembling lips."[19]

This great peasant act of kindness profoundly comforted Fyodor. We will return to this recollection shortly, but first I want to stress the importance of memory to Dostoevsky's understanding of the ethical, for I believe it was foundational. When all is said, he sought to combat a profoundly fragmented modern age with a vision of transcendent connectedness, temporal and otherwise. That included a strong connection with the past, examples of which abound in his literary work. They include the vital role played by memory in "The Peasant Marey."[20]

For Dostoevsky, our ethical lives start with a prior memory, though the act of remembering can take radically different forms. In *The Brothers Karamazov*, for example, Father Zosima's conversion as a young man occurred after he recalled the rudeness with which he had previously treated his own loyal servant. In that same repentant moment, Zosima recollects the conversion of his older brother, Markel, who died tragically in the full flower of his youth.[21] Similarly, the young Zosima once encountered a "mysterious visitor" who confessed that much earlier in his life he had murdered someone who had romantically rejected him. Though he had escaped formal punishment for that crime years ago, he had proven to be like Raskolnikov in his inability to cut himself off from this past deed.[22] He now felt compelled to confess, even if it meant his own total destruction. Diane Oenning Thompson has pointed out how all of these recollections of conversations with Zosima are themselves recollected later on—years later, in fact—by Alyosha.[23]

We have already seen, in *Crime and Punishment*, how Raskolnikov cannot erase the memory of the brutal murders he committed, nor can Sonya when she hears Raskolnikov's confession, for which she begs him to "bow at the crossroads." Nor can Raskolnikov forget a Bible story he remembers from long ago. Thus, he approaches Sonya in the midst of his ethical turmoil over whether he should confess his double murder to the authorities. In the course of a long and sometimes rambling conversation, Raskolnikov stops when he observes a copy of the New Testament in her modest flat. He picks it up, hands it to her, and asks her without warning to read "the part about Lazarus."[24] He remembers this story even if he does not know exactly where in the New Testament it is found. She *does* know, and she immediately opens the book to it. She passionately reads this account from the Gospel of John, which Dostoevsky considered important enough to include verbatim in his novel. This is a pivotal scene in the novel, for in this account of Christ's power over death there is reason for Raskolnikov to believe that his own death and assorted humiliations may also one day be overcome by some sort of new and resurrected life in Christ. That, at least, is the only way to explain the obviously salvific power this story has for him, let alone for Sonya, whom we are told "knew by heart what she was reading." Thus, she read "with an iron ring to her voice; joy and triumph sounded in it and strengthened in it."[25] Nor are we done with this account of Lazarus's resurrection: Dostoevsky will rely on the reader's memory of this reading when he returns to it at the end of the novel.

For Dostoevsky memory is vital, both to his narratives and to his ethics. In *Crime and Punishment*, Svidrigailov finds himself ultimately unable to escape horrific memories of past misdeeds. In *Demons*, Stavrogin is haunted by the memory of a sexually violated adolescent's pathetic suicide. In *The Brothers Karamazov*, Mitya acknowledges more than once that his whole life has been a disorder; he can say so only because he remembers his prior life in a way that no amount of alcohol can mask.[26]

Good memories and bad memories are scattered throughout Dostoevsky's writings. But it is clear that Dostoevsky saw memories themselves as something more than mere and present recollections; for him, they also had an eternal element. In a sense, he believed that our memories precede even our remembering of them. They have the power to precede our existence, and this is a crucial element in his construction of the ethical. Furthermore, they will continue long after we have left this earthly domain.

Thus, in *The Adolescent*, Arkady desperately yearns to make a quick financial fortune, for he believes that it will bring him true happiness. He sets out for the gambling halls, where, as wondrous as it is strange, he amasses a great pot of winnings—that is, until he is blatantly cheated out of them by a scoundrel sitting nearby. Defeated, humiliated, and enraged, he leaves the gambling hall and ponders his own suicide until he fastens onto the idea of murderous revenge instead. He decides to destroy the whole town if need be—to "blow it all sky high, destroy everything."[27] He sees his opportunity when he comes across a massive stockpile of lumber that lines both sides of the narrow road, as long as a hundred paces and as high as a stone wall. It will burn quickly, he knows, but in a manner that will allow him an easy escape. He sets out to destroy all but suddenly slips badly and falls with a crash from the woodpile.

As he lies there in a daze, he recalls a moment at Touchard's Boarding School in Moscow in the days of his youth. It was the week after Holy Week, the leaves were already budding, and the slanting rays of the evening sun entered the classroom. He remembers that this was the first time he had seen his mother in years. In that moment of recalled reunion, he also recollects the last time he had been with her—when she had taken him as a youth to the local church for communion, and a dove flew across the cupola.[28]

At first glance this recollection seems bounded by time, as does the one involving the peasant Marey—each is a memory within a memory, all within the lifetime of the narrator. But in fact it is profoundly different: Arkady's recollection that this took place in the week after Holy Week contains a memory of the entire Christian story. For Dostoevsky, Holy Week is meaningless if it does not point directly to the inexpressible timelessness of the eternal, triune God. God's incarnation in the person of Christ led directly to the events of Holy Week, which include the commemoration of

His crucifixion and subsequent resurrection, by which death was destroyed in death.

Mention of spring in Arkady's remembering propels us also to the Christian season of Pentecost and the assurance that God's Holy Spirit will henceforth be present for all humankind. The dove, which Arkady recalls with such clarity in its beauteous flight across the cupola, is the sign of the Holy Spirit itself. This account has such a profound impact on Arkady that he recalls it one other time with his mother.[29] The slanting rays of the sun are a favorite device for Dostoevsky, used to capture something of the moment when the transcendent and eternal intersect with the here and now. The sight of Arkady's mother in this moment cannot help but suggest an allusion to Mary, the Theotokos, or Orthodox Mother of God. This memory after the fall from the woodpile might be bounded by Arkady's lifetime, but it contains an eternity of meaning for him.

At the other end, the eternal future is itself already contained within our lives and beyond our dying. So Dostoevsky tells it. We sense this link between the mundane and the eternal in the final exchange between Arkady and Makar Ivanovich, the peasant who is the legal husband of Arkady's mother and whose patronymic Arkady himself bears, even though his biological father is the incessantly self-distracted Versilov. On his deathbed, Makar Ivanovich assures a deeply moved Arkady that even death will not serve as a barrier between them. He confidently declares that he will continue to pray "even when he is dead" for Arkady, for "there is love after death."[30] It will not surprise, given this extraordinary declaration, that the first words Arkady hears Makar Ivanovich say in *The Adolescent* are equally clothed in eternal memory. They are none other than "Lord Jesus Christ, our God, have mercy on us," spoken in the midst of a deep silence of late afternoon as the "slanting rays of the sun" are about to shine directly into Arkady's room.[31]

Nor is Makar Ivanovich's eternity-filled promise an isolated example, for Dostoevsky portrays a future memory at the end of *Demons* through the person of Stepan Trofimovich. Though we have followed this aging liberal's existentially empty meanderings since the start of the novel, we see him in a new light at its conclusion. Much has changed. His 1840s liberalism is dead and buried in the charred ruins of a nihilist fire and the heartless murders masterminded by his long-abandoned son, Pyotr. With his life's beliefs in shambles, Stepan Trofimovich sets out on a pilgrimage, which does not go as planned, mainly because there is no plan and no goal. He is a modern-day pilgrim.

Yet despair will not be Dostoevsky's last word here, for in a life filled with regret, Stepan Trofimovich has the good fortune near its end to be accompanied by a widow, Sofya Matveevna, who sustains herself by selling Bibles in rural Russia. Their lovely and unexpected encounter prompts Stepan Trofimovich to remember reading that sacred Christian canon in his youth. He longs to reread it after a hiatus of thirty years. But by now he is too ill to read for himself, so he asks his newfound companion to read it to him. It is for good reason that Boyce Gibson has referred to this itinerant Bible seller as a "pin-point of light" in *Demons*. It is as if Dostoevsky is suggesting, in the aftermath of the destruction of all those "possessed" by atheistic ideologies earlier in the novel, that it is from the likes of her that "the new Christian society is to be built on the ruins."[32] Sofya Matveenva decides to read first from the book of Revelation, and in that rendering Dostoevsky draws the reader into a memory that is at the heart of the Christian faith: the assurance that the end of time itself is certain to be joyous, for it has already been realized in Christ's death and resurrection.[33] It follows that Dostoevsky's readers could already begin to think of their future as a memory, for they could approach it by looking backward to the cross and resurrection of Holy Week. Nor does it end here. Minutes later, Stepan Trofimovich suddenly says to Sofya Matveevna, "Now read me one more passage . . . about the swine."[34] She then reads the text from the Gospel of Luke that forms the novel's epigraph. It concerns an occasion when Christ heals the demoniac and sends his demons into a herd of swine. At the end of the Lucan passage, the sick man has been cured and is sitting at Christ's own feet. As if to hammer home the point of the novel, Dostoevsky includes this entire Gospel account in his own text, just as he has included the entire reading from Revelation a little before. Stepan Trofimovich's response is to apply the Lucan text to the Russia of his day. In effect, Stepan Trofimovich dies knowing that a certain memory of the future has already been granted him, for just as the healed demoniac was found at Christ's feet, so one day will liberal and nihilist Russia be vanquished.[35] The timeline may be unknowable, but the outcome is not. Stepan Trofimovich can remember this final Christ-led victory as if it has already happened. In the only sense that matters, as far as Dostoevsky is concerned, it has.

Icons and Crosses

Dostoevsky suggests two important ways in which a transcendent memory will allow his readers to order their lives properly and hopefully. Both allow the beauty of Dostoevsky's prose to shine forth.

We have already mentioned Dostoevsky's liberal use of icons in his works. These icons are a vital component in Dostoevsky's Orthodox "semiosphere." He deemed them to be a constant reminder of Christ, of the divine image in which all had been formed, and of the divine likeness toward which all might move. This perspective is entirely consistent with Mikhail Bakhtin's depiction of Dostoevsky's characters as "inherently un-finalizable."[36] Bakhtin could easily have said the same about icons in the Russian Orthodox tradition, past and present. Even death need not hinder his readers in their dynamic movement toward ethical perfection, as Dostoevsky reasons out.

Icons are everywhere present in Dostoevsky's writings, and never by happenstance. Sophie Ollivier has demonstrated how the Mother of God icon is especially prominent in Dostoevsky's world.[37] Even nonbelievers, such as Stepan Trofimovich in *Demons*, are tempted to enlist the support of icons in the dead of night and similar moments of vulnerability. But in this context I wish to comment on the essential dynamism of icons within Orthodoxy. Let us begin by distinguishing between Orthodox understandings of *image* and *likeness*, or *face* and *countenance*. We read in Genesis 1:27 that in the beginning, "God created humankind in his image, in the image of God he created them; male and female he created them" (NRSV). Joseph Woodill succinctly summarizes the Orthodox understanding of this verse. The earliest church fathers established that humankind is born in the *image* of God but with the free-willed opportunity to grow into the *likeness* of its Creator. The great Russian theologian and Soviet martyr Pavel Florensky described the image as the spiritual groundwork of each created person, whereas the likeness is the potentiality given to every person to attain "spiritual perfection."[38] Nor are we on our own in the attempt, for in the words of St. Athanasius of Alexandria (ca. 300 CE), "God become Man so that man might become god." Dismiss or conflate this vital distinction between *image* and *likeness* and Orthodoxy suddenly becomes nonsensical; religious icons themselves become little more than religious images or symbols. But make the distinction—as Dostoevsky inescapably would have done—and suddenly icons become a vital component of a religious faith that is overwhelmingly intent on the divinization of humankind. Thus icons function as a liminal point between visible humanity and the invisible God.[39] Christ Himself became for Dostoevsky nothing less than the incarnation of that otherwise invisible God. In Paul Evdokimov's words, "The beauty of Christ is in the coexistence of divine transcendence and immanence. . . . The face of Christ is the human face of God."[40]

Dostoevsky utilizes a second, profoundly Orthodox practice when he repeatedly has individuals make the sign of the cross on themselves or on others. Still others wear the cross, or even, like Raskolnikov and Sonya at the start of this chapter, exchange crosses. Antony Johae has argued persuasively that Raskolnikov's willingness to wear the religious symbol that he had previously refused reflects the murderer's willingness, at long last, to make public confession and to enter onto the path marked by suffering.[41] Or consider "The Peasant Marey." In my retelling of it, I left off with Marey gently pressing his earth-blackened finger against young Dostoevsky's trembling face. What I did not recount is that Marey then addresses young Fyodor: "'Off with you, then, and I'll keep an eye on you as you go. Can't let the wolf get you!' he added, still giving me a maternal smile. 'Well, Christ be with you, off you go.' He made the sign of the cross over me, and crossed himself. I set off, looking over my shoulder almost every ten steps. Marey continued to stand with his little filly, looking after me and nodding every time I looked around."[42]

Dostoevsky credited this tremendously reassuring memory with transforming his appreciation for the peasant convicts with whom he lived during his Siberian imprisonment. He suddenly realized that even the most disordered of them, the most grotesque, might be akin to Marey, who had once comforted him, a comfort that was commingled with the sign of the cross.

Image and *likeness*. Similar examples abound. In *The Adolescent*, Arkady's mother repeatedly blesses her son with the sign of the cross. Raskolnikov crosses himself, as we have observed, before he confesses to his great crime, and in an extraordinarily moving scene in *Demons*, Shatov welcomes back his wayward wife, who is pregnant with another man's child. She is worn out when she returns to Shatov and expects only condemnation and rejection from him. Yet Shatov receives his prodigal wife and this child with deep joy. At its birth, he abruptly crosses himself. At the end of this same novel, the Bible seller Sofya Matveevna makes the sign of the cross "in hope" on her person after Stepan Trofimovich awakens from delirium.[43]

This is not to suggest that the meaning of the cross itself is always self-evident, for Dostoevsky never settles for the stultifyingly obvious. We see this in *Notes from a Dead House*, his prison novel set as a memoir. At one point he describes the death of a consumptive prisoner named Mihailov, who remains shackled to the end even though the chain's weight and encumbrance become increasingly oppressive. By the end he has cast off all of his clothing so as not to constrict what is left of his breathing. Then, just before death, Mihailov's "wandering and shaky hand found the [cross] on his chest and began tearing it off, as if it too, was a burden to him, bothered him, weighed him down."[44] His fellow patients help him remove it, and within ten minutes he dies. Does this removal carry some greater portent? Is it possible that the cross had never meant anything to him, and that he only then found the courage to be rid of it, as Robert L. Jackson suggests?[45] Or did he regard it as salvific to the end, even after its removal? We are never told. But we *are* told that one of the convicts approaches Mihailov after he has died and places the cross around his neck again. This convict then makes the sign of the cross on his own person, as does the sergeant of the watch who arrives shortly afterwards to collect Mihailov's remains.[46]

A no less puzzling account is found in *The Idiot*, immediately after the prince has seen Rogozhin's copy of Holbein's *The Dead Christ*. The prince is overwhelmed by this bleakest of portrayals and hastens to respond with several vignettes, in each of which the cross is central. Of these, the strangest involves two peasants, longtime friends, who once shared a room at an inn. On this occasion the one spied the other's watch and coveted it. The one who coveted was otherwise honorable, and yet despite the depth of their friendship, he was overwhelmed with temptation. The prince continues his narrative, saying of the covetous one, "He pulled out a knife and, while his friend was looking the other way, went up to him cautiously from behind, took aim, raised his eyes to heaven, crossed himself, and, after praying bitterly to himself: 'Lord, forgive me for Christ's sake!'—killed his friend with one blow, like a sheep, and took his watch."[47]

Again, the reader is left wondering what Dostoevsky wanted us to take from this account. We do not know, because the prince immediately moves on (and shortly receives an unexpected blessing and the sign of the cross from Rogozhin's mother).[48] Regardless of the questions left to the reader from these accounts, it is clear that wearing the cross and making the sign thereof are transcendent acts in Dostoevsky's world. At the very least, they raise the question of transcendence itself. Such signs are variously evident in his works as blessings between individuals, from one to the other, or between life and death. Even more mysteriously, they bridge whatever gap exists between the world that Dostoevsky regarded as here and now and an eternal world that he deemed no less real or immediate, even if it seemed less evident. Perhaps Johae is correct when he suggests that Dostoevsky's repeated reference to people encountering each other "at the crossroads" is nothing less than the crucifix made manifest over the whole world.[49] To read even this much is to recall Sonya's plea to Raskolnikov that he bow at the crossroads and confess his crime. Was it the cross writ large that Dostoevsky was trying to get at with this reference? Perhaps. None of this need be fully grasped to be true in Dostoevsky's world, for how can such transcendence be fully grasped in the first place?

In so many ways, then, Dostoevsky reminded his readers that they need not settle for a world of profound fragmentation and finite possibilities. On the contrary, he maintained that there were signs of coherence everywhere and in a manner that death itself could not overwhelm. Whatever the worst fears of Ivan Karamazov, Nikolai Stavrogin, Arkady Dolgoruky, and countless others, we do not come from nothing, nor is our world destined to return to some dull void in the end. If only we could remember as much.

The Necessity of Belief in Immortality

Icons, crosses, and assorted biblical texts give assurance in Dostoevsky's universe that our memories can be trusted, even when they extend beyond our ability to understand them. In the end, as in the beginning, our memory comes to include all that has ever been and ever will be. More than that—if there was a "more" after that—Dostoevsky believed that such a boundless memory was also the bedrock of the ethical life. All of this was entirely dependent on a corresponding belief in immortality. No wonder, then, that Kirillov, the tragically rational suicide in *Demons*, declares that humankind cannot exist without a belief in God, a belief he struggles in vain to claim for his own.[50]

One cannot encounter Kirillov's anguished yearning to believe in the transcendent without pondering the degree to which Dostoevsky himself may once have shared that same existential angst. Surely his earlier flirtation with socialist circles in the late 1840s hinted at his willingness to embrace a materialist worldview. But he did not stay in that place; he abandoned a world of finite limits for one that was boundlessly eternal, even unreasonably so.

Dostoevsky's reflections immediately following the death of his first wife, Marya, seem to provide the first sign of his own inner transformation. Joseph Frank is one of many who see these ruminations as foundational for all that Dostoevsky would subsequently write.[51] We need to pause briefly here to ponder these words, especially given their utter directness to the theme at hand.

Like the grief-filled husband he will later create—the one who ponders before the body of his recently deceased wife in "The Meek One"—Dostoevsky was also staring death in the face. Marya (Masha in the diminutive), his first wife, had died the evening before, on April 15, 1864. In the Russian custom, she had been laid out in their modest flat, and faced with this lamentable departure, Dostoevsky opened his journal and began to pour out his heart. His thoughts do not go where we would expect them to go—that is, unless it is clear to the reader by now that Dostoevsky rarely delivers the expected. Instead, he begins here:

> Masha is lying on the table. Will I ever see Masha again? To love a person *as one loves oneself*, according to Christ's command, is impossible. The law of the personality on earth binds us. The *"I"* hinders us. Only Christ is able to do so, as Christ was from ages unto ages the ideal to which a person strives, and to which, according to the laws of nature, a person must strive. Besides that, since the appearance of Christ, *as the ideal person made flesh*, it has become clear as day, that the highest, final stage of development of personality must reach that point (at the very end of development, at the very point where the goal is reached) whereby a person

would find, and recognize with all the strength of his nature, that the highest requirement to which it is possible for a person to move with his personality, and of the complete development of his *"I"*—would be to destroy that *"I,"* and to give it entirely to all and to everyone undividedly and unselfishly. And this is a great good fortune. Thus, the law of the *"I"* is merged with the law of humanism, and in essence both the *"I"* and the *all* (which appear to be two opposites) are each mutually destroyed one for another, and at that very moment they reach the highest stage of individual development in the development of the common.

This is the achievement of Christ. All of history, as that of humankind, in total and for each person, is only the development, the struggle and the aspiration to the achievement of this goal.[52]

At the outset, two things are clear for this vigil-keeping writer. By the one, we are all driven by a powerful ego, the "I," the one that actually militates against the common good. Yet deep within each "I" is a profound aspiration to seek the common good and to strive for ever-higher stages of development until we reach the highest. But we never seem to arrive at that final stage and instead are constantly compelled to choose between our individual fulfillment and that which serves the common good. That, he writes, is the human condition. In fact, in all of history only Christ has accomplished the ideal to which we all individually strive, whereby the "I" and the "we" dialectically destroy each other, to the astonishing fulfillment of both. This is why Dostoevsky goes on to say that Christ is the "great and final ideal in the development of all of humankind."[53] Dostoevsky further reasons that this aspiration, contained within each of us, would be cruelly placed if we did not possess any hope of realizing it, if we were always to be never quite reaching the place where both "I" and "we" are fulfilled in each other. It would be no less cruel to our moral struggling now if, in the end, there was nothing. If we believed that nothing was our reward, we would have to conclude that the desire to reach our final goal of becoming an elevated or ethical human being was cruelly placed within us. In that case we would do well to ignore it and to settle for immediate gratification and endless diversion.

Dostoevsky deems this bleak conclusion to be senseless. If we aspire to merge the "I" with the common good, it must be because such a goal can be reached, if not in this world, then in the world to come, which must surely be. In the directness which that moment in his life demands, he writes simply, "It follows that there is a future life of paradise. What is it exactly, on what planet, what is at the centre, and what does the centre consist of, that is, what is in the bosom of this universal synthesis, that is, who is God? We know none of this. We only know one distinguishing feature of this future nature of our future existence. . . . This distinguishing feature was foretold and foreseen in Christ."[54]

Thus Dostoevsky counterbalances two radically different notions: he is able to affirm the ethical necessity of immortality without needing to know anything about it. His questions can always, it seems, outweigh his answers. With one great exception, of course, and that pertains to Christ. The more he relies on Christ as the ideal he might one day become, the more he is able to name the ultimately unknowable nature of what lies beyond the grave. In the language of his immediate situation, and in answer to the profoundly existential question that begins his musings, Dostoevsky reasons out that he will see Masha again, even if he cannot grasp how. Travis Kroeker and Bruce Ward emphasize that Dostoevsky's understanding of Christ as the eternal ideal, as absolute truth, is entirely consistent with Orthodox understandings of the divine. It also points us, through the earliest Hellenist theologians mentioned above, to the understanding that Christ alone is "the model of the human life in the divine likeness."[55]

By this means, Dostoevsky beautifully combines Orthodox understandings of the divine as simultaneously apophatic and cataphatic. Orthodox Christians by the former confess that the divine is understood to be a great and incomprehensible mystery, the divine darkness. He is beyond our ability to know or to grasp, and beyond all human reason, such that even to name the divine is futile. Simultaneously, the Orthodox maintain that the unknowable divine can be at least partly grasped to the extent that He has revealed itself to us in creation. Orthodox Christians believe that the divine is nowhere more clearly presented to us than in Jesus Christ, the divine word made flesh. Through Him, and by the power of the Holy Spirit, we have access to a God who is simultaneously one and eternally triune, as Father, Son, and Holy Spirit.[56]

I can recall only one time when Dostoevsky uses this trinitarian formula. It arises unexpectedly near the end of *The Brothers Karamazov* as the murdered father's former physician, Dr. Herzenstube, is called to testify at

Mitya's trial. Herzenstube, who until this moment has been portrayed as somewhat given to quackery, suddenly recalls how Mitya was abandoned by his father in childhood. It was so dreadful that the physician himself came to pity the child, so Herzenstube once brought Mitya some nuts. No such present, no such kindness, had ever been given to the boy before. As Herzenstube handed the nuts to the boy he coaxed him to say, in German, "God the Father, God the Son, and God the Holy Spirit." All of this clearly moved the young Mitya then, as it does again in the retelling during the trial. The physician's simple act of kindness, bathed in a trinitarian incantation, had made a lasting impression.[57]

That one trinitarian reference aside, it should already be clear that references to Christ are everywhere in Dostoevsky's writings. He believed, moreover, that there was something distinctive about the Russian understanding of Christ that the whole world desperately needed. It follows that we will understand more about Dostoevsky's vision for the ethical if we understand more fully what he meant by "the Russian Christ." Thus, for example, Christ's example of self-abasement, of profound humbling, contains for Dostoevsky the assurance that Russians, and people everywhere and through all time, will become more fully divine as they embrace the assorted sufferings and humiliations of their lives.[58]

In a similar tone, but by different means, we have already observed how a dying Stepan Trofimovich asks Sofya Matveevna to read from the Gospel in *Demons*. Liza Knapp has demonstrated how even Dostoevsky's construction of this final chapter in Stepan Trofimovich's life defies those who wish for a true "conversion" of his erstwhile agnostic liberalism to a renewed Orthodoxy.[59] Sofya Matveenva reads the Sermon on the Mount to Stepan Trofimovich. In that section of the Gospel of Matthew, Christ radically overturns contemporary understandings of power and powerlessness. In Matthew's gospel, it is the powerless who are truly blessed. It is the persecuted. It is those who are poor in spirit. All of these words flowed from Christ, who was for Dostoevsky the window onto our own promise of immortality, even as Christ was simultaneously the measure of his readers' own present goodness, here and now. Dostoevsky regarded Him simply as a "marvelous and miraculous Beauty."[60]

But how is it that immortality provides the means for our emergence as ethical beings?

A Radical Freedom . . . to Do What?

Nikolas Berdyaev once suggested that freedom was at the heart of Dosto-evsky's view of the world.[61] But this was no ordinary freedom. Berdyaev observed that Dostoevsky wrestled with two contrary conceptions of free-dom, which he differentiated variously as "initial" and "final" or as "the freedom of the first Adam" and "the freedom in Christ." He likened it to Augustine's famous distinction between the lesser freedom (*libertas minor*) and the greater (*libertas maior*).[62] This conception of freedom(s) seems especially difficult to grasp in Dostoevsky's time, given the modern con-ception of freedom as almost exclusively the first in these dyads. By this freedom, Dostoevsky's readers were individually free to do what they wanted. We can choose, for example, to eat a lettuce salad instead of a hamburger and fries for lunch, just as it is my individual right to wear a blue shirt or a black one, and to carry a gun if I choose to do so. We can choose to do the right thing, or the wrong; we can even choose to reject the no-tion of absolute right and wrong.

Dostoevsky understood that there were problems with this lesser freedom. What happens, for example, if we decide that the decision to at-tack someone whom we feel has harmed us is equally mine, as is the deci-sion whether to drink vodka or water? What if I end up thinking I have a choice between two seemingly equal options: to respond to the poverty of my neighbor or a stranger, or to ignore it; or to nurture my infant children, or not to do so, as the elder Karamazov clearly chose?

Dostoevsky concluded that this definition of freedom was meaning-less if it did little more than permit his readers to view any and all choices as equal. Surely the greater freedom was not one that allowed his readers to choose between good and evil, for what sort of freedom is that in the end? Rather, it was one by which they willingly surrendered themselves to the absolute good. We might say, following Berdyaev's own formulation, that it is not enough for Dostoevsky's readers to have the freedom to choose the truth; surely they have reached the final stage when they freely choose to live in and surrender to absolute truth itself.[63] I concur fully with Berdyaev's conclusion that Dostoevsky repeatedly explored this lesser and initial freedom, taking it to its bleakest conclusion, for he believed that his readers' moral selves could only be realized through their embrace of, or surrender to, the greater truth, the final one. I will briefly spell out, in three stages, how Dostoevsky reached that endpoint.

Choice Matters above All

In *The Adolescent*, Arkady, the restless and rootless youth from a contemporary "accidental"[64] family, cannot stand the predictability of the earth's daily movement. As he lies recovering from the fall he suffered while trying to burn down the village, he dreads that the sun will soon set, as it always does at this time of day. "I knew it from the previous days, and the fact that it would unfailingly happen in an hour, and, above all, that I knew it beforehand, like two times two, angered me to the point of spite."[65] For him, life is most maddening when individual choice is removed from it, for where will freedom then be found? Later, while reflecting on another's fate, Dostoevsky concludes of Arkady, "He refused the *fatum* of life; what he needed was freedom, not slavery to the *fatum*."[66]

Dostoevsky constantly railed against the notion of fate/*fatum*. Decades earlier, in *Notes from a Dead House*, he had observed that prisoners longed for any means of self-expression possible, anything that could assert their simple freedom as individual human beings. When that freedom was taken from them, they refused to relinquish the *dream* of freedom: "From the very first day of my life in prison, I began to dream of freedom. Calculating when my prison term would be over, in a thousand different forms and methods, became my favorite occupation."[67] By contrast, prisoners painfully realized that the notion of a life that was entirely mandatory was its own curse — especially a compulsory life lived in common with others who had been similarly detained.[68] *Notes from a Dead House* is filled with accounts of prisoners who exploited what freedom they had to assert their own personalities, whether in sewing or bootlegging vodka or acting in a remarkably staged prison camp Christmas play. Even earlier, the Underground Man repeatedly rails against the inevitability of "two times two," whereby individual choice is overcome by the laws of nature, or by fate. At one point he declares, "I will answer for this, because the whole human enterprise seems to consist in man's proving to himself every moment that he is a man and not a sprig."[69] This needs to be so for him because, unlike a small plant, humans have a freedom to assert themselves, and much depends on it.

Simple Freedom May Free Us Only to Do Evil

Dostoevsky believed it was not enough to assert one's will, for how would his readers know whether they had asserted it in destructive ways? He was unimpressed by personae whose wanting rarely reached beyond wanting to choose. No wonder so many ended up choosing badly. As the Underground Man declares, a human "needs only independent wanting, whatever this independence may cost and wherever it may lead. Well, and this wanting, the devil knows."[70] The devil knows indeed. At one point, the Underground Man describes his need to choose between cheap and immediate happiness on the one hand and lofty suffering for a just cause on the other. "Well, which is better?"[71]

This question was not mere rhetoric: Dostoevsky was inviting his reader to answer it on his behalf. Perhaps it did not matter, especially if Dostoevsky's moderns chose not to give any one thing value over another. That is the view of Varvara Petrovna, the benefactor of Stepan Trofimovich. She informs him at one point that moderns regard paintings of the Madonna, who is the embodiment of the human ideal for Orthodox Christians, as less valuable than a mug of tea. The latter is at least useful.[72] And there are countless other choices in *Demons* alone. Shatov decides to trade his revolver for the services of a midwife when his wayward wife comes home, and he chooses to embrace his wife in love rather than flagrantly reject her, as would have been his right. Moments later he chides the midwife, for she sees this birth in strictly biological terms, as one more "unnecessary" birth. He chooses to see this birth as "a great mystery and an inexplicable one."[73] Sometime later, Pyotr Stepanovich Verkhovensky chooses to have Shatov murdered so as to galvanize the allegiances of the other young radicals in their town. In *The Idiot*, it seems that the prince must choose between two romantic interests, both of whom must make their own choices when it comes to the expressed desires of still other suitors.[74] And in *Crime and Punishment*, everything revolves around the freedom to make choices, from murder to sexual assault to abject confession.

Clearly, Dostoevsky saw his time as one in which people were obsessed by the variety of choices in their lives. Yet too often they seemed content to stay with "simple" or "initial" views of freedom, which essentially meant the freedom to ignore the good, the freedom to undertake evil. He laments as much in an 1873 issue of *Diary of a Writer*, where he reviews a new stage play with the intriguing title *Strong Drink Every Day Keeps Fortune Away*. He regards this play, whose theme is vodka's ubiquitous appeal, as a sign of the moral disorder that has gripped Russia.[75] It is a world in which some know the difference between vice and virtue and yet choose the former over the latter. Sisters are sold from peasant villages to pay for new clothes or a new accordion.[76] In a world of superficial choices, the most outrageous can become normal, as in the following excerpt from the play as Dostoevsky recounts it: "When [the protagonist] and Matryosha manage to get the mother to come to the tavern where they can be free to cajole her into giving permission to sell her own daughter to be raped by the business man, he first serves her sweet vodka and offers her a seat."[77] Surely there must be a freedom in Dostoevsky's moral universe that is worth more than this one.

The Freedom We Seek Is a Final One

A life lived with only a simple vision of freedom is for Dostoevsky hardly a life at all. More often than not, those caught up in such a life end up in desperate straits. We see it in the grand, pathetic patriarch of the Karamazovs, Fyodor Pavlovich, who has lived a life of alcohol-inflamed orgies and assorted dalliances. But we could substitute his name for that of his son Dmitrii (Mitya). Mitya's brother Ivan certainly fits here as well, as does Smerdyakov, and on to Raskolnikov, Svidrigailov, and on and on. No wonder those most aware of what is going on here, including Ivan in *The Brothers Karamazov* and Kirillov in *Demons*, decide to take an early exit from lives that have ended up in a meaningless cul-de-sac.

More gently, we encounter Madame Khokhlakov, in a chapter of *The Brothers Karamazov* aptly titled "A Lady of Little Faith." She confesses to Father Zosima that during her childhood years she believed in God, and even in immortality, but only mechanically so. Now she knows that, as an adult, she has to decide whether to believe in anything. Yet the divine cannot be proven, and when she looks around at others, all she sees is a profound indifference to this question.[78] Father Zosima's kind response points to his awareness that Madame Khokhlakov is stuck in the wearying ambivalence of her new freedom not to believe in anything if she so chooses.

By itself, then, freedom of this kind seems oppressive, but what alternatives are there? One such is offered by the Grand Inquisitor. During his prison-cell diatribe he is especially vexed that Christ did not release humans from the burden of their freedom, "for nothing has ever been more insufferable for man and for human society than freedom!"[79] Why? Because this freedom is ultimately dispiriting and self-destructive. It is so because humans cannot bear to live with options made available to them in a universe deemed meaningless once they sense that the divine is removed. In these circumstances, it is no longer freedom we want, he warns, but enslavement. "Know then," he declares to the imprisoned Christ while the fires of the Inquisition rage outside, "that now, precisely now, these people are more certain than ever before that they are completely free, and at the same time they themselves have brought us their freedom and obediently laid it at our feet."[80] Henri de Lubac has shown persuasively how the Grand Inquisitor's greatest reproach against Christ is that He placed too much confidence in humankind; in doing so, He burdened all of us with "this intolerable burden of freedom."[81] What then is the Inquisitor's solution? It is to implement Shigalevism, as outlined in chapter 2, whereby the vast majority of people will willingly enslave themselves fully—their very souls, in de Lubac's stark summary[82]—to the select few.

Ironically, it seems that Alyosha, the declared hero of *The Brothers Karamazov*, unwittingly is prepared to sacrifice his freedom to another at the novel's outset when he repeatedly regards Father Zosima as his savior. Alyosha seems intent on placing his own freedom in the hands of this person who has become, for him, a substitute for the divine. That at least is how Alyosha reacts when he is overwhelmed by the darkness of his brother Ivan's heart. As they part, with Ivan going to the left—always a sign for Dostoevsky of evil intent—Alyosha longs for nothing but to race back to the monastery, to his beloved Father Zosima, who presumably will save the young novice.[83]

The dying father will do no such thing, nor can he. Neither will Ivan's Christ when confronted with the Inquisitor's outrages in a Spanish prison. Christ refuses the easy way out, the way demanded by his accuser, of "miracle, mystery, and authority."[84] He will not go that route because, for Dostoevsky, the way forward to an ethical world can never involve coercion or an assorted grab bag of metaphysical tricks and trinkets. So Alyosha will need to look elsewhere for his own salvation. In terms of our investigation here, we might say that Alyosha *needs* to look elsewhere for the foundation of his ethical life, just as his biological father, Fyodor Pavlovich, *needs* to look beyond his vodka or Grushenka's sensuous intrigue.

That is, some say, the key to understanding Dostoevsky's tragedy. He was so committed to human and moral freedom, in its initial *and* final manifestations, that he would not countenance an alternative of ethical compulsion. Nor did he allow us to deceive ourselves with any illusions about where his readers' lives, or their world, would go if they never made it past an initial or lesser view of freedom. They must not stay with the freedom of Adam. They needed to strive for something more. They had no choice if they wanted to be individually free and ethical. It was precisely this dynamic yearning for something more complete, more whole, that had so captivated Dostoevsky as he pondered Masha lying on the table in 1864. That is how much the dynamism of Orthodoxy's rich iconic imagery appealed to him in that moment, as did the image of the eternally dynamic and engaging Christ. That is, of course, if his readers were not already paralyzed by a sense of ethical indifference or fears of failure.

Perhaps most surprising of all, he believed that the truly ethical life was most likely to be founded on an edifice of exhausted alternatives, even in the shadow of death itself.

Seeking Wholeness Where Brokenness Resides

Dostoevsky's writings overflow with examples of those who find their way back to a life well lived, and in every instance it is akin to a resurrection.[85] We see it in Raskolnikov in *Crime and Punishment* and Stepan Trofimovich in *Demons*, though it is equally evident in Grushenka, Mitya, Zosima, Markel, and the so-called mysterious visitor; and all of these are from a single novel (*The Brothers Karamazov*). Still others struggle to find their way back, to reach the peace and joy that Dostoevsky associated with true and final freedom. The list here is equally long, though pride of place must surely go to Nastasya Filippovna in *The Idiot*, Kirillov and Stavrogin in *Demons*, and the tormented Ivan in *The Brothers Karamazov*. The shortest list of all may well be that of characters in Dostoevsky's works who do *not* seek their return to moral wholeness.

It seems possible to identify the main aspects of what these personae seek and of what the moral life consists, though we must do so with caution, lest we reduce the dynamism of Dostoevsky's own writings to a scientific certainty. It bears repeating that he was always hostile to lives lived as equations. He was taken instead by the beauty of gestures, symbols, the slanting rays of the sun at sunset, a dove in the cupola—and, above all, by love. None of this is given to unambiguously formulaic summaries. Nevertheless, we begin.

The Illusion of Moral Progress

Raskolnikov experiences a lovely moment in Siberia. It comes after he has bowed in the Haymarket and been sentenced to a Siberian confinement. He is now serving an eight-year prison term for the murder of the elderly pawnbroker and her sister (his sentence having been reduced after he willingly confessed). We are told that the prison fortress is on the banks of a wide and desolate river.[86] While there he falls deliriously ill. During his slow recovery Raskolnikov walks one day to the riverbank and looks out onto that wide river and beyond:

> From the high bank a wide view of the surrounding countryside opened out. A barely audible song came from the far bank opposite. There, on the boundless, sun-bathed steppe, nomadic yurts could be seen, like barely visible black specks. There was freedom, there a different people lived, quite unlike those here, there time itself seemed to stop, as if the centuries of Abraham and his flocks had not passed. Raskolnikov sat and stared fixedly, not tearing his eyes away; his thought turned to reverie, to contemplation; he was not thinking of anything, but some anguish troubled and tormented him.[87]

What doubtless torments him is the idea that he has long deemed himself a superman who stands above the splendid timelessness here spread out before him. Now he knows differently. There are no superhumans, only those deluded as such, and there is likely no moral progress either. The "progressive" society that birthed a Napoleon has lost much more than it has gained. In search of a new goal for his life, Raskolnikov finds himself staring out at "a different people" for whom time seems to have stopped, as if it is no more. De Lubac has called this moment in Raskolnikov's life the birth into a new reality, "the entry into a new world," for in that moment he overcomes the schismatic divisiveness at the core of his name; recall that *raskol* points to a schism, a division, in Russian. This moment of awareness coincides with his recognition that there are no advanced or superior supermen and will, coincidentally, end his existential isolation from all around him, including Sonya.[88]

Similarly, Father Paissy rejects the notion of progressive societies in any substantive sense when he cautions Alyosha about Europe in *The Brothers Karamazov*. The continent may have developed a brilliant ability to examine the parts of things, but always at the expense of understanding the whole, he declares.[89] Ivan Karamazov tells his youngest brother, Alyosha, that he longs to go to Europe, even though he knows it is but a precious graveyard.[90]

By contrast, the timelessness of the Russian People draws Dostoevsky's warmest praise, as does the enduring landscape itself in Raskolnikov's gaze across and beyond a Siberian river. In *Notes from a Dead House*, regarding the Christmas play put on by the convicts, Dostoevsky considers that "the People" have much to teach society's so-called "wise men" but little to learn from them.[91] This is so even though Jackson is correct to conclude that the peasant convicts were not at all pious by nature. They lived most of the year in the most profane manner possible. Then came the splendor of the Orthodox feast days, and it was in those moments that simple Russian convicts found themselves entranced by the moment of ritual purification associated with the birth of the Christ-child. In a sense, they rediscovered their own human image—their iconic form—in a way that even centuries of barbarism could not conceal. That, as Jackson sees it, is how Dostoevsky understood the true greatness of the Russian People.[92] Similarly, it is a peasant who plays such a pivotal role in Stepan Trofimovich's conversion in *Demons*.

Two separate contrasts capture Dostoevsky's portrayal of the salvific role that the People could yet play for Russia. Concerning the first, recall the prince's devastation in *The Idiot* when he sees Rogozhin's copy of Holbein's *The Dead Christ*. In his challenge to it and to the atheism it generates, the prince declares that Russian peasants are the best hope not just for Russia but for the world. This is so because they keep within themselves the essence of religious feeling in its utter unreasonableness.[93]

The second contrast is from *The Brothers Karamazov* and occurs when Father Zosima leaves the feuding Karamazov entourage to meet with the women who have gathered for blessing or counsel from him. They are in two groups: the peasant women and those barely removed from that social estate gather in an open area, and the noblewoman, Madame Khokhlakov, and her daughter Lise are on a specially constructed porch. Dostoevsky titles the chapter on the peasant women "Women of Faith," whereas Madame Khokhlakov's chapter is the already-mentioned "A Lady of Little Faith." The language of the former is intimate and tender: Zosima and the peasant women speak in the familiar second-person singular—a point lost, unfortunately, in translation, which uses the generic English-language "you" throughout. With Madame Khokhlakov and her daughter, however, the language is formal, using second-person plural, and borders on the insincere at times—that is, insincere as spoken by Madame Khokhlakov and her daughter, never by the Elder.

All of this is consistent with Dostoevsky's appeal in *Diary of a Writer*, in which he affirms directly that his own salvation came while in exile, through the Russian People.[94] The reader hears these words and immediately is able to link them with "The Peasant Marey." The Russian People, Dostoevsky writes, remain constant to the old truths of the Christian faith, and that gift will one day save all of humanity: "Does not Orthodoxy, and Orthodoxy alone, contain the truth and the salvation of the Russian People, and in ages yet to come the salvation of the whole of humanity? Has not Orthodoxy alone preserved the divine image of Christ in all its purity? And perhaps the principal, preordained mission of the Russian People, within the destiny of humanity as a whole, is simply to preserve within it this divine image of Christ in all its purity, and when the time comes, to reveal this image to a world that has lost its way!"[95]

When we recall that "the Russian People," the *narod*, refers directly and specifically to the Russian peasantry, we see here Dostoevsky's bold declaration of where moral truth could be found within the empire and where it was absent. Whatever else, it was clear that for Dostoevsky there were no elites to be found in modernity, in the West; even the West's belief in moral progress provided much less than many imagined. Sadly, the West's fixation on the momentarily particular had left it incapable of understanding the whole. We will return to this theme in the next chapter, but for now Dostoevsky's good news was that those readers who realized this great truth were on the way to the moral life.

In Search of Wholeness and the Grand Idea

If Dostoevsky characterized modernity as an age of disassociation and fragmentation, it followed that the moral life was marked by a profound sense of wholeness, even if unexpectedly realized. Many of his characters, such as the relatively modest persona of Lebedev in *The Idiot*, identify our need for a binding idea. On one occasion, Lebedev entertains the prince and his companions with a ghoulish account of how an elderly twelfth-century man willingly confessed that he had eaten "sixty monks and several lay babies" during a long life marked by periodic famine in his region.[96] In his reflections, he contrasts that time with his own "modern" era of "science, industry, associations, salaries, and the rest."[97] People did horrific things to one another then, as now. But Lebedev argues that at least then, people lived under a grand idea that bound them together in a way that no longer exists in this time of railroad-driven modernity. People possessed a binding idea back then—one that arched over everything else. That is what allowed them to survive and to flourish. It was the old man's belief in a binding idea that later compelled him to confess his cannibalistic crimes. Lebedev concludes, "Show me an idea able to bind humankind together that is even half as strong as existed in those centuries."[98]

Stepan Trofimovich seeks no less in his final words, a joyous deathbed farewell:

> The one constant thought that there exists something immeasurably more just and happy than I, fills the whole of me with immeasurable tenderness and—glory—oh, whoever I am, whatever I do! Far more than his own happiness, it is necessary for a man to know and believe every moment that there is somewhere a perfect and peaceful happiness, for everyone and for everything. . . . If people are deprived of the immeasurably great, they will not live and will die in despair. . . . My friends, all, all of you: long live the Great Thought! The eternal, immeasurable Thought![99]

In Stepan Trofimovich's case, peasants are the midwives to this great thought, for it is a peasant-filled cart that stops to pick him up as he sets out on his wandering way at the end of *Demons*. Though this encounter is all too fleeting, Knapp has suggested that it is nevertheless sufficient for

Stepan Trofimovich to experience what he calls "the *vrai* people" (the real people). He even eats *bliny* (Russian-style pancakes) for the first time in his life.[100]

Both Stepan Trofimovich and Lebedev seek a wholeness that ultimately seems to transcend all of time and space. Arkady longs for something more modest in scale, though hardly less significant: his biological father's love. Most certainly he does not want to settle for Versilov's noble lineage. In Arkady's own lament, "And can it be that [Versilov] wasn't faking, but was indeed unable to guess that what I needed was not Versilovian nobility, that it was not my birth that I couldn't forgive him, but that all my life I've needed Versilov himself, the whole man, the father, and that this thought has already entered my blood?"[101]

It is clear that what Arkady needs is a love that transcends generations, one that will somehow confirm and justify his own existence. This, however, also makes him sensitive to the need for a larger binding narrative. Though his own obsession initially is for financial wealth, he is reminded early on that society will collapse without a lofty idea.[102] The cautionary tale, again, is Europe, where we are told that people have been equalized by rights but at the expense of so much more: "Egoism has replaced the former binding idea, and everything has been broken down into the freedom of persons. Set free, left without a binding thought, they have finally lost all higher connection to such a degree that they have even stopped defending the freedom they obtained."[103]

Perhaps Arkady's greatest tragedy is that Versilov, whose love he so desperately seeks, is himself lost when challenged to identify such a "great thought" for his own life. In its stead, he confesses that he yearns only for amusing distractions and assorted diversions.[104]

Dostoevsky's call for wholeness often transcends a narrow view of logic. We see this in two distinct reflections from *The Idiot*, both of which open us up to the writer at his most intimate. The first occurs early in the novel, when the prince reflects on a public execution that he observed in Switzerland—an account that surely would have caused Dostoevsky to reflect on his own near-execution in the late 1840s. The prince's audience, primarily the three daughters of General Ivolgin, is captivated by his account, during which he stresses how a person can live an eternity within a finite amount of time. In those conditions, even a single week before a convict's execution can seem almost endless if lived well by the condemned;

so can the last morning that this doomed individual will see; and so can the final route through dark city streets to the place of execution. Why, even the final moments can seem like an eternity if well lived, even the final quarter-second when the guillotine has been released but has yet to strike his head. And what about when it does strike the head, the prince wonders? "And imagine, to this day they still argue that, as the head is being cut off, it may know for a second that it has been cut off—quite a notion! And if it's five seconds!"[105]

On the second occasion, later in the novel, the prince, who shares Dostoevsky's epileptic condition, reflects on the onset of such an attack. It is for him a time of extraordinary richness: "The sense of life, of self-awareness, increased nearly tenfold in these moments, which flashed by like lightning. His mind, his heart were lit up with an extraordinary light; all his agitation, all his doubts, all his worries were as if placated at once, re-solved in a sort of sublime tranquility, filled with serene, harmonious joy, and hope filled with reason and ultimate cause."[106]

The prince sees these epileptic attacks as much more than a mere medi-cal ailment, for they open up to him a transcendent sense of being. It is after one such episode that he mentions to Rogozhin, whose copy of Holbein's *The Dead Christ* haunts the novel, that the onset of a fit allows him "to un-derstand the extraordinary phrase that *time shall be no more*."[107] This reference to Revelation 10:6—to the last book of the New Testament—suggests how Dostoevsky utilized even chronic physical illness to reveal moments of profound existential insight and deep peace—insight that can also come to someone doomed to certain death. Both point to the degree to which the grand and transcendent idea is a lovely vision in all of his works.

The Ethical Life Is a Thing of Joy and Beauty

That which binds us together, which transcends here and now to con-tain within itself the whole, is always synonymous with beauty and joy for Dostoevsky. This beauty is found in the briefest of moments and tiniest of places in *The Idiot*—for example, when the man on the way to his execu-tion is awestruck by the sun's rays glancing off the gilded dome of a nearby cathedral.[108] We read these words and recall the rays that grace the Mother of God icon in Alyosha's memory in *The Brothers Karamazov* and in Arkady's parallel recollection in *The Adolescent*.

Demons turns on an expressed appreciation of beauty in words brought
to life by Stepan Trofimovich. He declares this boldly at a liberal fundrais-
ing gala for the disadvantaged that is being held with the governor's full
support in the local town. The event is hijacked and then sabotaged by
more radical elements and ends with murderous arsonists setting the town
aflame. Stepan Trofimovich's appearance on stage coincides with this
mounting catastrophe. Had things gone according to plan, he would have
recited a bit of liberal fluff, the pure doggerel of the mindless intellectual
he happens to be. Yet as things transpire, he mounts the stage realizing
that his liberal dreams have given birth to a socialist nightmare. Thus he
unexpectedly declares to the assembled that the rigors of their scientific
socialism will never save the world, or Russia: "And do you know, do you
know that mankind can live without the Englishman, it can live without
Germany, it can live only too well without the Russian man, it can live
without science, without bread, and it only cannot live without beauty, for
then there would be nothing at all to do in the world! The whole secret is
here, the whole of history is here! Science itself would not stand for a
minute without beauty."[109]

Stepan Trofimovich's denunciation in that moment does not exorcize
his radicalized audience of their own demons; that, however, does not rob
his insight of its power. For him, this is not a return to anything remotely
Orthodox so much as a return to the splendor of beauty itself, which coincidentally matches it with the greatest longings of the 1840s generation.[110]
Later on, Kirillov declares much the same when he hears Shatov describe
his joy at his wife's return: "There are seconds, they come only five or six
at a time, and you suddenly feel the presence of eternal harmony, fully
achieved. It is nothing earthly; not that it's heavenly, but man cannot endure
it in his earthly state. One must change physically or die. The feeling is clear
and indisputable. As if you suddenly sense the whole of nature and suddenly say: yes, this is true. . . . In those five seconds I live my life through,
and for them I would give my whole life, because it's worth it."[111] Thus we
can see that Kirillov grasps something of the infinite beauty that has seized
Shatov in that moment. Though neither will survive that very night, Dostoevsky seems to suggest that the beauty that has so captivated them will.

Even the most superficial appreciation of Orthodoxy will help account for at least a portion of Dostoevsky's unwavering belief in beauty's

enduring transcendence, and in a manner that the romantics of the 1840s generation could not have imagined possible. The Primary Chronicle of ancient times, after all, declared that the great Prince Vladimir had been drawn to Orthodoxy in the first place because of its transcendent beauty: a beauty kept alive in a host of ways in the Orthodox practices of Dostoevsky's time. It was transcendentally evident in the unreasoned beauty of Russian iconography and in a theological approach that stressed God's mystery—a mystery best expressed as inexpressible light, joy, and beauty.

In one of the great Russian Orthodox reflections on iconography, *The Art of the Icon: A Theology of Beauty*, Paul Evdokimov begins, "'Beauty is the splendor of truth.' So said Plato in an affirmation that the genius of the Greek language completed by coining a single term, *kalokagathia*. This word combines goodness and beauty together as if they were the two slopes of one mountain. At the highest degree of synthesis, that which is found in the Bible, truth and goodness offer themselves for our contemplation. Their living union, symbiosis denotes the integrity of being from which beauty springs forth."[112]

Orthodoxy inextricably links goodness and beauty. Both flow in and out of the incomprehensibly divine, as do joy and love. Such was certainly the case as Dostoevsky understood it. We see this confirmed in one conversation between the peasant Makar Ivanovich and his de jure son, Arkady, in *The Adolescent*. They are discussing everything from education to wisdom to godlessness when the conversation turns to the anguish of boredom faced by the moderns. Makar Ivanovich continues, "But the big man drinks too much, eats too much, sits on a heap of gold, yet there's nothing but anguish in his heart. Some have gone through all learning—and are still anguished. And my thinking is that the more one learns, the more boredom there is. Take just this: they've been teaching people ever since the world was made, but where is the good they've taught, so that the world might become the most beautiful, mirthful, and joy-filled dwelling place?"[113]

As one might expect, Dostoevsky interwove the all-embracing beauty of joy and goodness throughout his final novel, *The Brothers Karamazov*. One scene stands out: in some ways, the entire novel hinges on the chapter titled "The Wedding at Cana," for it is here that Alyosha confronts the decomposing remains of his beloved Father Zosima. Those who had taken the Elder for a saint, whose remains would thus never face corruption, had

abandoned him with scorn as the unmistakable odor of corporeal decomposition set in. Alyosha himself had already fled in profound disillusion-
ment, hoping that Grushenka would have her way with him sexually and
thereby grant him at least some modest diversion. Yet she did not deliver.
Instead, she had her own conversion to goodness in the moment she realized that Zosima was dead. Now, through her conversion, comes the possibility of Alyosha's own rebirth. With renewed hope, Alyosha returns to
kneel before the deceased Elder, whom all in the monastery have abandoned save for Father Paissy.

Paissy, who is reading the Gospel over the rotting corpse, has reached
the wedding at Cana[114] in the Gospel of John. Cana was the site of Christ's
first miracle, where He turned water into wine. This passage has profound
significance for the Orthodox Church, as it did for Dostoevsky's first
readers, for it symbolizes the joy that Christ brings to human endeavors.
Sublime goodness and joy flow together in the miraculously created wine,
and as Alyosha hears these words he no longer knows where he is. Suddenly he sees Father Zosima himself standing before him. *But surely he's
dead,* Alyosha wonders in amazement. The deceased but seemingly alive
Elder tells his former novice that he is now rejoicing, for he is drinking
"new wine, the wine of a new and great joy."[115] With these words, Dostoevsky links Alyosha with the joy of the new wine, itself a clear link to the
Orthodox observance of the Eucharist, whereby the wine becomes the
blood of Christ for the believer's joy-filled salvation.

Sound bizarre? Perhaps, but not to Alyosha. For in that instant he realizes that somehow Zosima is again prone before him in his coffin, and
Father Paissy's words again drone on. But Alyosha has been forever transformed. He gets up, walks into the night, and looks up in joyous wonder at
the starlit sky. It is as if he suddenly sees something grand in its entirety:
"Some sort of idea, as it were, was coming to reign in his mind—now for
the whole of his life and unto ages of ages. He fell to the earth a weak
youth and rose up a fighter, steadfast for the rest of his life, and he knew it
and felt it suddenly, in that very moment of his ecstasy."[116] In that moment
Alyosha has experienced the whole within his own previously shattered
being. Even as the tragedy of Zosima's death has been overwhelmed by
joy, so is Alyosha able to see that goodness and joy are forever intertwined
in Christ, for ages unto ages. Alyosha leaves the monastery as Zosima had
called on him to do and sets out to live in the world. He is able to do so be-

cause, according to Frank, the "unnamed Christ" has become "awesomely present and triply praised" in Alyosha's vision. He is able to leave the monastery because the joy that had overwhelmed him at the dead father's side has become incarnate and transcendent in love.[117]

But how would Alyosha live that life? What are the primary components of the life deemed ethical? We turn, finally, to these vital questions.

The Call to Shame, Suffering, and Forgiveness

Vladimir Sergeyevich Soloviev, the philosopher and theologian, developed a close relationship with Dostoevsky in the final decade of the latter's life despite the more than thirty years that separated them in age. So it was fitting that Soloviev paid tribute to his great mentor when he delivered three public addresses shortly after Dostoevsky's death in 1881. In the first of these, he distinguished his mentor from the other great writers of his day, notably Tolstoy and Turgenev. He suggested that Dostoevsky's great strength lay in the dynamic nature of his writing; and here, again, we are back to the limitless dynamism found in the Russian icon, of image and likeness. Never content simply to portray Russian society as it was, Dostoevsky always sought to divine where it might yet go—where it *must* go.[118] Soloviev maintained that Dostoevsky could do this precisely because he had lived through all of the deviations that he later dissected so skillfully, even as he had also come to accept the moral right and truth associated with Orthodoxy.

Dostoevsky's hold on Soloviev did not end there. We see this clearly in the eminent philosopher's magnum opus on the moral life, *The Justification of the Good: An Essay on Moral Philosophy*, in which he argues that one of the great distinguishing features of humans is their ability to feel shame. From shame we gain two vital insights: we see clearly where we are now, and we become aware of a higher level to which we might aspire morally. Soloviev concluded that those who had never experienced shame had had their life's senses dulled; they had allowed themselves to become less than what it meant to be human. Reflecting on the biblical account of the fall of humankind in the Garden of Eden, a fall in which all except Christ participated, Soloviev writes, "At the moment of fall a higher voice speaks in the depth of the human soul asking: Where art thou? Where is thy moral dignity? Man, lord of nature and image of God, dost thou still exist? And the answer is at once given: I heard the Divine voice and I was afraid of laying bare my lower nature. *I am ashamed, therefore I exist*; and not physically only, but morally."[119]

These reflections, though Soloviev's,[120] open us up to Dostoevsky's own understanding of the primary shape of the ethical life, starting with the necessary—though always voluntary—embrace of shame. At the same time, "I am ashamed, therefore I exist" serves as the boldest of counterpoints to the Cartesian tradition built on "I think, therefore I exist." They alert us to new, if uncomfortable, ethical approaches. As Deborah A. Martinsen suggests in her own study of Dostoevsky and the dynamics of shame, Dostoevsky reminds readers that shame is the appropriate response for everyone to feel in a postlapsarian world (i.e., for Orthodox Christians, the time that followed humankind's fall, after Adam and Eve ate the forbidden fruit in the Garden of Eden). Nor is shame's effect easy to limit, for our exposure to the shame of another has the paradoxical effect of making us reflect on our own shame. Thus shame isolates the individual while making it possible to create a new community as intersubjective boundaries collapse. Martinsen believes that for Dostoevsky, shame was an essential device by which Europeanized, individualized Russians would return to a new identity grounded in the interdependence of the People.[121]

We Become Ethical Beings
When We First Embrace Our Shame

An awareness of shame is omnipresent in those of Dostoevsky's characters who seek to rediscover their full humanity. Grushenka, the seductress who wants to despoil Alyosha's virginity, suddenly backs away when told of Father Zosima's recent death, despite Alyosha's willingness to be sexually intimate. She is, after all, sitting on his lap. But her first reaction to that death is to cross herself piously, then rise from Alyosha's lap. When praised by Alyosha for her integrity in that great moment of amorous temptation, Grushenka responds, "And don't praise me after that, Alyosha, don't think I'm good. I'm wicked, wicked as can be, and if you praise me you'll make me ashamed."[122] Thus, her shame is vital—she herself knows the degree to which she is unworthy of praise. Somewhat later, as a bloodstained Mitya comes to her one last time to say good-bye before blowing his brains out, Grushenka again responds, "What shame, Mitya! Oh, I'm ashamed, Mitya, ashamed, so ashamed for my whole life! Cursed, cursed be those five years, cursed!"[123]

Mitya's moment of shame comes only a few moments later, in a two-fold manner. He feels immense disgrace after his arrest, when he is compelled to remove his clothing to be searched for clues to the murder of his father. The language of disgrace, guilt, and shame is everywhere here[124] and signals a dawning awareness that Mitya's degenerate lifestyle has brought him to this moral dead end. We see this clearly, just as he himself does during the interrogation that follows, during which he is forced to confess that he stole and then hid money from his now-abandoned fiancée, Katya. He acknowledges before the authorities that he knows he is nothing but a common thief—a term he repeatedly uses as self-description, with obvious shame.[125] Indeed, Mitya considers this theft so base that it will put to shame those officials who must listen to his confession: "I'll tell you everything, so be it, I will now confess all my infernality to you, just to put you to shame."[126] This sense of a shame felt for others hearkens back to *The Idiot*, when Ganya strikes the prince in the face. The prince responds immediately with tearful sorrow, not for the wound inflicted on his own person, but for the impact this will have on Ganya. The prince says with a faltering voice, "Oh how ashamed you'll be of what you've done!"[127]

In all of this, Dostoevsky is relentless in his pursuit of shame's diverse manifestations. We see this in his depiction of a still-unrepentant Raskolnikov, who languishes in a Siberian prison. Raskolnikov has adjusted well enough to prison food and is not shamed by his shaved head and convict's clothes. Even the work is bearable. What he *cannot* bear is the pitying love of Sonya, who has followed him to this desolate landscape and will not abandon him. He is ashamed before her, and he responds by persistently tormenting her, so much so that she comes to fear him. Yet even then she will not abandon him. Raskolnikov was initially ashamed because he had allowed himself to admit to a crime for which he could have escaped punishment, thereby proving himself to be a superman. Martinsen argues that this is one clear instance in which Raskolnikov's awareness of his own shame is essential for his return to community.[128] As always, there are layers of meaning in Dostoevsky: the reader is compelled not merely to accept the notion of shame, as in this instance, but also to wrestle with what that state reveals.

Shame Opens Up the Possibility of Repentance

Dostoevsky almost never presents characters who have placed themselves beyond the realm of a new beginning; almost all of them find it possible to repent and begin anew. Confession and the new life that awaits are at the heart of Raskolnikov's encounter with Sonya, recounted at the opening of this chapter. It is the act of public confession that moves Raskolnikov to "bow at the crossroads" as his first repentant act.

The list of those who follow Raskolnikov through the gate of repentance is a long one. It includes major characters such as Grushenka and Mitya, and even Alyosha, who abandons his attempt to seduce Grushenka for the new life symbolized by the wedding at Cana (which lends its name to the chapter that immediately follows). Distinct patterns emerge across Dostoevsky's writings. Repentance must come out of suffering, as it clearly does for Raskolnikov, whereas Alyosha's own fall can be tied directly to the death of his beloved mentor, Father Zosima. He is never lower than when Grushenka is there on his lap. In the chapter of *Demons* initially banned by censors, Stavrogin sexually assaults an adolescent girl who subsequently commits suicide; Stavrogin then goes to Bishop Tikhon in confession. Almost immediately, Bishop Tikhon urges Stavrogin to repent and embrace the suffering that lies before him, knowing that Christ, too, will forgive.[129]

Dostoevsky also links repentance directly to the transcendent, as when Stavrogin doubts whether the divine, in whom he really does not believe, can forgive his great atrocity, despite Tikhon's assurance that such forgiveness is possible. Stepan Trofimovich encounters his new life through a reading of Christ's Sermon on the Mount, whereas Grushenka finds her way back through a Russian folktale about how a simple onion made possible a release from hell.[130] In every way, then, Dostoevsky's readers were always more than here and now, if they but realized it.

Lastly on this theme, Dostoevsky privileges peasants, the great Russian *narod*, as the primary agents of repentance. On Mitya's mad journey to Grushenka and his anticipated suicidal act, his simple-hearted driver prompts him to conceive of a new beginning. Zosima, in his youth, had his own crisis when he impatiently struck his servant one day. On reflection, he recognized the shamefulness of this act even though the servant himself had regarded that action as acceptable.[131]

One story captures all of these elements: that of Vlas, whom we meet in an 1873 edition of *Diary of a Writer*. Vlas was a peasant full of bravado who wanted to prove to his friends that he could live without restraint. One of them challenged him to follow through on his dare. Lent was approaching in their village, and the challenger told him that the next time he was in church for Eucharist, he should not consume the bread when given it by the priest, but instead leave the church with it. So he did just that. The challenger took Vlas out of the village into the garden. He asked for the bread—which Orthodox Christians believe is, in that moment, the body of Christ, given for all creation, given for Vlas. The challenger put it on a stick, then handed Vlas a gun and dared him to shoot the Host. So Vlas took the gun and loaded it and was preparing to shoot when he suddenly saw a cross before him with the crucified Christ on it, in the place where the bread had been. Vlas fell unconscious.[132]

Dostoevsky tells this story through the eyes of the priest to whom Vlas had come crawling on his knees in search of a release that he feared would never come. Dostoevsky concludes that Vlas's exact identity is not really known. What we do know, he writes, is that Vlas had overstepped the moral bounds and came looking for a release from his great suffering, even though suffering is what Vlas had long embraced. Would he find the release he needed in repentance? We are not told, though the road map set for us by the fictional Vlas's creator is clear, even as the story itself arouses strong feelings of compassion in those who read it.

It seems that shame opens the door to repentance, but why? We come close to an answer if we adopt Martinsen's findings. At the end of her examination of this subject, she suggests that Dostoevsky employed shame in his writings to reflect his "ethical commitment to universal brotherhood." This is because the recognition of shame coincides with the recognition of separation and disunion. Thus an individual is always, in Martinsen's words, "isolated *from*."[133] It is only once that separation is recognized, and shamefully so, that one is ready to begin the way back toward union and wholeness.

A Life of Active and Limitless Love and Compassion

There is a moment in Father Zosima's encounter with the "lady of little faith," Madame Khokhlakov, when she confesses her inability to believe in any sort of life after death. She is distraught, for she wants proof of im-mortality yet knows she cannot obtain it. Zosima agrees that life after death cannot be proven. But there is no doubt, he adds, that it is possible to be convinced of it. How? she wonders. Zosima answers, "By the expe-rience of active love. Try to love your neighbors actively and tirelessly. The more you succeed in loving, the more you'll be convinced of the existence of God and the immortality of your soul. And if you reach complete selflessness in the love of your neighbor, then undoubtedly you will be-lieve, and no doubt will even be able to enter your soul. This has been tested. It is certain."[134]

This is not the answer that Madame Khokhlakov is seeking, for it raises another stumbling block for her. She tells Zosima that she has no difficulty loving humankind in general, in the abstract. On that level, she often closes her eyes and imagines herself among the destitute and able to comfort all, even to kiss the most appalling sores. The problem for her is that she realizes she depends greatly on the reaction of the one being nursed, for if that person were anything but profoundly grateful to her it would simply fill her with resentment: "In short, I work for pay and de-mand my pay at once, that is, praise and a return of love for my love. Other-wise I'm unable to love anyone!"[135] Zosima replies with a recollection of his own, concerning a physician who came to see him years ago. This physi-cian had also declared his love of all humankind to Zosima, and his will-ingness to give all for those in need, even his own life. The problem, though, was that he struggled mightily as soon as anyone in particular ap-proached him for assistance: "I become the enemy of people as soon as they touch me. . . . On the other hand, it has always happened that the more I hate people individually, the more ardent becomes my love for hu-manity as a whole."[136]

Father Zosima ends his reflections with words of profound encour-agement for the still-struggling Madame Khokhlakov. He urges her to love without regard for her own state and status. If she does that, even through tears and massive disappointments, she will sense the "wonder-working power of the Lord" and the certainty of the immortality she seeks.[137]

In some ways, this brief encounter encapsulates the centrality that Dostoevsky attached not only to an ethic of love but also to its divine manifestation in our world. His position was entirely consistent with the

Orthodox proclamation that God is love. This transcendent love had preceded Dostoevsky's readers in the person of Christ. Their calling, in response to this gesture, was to follow Father Zosima's counsel. They were henceforth to love all and everything without distinction. Even more specifically, readers were called to love people individually, actively, just as they were. Each of these segments deserves comment.

Dostoevsky believed that his readers were called to love because an embodied love in Christ had preceded them; for that matter, it also awaited them in the end. He linked this to immortality because, in essence, true love is indistinguishable from immortality itself. We have already commented on this with reference to the use of icons. In his oeuvre, the Theotokos (Mother of God) is most prominent in the salvific memories of Alyosha in *The Brothers Karamazov* and Arkady in *The Adolescent*. The Theotokos icon is also the one clasped by "the meek one" in Dostoevsky's story of the tragic young suicide. In their contemplative and transcendent power, these icons contain powerful assurances of love-filled immortality. This is why, even though Alyosha's "shrieking" mother, Sofia Ivanovna, has died, the memory of her lifting Alyosha up to the Theotokos icon has endured. And that endurance does not depend on Alyosha's remembrance of it. Orthodox believers of Dostoevsky's time maintained that Mary, the Mother of God revealed in the icon, was eternal. They also understood that she had become Arkady's spiritual mother once and for all, just as she was the eternal mother of all believers. Moreover, the relationship of Mary to Christ in Russian icons suggests an unbreakable link of "loving-kindness" for Dostoevsky, for it is through her that Christ becomes our brother.[138] In short, icons vouchsafe what all Orthodox Christians know: love endures even after death, as Makar Ivanovich joyously affirms before his own earthly end in *The Adolescent*.[139]

Love precedes us; nothing is higher. So says Stepan Trofimovich as he lies dying in *Demons*.[140] Writing directly to his readers, Dostoevsky declares that the link between love and the divine was most directly evident in the person of Christ, who was for him the visible sign of the divine love made manifest.[141] But this love was more than a divine gift: its adoption required humans to respond with compassionate love for all humankind. Dostoevsky affirmed no less in his intimate reflections as he kept vigil with his deceased wife Masha in 1864, when he observed that each one needed to strive toward sacrificial love because our beings were created in love, as was manifest in Christ. Thus readers are urged to love all, to have compassion for all. To do less is to deny something profound about what they were meant to be.[142] Nor is it enough for his readers to love those who were close at hand, for even a love-filled marriage or a love of nation could simply be another manifestation of egoism. If love is a true and timeless reflection of the divine spark, his readers have no option but to freely love all and everything.

At the same time, Dostoevsky never settles for love in the absolute and abstract: it must be manifested actively in the individuals his readers encounter, even at the expense of their personal joy. That is a small price to pay. Liza tells the Underground Man that "with love . . . one can live even without happiness. Life is good even in sorrow."[143] In some ways, *The Idiot* is where this notion of a universal love expressed in countless individual instances is most clearly embodied, for the prince's seeming idiocy is this: he openheartedly accepts all whom he encounters. He loves madly, and he is especially drawn to love those who struggle in sorrow, including above all Nastasya Filippovna, who is a ravishing beauty and a trophy of sorts to many. Yet the prince is more drawn to the deep wounds she carries from past outrages. He feels "infinite pity" for her. Her face "had evoked in his heart all the suffering of pity; the impression of compassion and even of suffering, for this being never left his heart and had not left it now."[144]

It is no surprise that love was paramount for Dostoevsky. Irina Kirillova has recently observed as much simply by considering the writer's markings of his New Testament.[145] Dostoevsky recollected many of these biblical verses in Father Zosima's recorded "talks and homilies"—that is, as recorded by Alyosha long after the death of his spiritual mentor. Zosima urges that all of God's creation be loved, and that children especially be loved, though the same applies to the whole world.[146] The words themselves pour out from the New Testament commands of Christ, who remains forever the embodied ideal whom Zosima urges his own disciples to seek. But the words are no less a reflection of Dostoevsky's careful reading of the earliest church fathers, especially Isaac the Syrian, the seventh-century saint and mountain solitary acclaimed for his spiritual writings and severe asceticism. Isaac communicated an overwhelming sense of unsurpassable divine love, which called forth a response of humility and repentance.[147]

The Unreasoned Embrace of Suffering

Soloviev argues that the second characteristic defining our humanity is pity, which unites us with all living creatures. It simply does not matter whether someone's suffering is justified, in whole or in part: "For this reason participation in the suffering of others (even when they deserve it)— i.e., pity or compassion—can never be immoral. In commiserating with the one who suffers I do not in the least approve of the evil cause of his suffering. Pity for the criminal's suffering does not mean approval or justification of his crime. On the contrary, the greater my pity for the sad consequences of a man's sin, the greater my condemnation of the sin."[148]

Soloviev's encouragement that humans willingly pity and willingly suffer was yet another place of correspondence with his mentor, Dostoevsky, who wrote more than once that all Slavs were particularly gifted with the ability to enter into universal suffering for others. In one particular excerpt he concluded that "the majority of Slavic tribes have themselves been schooled and have developed only through suffering. We wrote above that we are amazed that the Russian People, in their slavery of serfdom, in their ignorance and oppression, never forgot their Orthodox duty, never sank irretrievably into bestiality or became gloomy self-absorbed egotists concerned only for their own advantage. But probably this is just their nature as Slavs; that is, to ascend spiritually in their suffering, to strengthen themselves politically in their oppression; amid slavery and humiliation, to join together in love and in the truth of Christ."[149]

Dostoevsky's reference to Christ's truth and assurance, of course, is the notion that life comes out of suffering and that a cross and a tomb will assuredly give way to endless joy. No wonder Sonya begs Raskolnikov to embrace suffering, or that she willingly takes upon herself the suffering of her whole family at the novel's beginning, as well as Raskolnikov's own suffering at the end. Sonya offers him the cross, the transcendent Christian symbol of suffering as well as of death's ultimate defeat. And we know that Raskolnikov had himself begun to understand the gift that suffering brings, for we are told that he looked with suffering on his own mother as she bade her convict son farewell for the last time.[150] None of this has to do with whether suffering can ever be justified. In Dostoevsky's world, all suffering is in fact unjustified—except, that is, for the suffering that individuals take upon themselves, as James Scanlan notes in his own investigation into the ethical significance of suffering for Dostoevsky.[151] Mitya, in the midst of his own suffering in *The Brothers Karamazov*, knows he is thereby redeemed. He embraces suffering, for he understands that there is a deep connection between one's ability to live, to love, and to suffer, out of which anyone can be resurrected.[152]

Perhaps the most poetic depiction of the embrace of suffering is found in *The Adolescent*. Arkady wants us to understand the person and personality of his nominal father, Makar Ivanovich, so he tells us a story this man told him, a story moving enough to warrant the reading of this entire novel. It concerns a merchant named Maxim Ivanovich who was cruel in every way. He was given to drink, and there was reason to believe he had murdered his first wife. A young merchant in that town had died destitute largely because of the unfair treatment he had received from Maxim Ivanovich. The widow's lot worsened further as Maxim Ivanovich seized what few belongings she had left. Then, in destitution, her little children began to die off until only one was left, a boy. Finally Maxim Ivanovich, a steady churchgoer throughout this entire time, decided to show some kindness for the lad—that is, until the child accidentally broke some of the merchant's fine china. Fearing Maxim Ivanovich's reaction, the boy rushed off and leaped into a fast-flowing river, in which he drowned.[153] Maxim Ivanovich eventually finds his way back to wholeness and marries the woman he had left a widow, whose children's deaths could have all been laid at his door.

I will not say here how this story ends, except to forewarn the reader that "happily ever after" is best found in the company of authors other than Dostoevsky. I *will* say that after a great and repentant struggle for wholeness, Maxim Ivanovich receives "the gift of tears: someone would start talking to him, and he'd just dissolve in tears."[154]

What of this so-called gift? We know from Orthodoxy, from Dostoevsky's world, that a rich patristic tradition surrounds the gift of tears. This is in no small part tied to the Sermon on the Mount, in which Christ declares, "Blessed are those who mourn, for they shall be comforted." For whom should one mourn? There seem to be two reasons why one should weep. First, for our sins, which in the case of Maxim Ivanovich were tied directly to the horrors he had inflicted on his second wife, her first husband, and their little children. This is also the gift of suffering, for it comes from the divine. But these tears are also tears of joy, for with them we begin the process of spiritual purification.

It is of great significance to Arkady's "memoir"—*The Adolescent*—that his biological father Versilov, whose pointless egoism is a constant feature for much of the novel, himself receives the "gift of tears" by its end. This is a sign that he has found his way to a point of ethical wholeness. He is no longer removed from the suffering of others.[155]

Forgiveness for All, Obligated for All

A modern classic study of Orthodox theology, John Zizioulas's *Being as Communion*,[156] would have resonated deeply with Dostoevsky, whom the theologian cites more than once. Zizioulas argues for a profoundly relational understanding of life. How can it be otherwise, he asks, when the divine is eternally one God, yet relational as Father, Son, and Holy Spirit? In Zizioulas's understanding, which itself is fully, almost timelessly Orthodox, humans enter relationally into the divine through the Son and by the working of the Spirit. There is simply no other way to approach the Father. Moreover, the divine's mode of existence is love freely offered and dynamically present to all. Thus Zizioulas stresses the extraordinary uniqueness of all, for once created, they can never really die. That said, we realize our true personhood by becoming like the divine as we ourselves become fully relational, first in the church and then well beyond. Zizioulas writes, referring to the church as "the ecclesial hypostasis": "Thus a characteristic of the ecclesial hypostasis is the capacity of the person to love without exclusiveness, and to do this not out of conformity with a moral commandment ('Love thy neighbor,' etc.) but out of his 'hypostatic constitution,' out of the fact that his new birth from the womb of the Church has made him part of a network of relationships which transcends every exclusiveness."[157] Readers may blanch with good reason at his identification of the person with an exclusively male pronoun, but they should blanch more at the suggestion that each person is compelled into a dynamic relation with every other person without exception. For no one is excluded when love transcends all.

It was Dostoevsky's gift to push that understanding to its logical conclusion. It meant that his readers were obligated for all, because they were, as if in communion, responsible for all. We see this in Shatov, the erstwhile revolutionary who seeks to abandon the socialist cause and whose subsequent murder in the attempt is the tragic focal point of *Demons*. It is he who welcomes his wife back, even though she has become pregnant by another. At the child's birth, Shatov suddenly exclaims, "We're all guilty, we're all guilty. . . . If only we were all convinced of it!"[158] Yet his words go unheeded until near the end of the novel, when a now-repentant Stepan Trofimovich declares, "Oh let's forgive, forgive, let's first of all forgive all and always. . . . Let's hope that we, too, will be forgiven. Yes, because all are guilty one and all before each other. All are guilty!"[159] We sense from this that the repentant life that yearns to be fully moral simultaneously accepts full responsibility for all. Perhaps it is because, as Bishop Tikhon counsels Stavrogin in the banned chapter of *Demons*, when we sin—that is, when we willfully violate the notion that being is communion—we really are sinning against all. Thus each one is at least partly responsible for another one's sin. Stavrogin comes to Tikhon to make confession for horrific past deeds, yet it is the father confessor who mysteriously seeks forgiveness from the "sinner."[160] That is how it is in Dostoevsky's world, where lines of responsibility ripple out to include, eventually, the whole.

There is no other conclusion to be drawn from *The Brothers Karamazov*. Surely all are responsible for the death of the father, including Ivan, who left the scene knowing that the calamity was about to unfold. But it includes Alyosha no less; his faith initially wavers in a novel that is as much concerned with the "death" of the divine Father in the minds of contemporary Russians as it is with Fyodor Pavlovich's tragic demise. All are responsible, Mitya declares before his trial and after dreaming about a poor innocent peasant child, a "wee one" who had been abandoned in the harshest conditions: "Because everyone is guilty for everyone else. For all the 'wee ones,' because there are little children and big children. All people are 'wee ones.' And I'll go for all of them, because there must be someone who will go for all of them. I didn't kill father, but I must go. I accept!"[161]

As is already clear from Stepan Trofimovich's plea, a universal call to forgive accompanies our acknowledgment of our collective guilt. Personae who exercise an all-embracing forgiveness abound in Dostoevsky's literature. They include Sonya, who not only forgives Raskolnikov his crimes but also follows him to the ends of the earth with a love that does not originate within her. Of course, one might argue that it was not her place to forgive the murder of another; that is why Makar Ivanovich is all the more compelling in *The Adolescent.* He is the one whose wife abandoned him for their former serf owner Versilov, with whom she lived a barely fulfilling life. She bore Versilov two children even though he was repeatedly unfaithful, and hardly a father to boot. As ironic humiliation on all sides, these children still bore Makar Ivanovich's name, giving them the oddest of lineages and him the strangest of legacies.

So what does the clearly wronged Makar Ivanovich have to say? In a conversation with his "son" Arkady (Arkasha), who is guilt-ridden over a past offense, Makar Ivanovich says, "Christ will forgive everything, Arkasha; he will forgive your abuse, and he will forgive more than that. Christ is our father, Christ needs nothing and will shine even in the deepest darkness."[162] Later on, Makar Ivanovich models the spirit of forgiveness he saw exemplified in Christ when he forgives Arkady's mother, Sofya Andreevna. It is near the end of his life, and Makar Ivanovich has come to her one last time. As innocent husband and unfaithful wife part, she suddenly says to him, "Well, Christ be with you." Then she leaves. But Dostoevsky's narrator, who is oddly the son of this union, himself concludes, "She left. All her life, in fear and trembling and awe, she had greatly respected her lawful husband, the wanderer Makar Ivanovich, who had magnanimously forgiven her once and for all."

Rowan Williams has recently linked the call to forgiveness in Dostoevsky's canon with the simultaneous call to live in community. For sinners who ask for forgiveness must themselves be ready to extend it, and there is no end to this action and reaction.[163]

The Brothers Karamazov is ultimately about our need to forgive and the self-inflicted wounds we receive when we fail to do so. It is a word of forgiveness that Father Zosima urges a peasant woman to utter to the deceased husband who had physically abused her in life.[164] In countless ways, from Zosima's final words to those of his brother Markel, whose death preceded his own, Dostoevsky's readers are gently, repeatedly, and relentlessly called to a level of forgiveness that is beyond their imagining. How could one forgive all, or be responsible for all? Are his readers not permitted to distinguish between their generalized responsibility for all on the one hand, and those who are truly guilty for specific misdeeds on the other? Dostoevsky did not answer these questions, though he made our engagement with them inescapable. He did leave his readers with a puzzle that was perhaps best expressed by an "idiot": "You know, in my opinion it's sometimes even good to be ridiculous, if not better; we can the sooner forgive each other, the sooner humble ourselves, we can't understand everything at once, we can't start right out with perfection! To achieve perfection, one must first begin by not understanding many things. . . . Let us become servants, in order to be elders."[165] In this way, Dostoevsky linked his readers' ability to forgive with their ability to achieve perfection. And if that linkage puzzled them, his call to embrace death itself with joy would have left readers thoroughly bewildered.

The Embrace of Death

Every topic raised in this chapter is worthy of a book-length investigation, and such is surely the case with death, which comes in various ways in Dostoevsky's writings. He provides us with countless variations. Innocent children die from disease or ill treatment. Fyodor Pavlovich, Shatov, the former criminal Fedka, and others are murdered as adults, and still more — many more — commit suicide. There is little solace to be found, except perhaps for what Zosima tells a grieving mother — that her infant child is now joyous in the presence of the divine.

There is, however, a way in which death loses its sting in Dostoevsky's prose, or, at the least, is nothing to be feared. Dostoevsky repeatedly declares that life itself comes out of death. The epigraph to *The Brothers Karamazov* speaks directly to the life that comes out of death, for it proclaims the words of Christ, Himself risen from the dead in Dostoevsky's understanding, once and for all in the Gospel of John: "Very truly, I tell you, unless a grain of wheat falls into the earth and dies, it remains just a single grain; but if it dies, it bears much fruit" (NRSV). These words point to a profound and hope-filled transcendence. They suggest that death is not an ending as much as it is a manifold beginning, and it is surely no coincidence that this particular verse adorns Dostoevsky's gravestone in St. Petersburg's Tikhvin Cemetery.

A similar vision of life out of death shapes the core of *Crime and Punishment*, where the account of Christ's resurrection of Lazarus is prominent in Raskolnikov's own rebirth. He only begins to live once he has embraced his own death, which is surely what he does when he bows at the crossroads. Could Dostoevsky be suggesting that the line between life and death is not as great as his own contemporaries assumed? Was he calling on his readers to understand both life and death in inverse proportion to what a post-Orthodox and modern world deemed to be the case? Certainly Father Zosima saw barely a loss at his own dying, for this marked nothing less than a time when heaven and earth touched each other. He declared as much in his own recollections, gathered together by Alyosha: "But what is here is this very mystery—that the passing earthly image and eternal truth here touched each other. In the face of earthly truth, the enacting of eternal truth is accomplished."[166]

Who can doubt that death is a mystery, and all the more so if one imagines that something awaits us after this world, as Dostoevsky had reason to hope in his own direct ruminations over Masha? No wonder Zosima was able to go to his own death "in joyful ecstasy, kissing the earth and praying (as he himself had taught) quietly and joyfully" as "he gave up his soul to God."[167]

At the end of *The Brothers Karamazov*—also the end of the last novel Dostoevsky would write—we again encounter life starting in the face of tragic death. This time it is the death of young Ilyushechka, whose father is wracked with grief and whose family is in utter disarray. Within that setting, Alyosha gathers his gang of twelve together to mark a new beginning, a sort of birth coming out of a tragic death. Alyosha is determined that death will not have the last word here. It is not even death, really. For even here there are signs of a great new birth and a memory that will last from ages to ages.

At this point we are ready to return, finally, to where this chapter began. We again see Raskolnikov before us. He is dying to his old self as he kneels at the crossroads, wearing a cross he has only just acquired. We see Sonya's heartrending decision to accompany him on this most dramatic journey toward confession and imprisonment, and we recognize that this act of surrender has the unexpected promise of new life all about it.

For even as Ilyushechka's tragic death mirrors Christ's own death, as has previously been suggested by Kroeker and Ward, so are reminders of death and humility everywhere in Dostoevsky's Russia. And all of them point to Christ—to the one whom Vladimir Lossky and countless other Orthodox theologians regard as the eternal self-emptying Son of the Father.[168] No words capture this kenotic act better than those of Philippians 2:5–8: "Let the same mind be in you that was in Christ Jesus, who, though he was in the form of God, did not regard equality with God as something to be exploited, but emptied himself, taking the form of a slave, being born in human likeness. And being found in human form, he humbled himself and became obedient to the point of death—even death on a cross" (NRSV).

As Kroeker and Ward note, however, for Dostoevsky, eschewing the ethics of violent self-assertion "requires that the death-dealing violent and retributive pattern of fallen desire be 'put to death,' in order for the self to be reborn into a community where even kinship relations are transfigured into nonrivalrous, nonegoistic relations of love. . . . At the motivating heart of this participation in the kenotic pattern of Christ is neither dazzling miracle nor forensic transaction—it is the transformation of all of life by holy, erotic, divine love."[169] This was the path that Dostoevsky, following an Orthodox faith tradition that clearly and profoundly shaped him, urged his readers to choose in an empire that was being pulled in a different direction. It had to be so because the only alternative he could envision was one that claimed power over weakness, with violence and self-assertion as its ethical engine.

There is no doubt that following this sort of death-embracing, life-giving ethic would have been profoundly difficult for Dostoevsky's first readers to imagine, let alone live out. Yet Margaret Ziolkowski has persuasively argued that Dostoevsky relied heavily on this kenotic tradition within Orthodoxy—a tradition that already had several centuries of development behind it by the time he began to write. It was from this kenotic tradition that some of the most powerful Dostoevskian characters emerged, in the persons of Bishop Tikhon from *Demons* and the Elder Zosima from *The Brothers Karamazov*.[170] It was a religious tradition rooted in the willful embrace of suffering, of moral responsibility for all, and of an almost mind-numbing willingness to embrace suffering and even shame. Above all, it was dominated by what Scanlan has called "the figure of Christ as the supreme ethical ideal and the Christian law of love as the supreme ethical principle."[171]

It seems likely that few would have embraced Dostoevsky's moral universe other than the Orthodox personae of Zosima and Tikhon. Yet many others aspire to join them, including Makar, Versilov, and Sofya in *The Adolescent*, and Aloysha and Mitya Karamazov in the *The Brothers Karamazov*. Stepan Trofimovich longs to embrace that new life in Christ by the end of *Demons*; that entire novel can be read as Nikolai Stavrogin's attempt to do the same, an attempt that sadly ends in his suicide. Or we can turn to Svidrigailov of *Crime and Punishment*, who seeks to embrace the grand ideal even as he takes his own life in despair. We see the same tensions fully at work in *Demons'* Kirillov, with an equally tragic end. Taken together, we can see why Ivanov once described Dostoevsky as the author of the novel as tragedy. For each can find his way into the icon's embrace; each can find his way to a life of supreme and unending beauty, if he but chooses to do so. Alas, the tragedy is that so often we make other choices.

Dostoevsky consistently argued that none of this ethical transformation was possible without a belief in immortality—more specifically, without the Russian Christ, who remained the great writer's eternal ideal. Of course, not all agreed, and many of his first readers rejected exclusively Christian ethical claims as anachronistic and intolerant. Dostoevsky battled against those challenges with ever greater ferocity in the last years of his life. We turn now to that debate as it unfolded in his time and under his watch.

CHAPTER 4

In Search of a Universal Reconciliation

Two Speeches, One Vision, and
"The Means to Save the World"

Dostoevsky advanced an argument with his readers in January 1877 that he deemed both sensitive and controversial: "Every great people believes and must believe, if it wants to survive long, that in it and in it alone is contained the means to save the world; that it lives in order to stand at the head of the nations, to bring them all to communion with it and to lead them, in a harmonious choir, toward the ultimate goal for which they are destined."[1]

He further claimed that it was precisely this faith in a world-changing mission that had elevated all past and present great powers to positions of "immense, global influence on the fate of humanity."[2] Such was unmistakably the case, for example, with ancient Rome, but it was no less the case with Catholic France after it inherited that ideal from Rome. Indeed, France had continued to see itself as "the leader of the world's advance and as guide to its future," morally at least, until its recent and devastating defeat by the Germans in 1871. Even then, Catholic France's humiliation had not resulted in the utter defeat of French universalist thinking. Quite the contrary, it had led to the full flourishing of French Catholicism's stepchild: socialism. What was the idea that bound Catholic and socialist France together? It was, Dostoevsky had written in a previous installment of *Diary of a Writer*, the forced pacification of society by an overarching state, with or without Christ.[3]

Dostoevsky contrasted the Catholic socialist idea of political hegemony with the German idea, one that emerged out of Protestantism. The latter stressed individual freedom over the more statist controls of the former. This was a belief in "endless freedom of conscience and enquiry set . . . against the universal Catholic idea and its authority."[4] Dostoevsky then turned his gaze to England, where he observed an English notion of what being English, and human, meant. In every instance he maintained that the egoism of each respective culture had a threefold expression, starting with "the faith that one wants to and can express to the world the ultimate word, that one *can* at least renew the world with the surplus of one's own living force; [second] the faith in the sanctity of one's own ideal; [and third] the faith in the strength of one's love and ardent desire to serve humanity—no, such a faith is the token of the very highest life of nations, and only through it will they bring all that benefit to humanity they have been destined to bring."[5]

Dostoevsky fully sympathized in *Diary of a Writer* with those Europeans who deemed themselves to be more than citizens of a state, for they always regarded themselves coincidentally as panhumans. He appreciated how Europeanized Russians had long regarded themselves as "panhumans" in their embrace of these broader European intellectual trends, and he sympathized with their desire to adopt a higher form of moral living. The problem—and it was of monumental importance for him—was that these European Russians had made a near-fatal error of judgment when they tried to elevate themselves morally through European understandings. For in the attempt they had bypassed a truly universal ethic of future harmony in the Orthodox Christ for one grounded in what was ultimately groundless and thus doomed to fail. How could it be otherwise when contemporary Europeans, in the shadow of statist France, had sought to unify the world with an ethic based on little more than positive science and porous moral boundaries defined by the freest of spirits? He marveled how anyone could honestly conclude that science was capable of determining those moral boundaries.[6]

Nor was that the end of this ongoing tragedy. Dostoevsky lamented the cost that Russia had paid for European acculturation. As he saw it, this aping of Europe had alienated Russia's elite from Russia's People. Unwittingly, it had also distanced these Europeanized Russians from Europe it-self. How could it be otherwise, he asked, when elite Russians had entered indiscriminately into the contemporary European intellectual scene, bor-rowing an ethical adage here and an intellectual movement there? They thought, he wrote, that they were thereby creating a universal and cosmo-politan type of European, but they were not. Instead, Europeans looked derisively upon these Russian Europhiles as "aliens and newcomers." That Dostoevsky often used the first-person plural to identify these European-ized Russians suggests the degree to which he understood his own com-plicity in this Eurocentric approach—during the 1840s especially, prior to his seemingly dramatic spiritual conversion in a Siberian prison.

By the late 1870s, Dostoevsky was contending that Europeanized Rus-sians had become the "universal wretches of Europeanism, liberalism, and socialism" at their own expense, and their homeland's. Their behavior had done harm to their previously servile population, whose lot had actually worsened since their supposed emancipation in 1861. After all, it was the peasants who were expected to pay for this elite pursuit of European mo-dernity. This was especially tragic given that a much more glorious ethic of the heart, an ethic of all-embracing love, was right in front of them.[7] In-deed, this readily available ethic was the only one that would win the day because it alone was founded on absolute truth. But all was not lost, for in order to triumph, this truly universalist ethic required only a change of mind among Europeanized Russians, who only needed to set aside their recently acquired European ethic of "isolation, dissociation, and the self-enclosed world of sectarianism" in favor of one unified "in the spirit of genuine, broad love."[8] This meant a change of mind, he wrote, not a change of heart, for their hearts had been in the right place all along. And in the end that would make all the difference.

What was at the heart of Dostoevsky's withering analysis, strident de-nunciation, and heartfelt appeal? Harriet Murav has argued that Dosto-evsky's literary approach began to change after 1876, for at that time he no longer saw himself as simply a chronicler of Russian society (if Dosto-evsky had ever "simply" been anything). Henceforth he was determined to restore or reimage Russia itself, for which he used the Russian verb *obrazit*. Murav observes that Dostoevsky explicitly used that word in an ar-ticle published in the January 1876 issue of the *Diary of a Writer*, in which he examined animal cruelty in Russia, though he acknowledged in a note at that time that he had often heard *obrazit* used by convicts during his Siberian confinement. Those who had been drinking too much were occasionally advised by the other inmates to go and "reform" or "reimage"— *obrazit*—themselves. Dostoevsky suggested in his 1876 article that *obrazit* implied the need to be re-formed in a human image. But Murav points out that *obrazit* contains another, deeper meaning: it alludes directly to the image or *obraz* of God, in whose image the Orthodox believed humankind was created. In this sense the word has an unmistakably iconographic connection. It was this human imaging in the divine made manifest in Christ that Dostoevsky feared was being cast aside by elite Russia's fascination with all matters European.[9] So he was determined to speak out directly. He wrote in January 1877 that "*each one* must say his piece as frankly and as directly as possible, without feeling any shame for naively laying bare certain of his ideas."[10]

"Lay bare" is exactly what Dostoevsky did as he countered those calling for the ongoing Europeanization of Russian culture with his own appeal that elite Russia turn again to the Russian Christ. This chapter investigates Dostoevsky's argumentation and approach on this vital matter. As is already evident in this chapter's introduction, we will be investigating Dostoevsky, the nonfictional publicist, for he did speak directly to the reader in *Diary of a Writer*, and with increasing urgency in the late 1870s. That said, an even greater public platform was presented to him in what may have been his crowning achievement, his speech on June 8, 1880, at the unveiling of a monument in Moscow to the "Russian Shakespeare," Alexander Pushkin. Though other literary greats also spoke at this major intellectual event, it was Dostoevsky's impassioned plea that Pushkin be seen as a distinctly Russian type—as someone who opened the door to the salvation of all humankind—that overwhelmed all others. The speech is of considerable significance for our understanding of Dostoevsky's critique of Europe generally and Europeanized Russians specifically; it also offers us a rare opportunity to observe Dostoevsky's own self-reflection, for he provided an introduction to his own speech when he published his remarks in *Diary of a Writer* shortly after delivering them. And even this was not the end of the story: a critical response to Dostoevsky by the liberal A. D. Gradovsky allowed Dostoevsky a final opportunity to articulate his own views. It is here, as much as anywhere, that we grasp the full flowering of Dostoevsky's contention that an ethical worldview built on a cocktail of atheism, science, and liberalism is doomed to fail. In a manner that occasionally bordered on caricature, he argued that such a Eurocentric worldview represented the weakest of conceptual parochialisms, one that relied on brute force to make itself known and accepted.

Dostoevsky did not fear that this sort of modernism would be the last word: he firmly believed that, in the end, a universal ethic would emerge triumphant. Contrary to Europeanized Russian opinion, this certain victory would come not from Europe's flawed Enlightenment but rather from a Russian People (the famed *narod*) who had long maintained their rich ethical and Orthodox beauty despite the worst excesses of Imperial Russia's Petrine revolution, regardless of their own assorted transgressions and abominations. Dostoevsky spoke to this certitude from the extraordinarily public platform afforded to him by the Pushkin Monument's unveiling in 1880. There, at the height of his powers, he argued that the only conceivable and universal ethic was one rooted in Russia's Orthodoxy as preserved by the Russian People, and in a "Russian" Christ who was ineffably beautiful.

The second half of this chapter focuses on a single novel, *The Brothers Karamazov.* Robert Belknap has documented how Dostoevsky had turned to this great project by the spring of 1877. Though his earliest notes are lost, a letter by Dostoevsky written in March 1877 makes it clear that he was working on a novel that he indicated would feature children—"particularly young ones, from 7 to 15." His writing was curtailed briefly and tragically in May 1878 by the sudden death of his beloved son, Alexei, from an epileptic seizure. But Dostoevsky continued on, and by June he had already sold the rights for this new novel to the journal *Russkii Vestnik.*[11]

I contend that Dostoevsky used *The Brothers Karamazov* in a manner unlike what he had previously undertaken. Now, more than ever, he was determined to "reimage" his Russian readership in a manner that dramatically differentiated Dostoevsky the novelist from the publicist. Regarding the latter, Gary Saul Morson has pointed to Dostoevsky's increasingly strident tone in *Diary of a Writer* by the late 1870s. Ironically, he now shared characteristics of the same intelligentsia by whose conclusions he was most appalled. Thus he also became increasingly unable or unwilling to give contrary views their due in his reportage. In fact, he appeared willfully to distort them on occasion,[12] and in doing so he obscured the depth and rhetorical persuasiveness of his own deeply held positions. At the same time, as Robin Feuer Miller has pointed out, he had been aware since at least 1861 that convictions uttered directly ran the risk of looking like "copybook maxims." He understood that his deepest convictions could be cheapened if he expressed them directly and without nuance, especially when they pertained to the ultimately inexpressible. Far better, he wrote, to "sweeten truth as though it were a bitter pill" through humor, satire, and the like.[13]

So it is that Dostoevsky's prose took on a dramatically different shape in the late 1870s, and nowhere more so than in the incomparable *The Brothers Karamazov*. As Bakhtin notes in his seminal study *Problems of Dostoevsky's Poetics*, Dostoevsky's true genius lies in his fiction, for it is there that he presents every thought as itself dialogic and internally unfinished, as is every person.[14] All voices need to be heard in this dynamic interplay of external (expressed) and internal dialogue. Dostoevsky wished to create a forum, or stage, which Bakhtin likens to the medieval carnival: "The main arena for carnival acts was the square and the streets adjoining it. To be sure, carnival also invaded the home; in essence it was limited in time only and not in space; carnival knows neither stage nor footlights. But the central arena could only be the square, for by its very idea carnival *belongs to the whole people*, it is *universal, everyone* must participate in its familiar contact. The public square was the symbol of communal performance."[15]

According to Bakhtin, Dostoevsky's radically dialogical stance recreates this public and carnivalesque square in literary form. The second half of this chapter considers Dostoevsky's depiction and utilization of this public square as located in *The Brothers Karamazov*. As a case study of sorts, it pays particular attention to how Dostoevsky spoke his moral truth about Christ when making his appeal, while boldly providing contrary views with sufficient space to make their voices heard.

So we begin with Pushkin, and Dostoevsky's first (and last) great public moment of ethical engagement.

Pushkin and the People: Dostoevsky and the Monument Unveiling

Dostoevsky's first great public appearance also proved to be his last. It occurred during the public unveiling of a monument to Pushkin in the early summer of 1880. Pushkin had long been a barometer of sorts for Russian society, and both liberals and conservatives claimed an intellectual linkage to this early-nineteenth-century Russian poet. His tragic death in 1837 (the result of a duel at the age of thirty-eight) only added to his mystique, while his foreshortened literary career added to the ambiguity of his legacy. Marcus C. Levitt has shown how the unveiling of this monument, which brought together the literary greats of nineteenth-century Russian culture, turned into an intellectual sparring match with Pushkin's literary legacy as the trophy. The Society of Lovers of Russian Literature, which had organized the event, sent invitations to such literary greats as Tolstoy, Saltykov, Goncharov, and Ostrovsky.[16] The biggest draws however, were to be Ivan Turgenev and Dostoevsky, who by the 1870s were viewed as bitter rivals. They were scheduled to address those assembled on consecutive days.

Turgenev spoke first, on June 7, 1880, and Levitt comments on Turgenev's paradoxical challenge at this time. Except for brief and infrequent visits, he had lived abroad for almost two decades before returning for the unveiling. Thus he was inescapably linked to Russia's emerging liberal movement and to the very developments that Dostoevsky regarded so skeptically. So Turgenev's challenge on this great occasion was to communicate the strength of that great liberal hope—one that called for greater freedom of speech and democratic pluralism along European lines—while acknowledging liberal concerns that Russia's peasant masses were not yet ready for either. Turgenev had worked behind the scenes to bar the conservative Mikhail Katkov from this monumental celebration, lest his views be given too much attention. Openness, it seems, had its limits.[17]

By the late 1870s, Dostoevsky's stature was so great that he could not possibly be excluded. Even so, he worried about his reception in Moscow that June and about the opposition he was sure to encounter. Joseph Frank quotes from a letter Dostoevsky wrote to a colleague en route to the Pushkin Festival: "I have prepared my speech about Pushkin, and precisely in the most *extreme* spirit of my . . . convictions, and therefore I expect, perhaps, a certain amount of abuse. . . . But I'm not afraid, and one should serve one's cause, and I will speak without fear. The professors there are paying court to Turgenev, who is absolutely turning into a personal enemy of mine."[18]

Dostoevsky's reference to "professors" captures well the revolutionary changes under way in Russia's universities in the second half of the nineteenth century. Writing a half-century later, Nestor Kotliarevskii looked back on this period as one that saw an explosion of secular reasoning in postsecondary institutions, including "a substitution of anthropology for religion, inductive method for deductive method, materialistic monism for idealistic dualism, empirical aesthetics for abstract aesthetics, and the theory of rational egotism for morality based on supersensory principles."[19] Historian Alexander Vucinich has called this "a period of national awakening" for Russia. It was reflected in the ballooning interest in the natural sciences, but no less in the growth of positivist thinking, which Vucinich suggests emerged at this time "on the ruins of religious and metaphysical thought."[20] Indicative of this, H. T. Buckle's *History of Civilization in England* became hugely popular among Russia's emerging professoriate, who viewed science as the primary agent of social progress. But even Buckle's history could not match the enthusiasm afforded the works of Charles Darwin, whose *On the Origin of Species* had been translated into Russian within two months of its initial publication in English in 1859. We are told that the educated public in Russia was "immediately receptive" to Darwinian thought.[21] Vucinich writes that the older professoriate continued to resist this intellectual revolution; that, however, began to change once a new generation entered the ranks in the 1860s and 1870s.[22] After all, as Dostoevsky himself put it in reference to the liberal Stepan Trofimovich in *Demons*, "there was something truly lofty here and, to use the newest language, almost a struggle for existence."[23] Russian academics were now enthusiastic about social Darwinism and its claims about an ageless struggle for existence, all of this unfolding within a universe deemed profoundly disenchanted. Kliment Timiriazev, a pioneer in the field of plant physiology, was one of the first scientists to link Darwin's thought on evolution to the empire's nascent liberal political thinkers, thereby contrasting it with the emerging community of radical Russian nihilists who were equally enraptured by Darwinian thought. One assessment concluded, "Under the influence of Timiriazev's popular writings on Darwinism, this scientific theory soon became a part of the political creed of all those persons who considered themselves progressive in social and political thought."[24]

None of this was lost on Dostoevsky, whose entire body of post-exilic writing can be viewed as an ongoing dialogue with proponents of these trends. As only a single example of such engagement for our purposes here, he published one of the first Russian critiques of Darwin's *On the Origin of*

Species in the journal *Time* (*Vremya*), which he had founded with his brother Mikhail in 1862. The critique, written by N. N. Strakhov, did not dispute the merits of Darwinist thought in accounting for certain developments in the natural sciences. But Strakhov strongly opposed applying it to the social sphere—something that the work's French translator had done in his preface. Strakhov deemed that application of Darwin's thesis inappropriate, an academic sleight of hand with little connection to Darwin's thesis. He argued that human sympathy for the poor and weak would disappear if ever the human race was divided into "superior" and "inferior" races.[25] Strakhov's views, though, were increasingly marginalized in an academic environment captivated by social and scientific positivism. No wonder, then, that Dostoevsky, whose own assessment followed from Strakhov's, viewed "the professors" with a mixture of suspicion and alarm as he anticipated his own presentation during the Pushkin Festival of June 1880.

Upon his arrival in Moscow, matters unfolded in rapid succession: the monument was unveiled on June 7, and Dostoevsky provided a reading that evening. He was not prepared for the wildly enthusiastic welcome and public adulation he received. Turgenev's reading that same evening was less well received (one cannot help but recall the readings associated with the imploding gala for provincial governesses in *Demons*). Dostoevsky's presentation to the assembled on June 8 was a sensation. An earlier biographer of his, Konstantin Mochulsky, later enthused, "This amazing day does not have a parallel in the whole history of Russian spiritual culture."[26] That evening, Dostoevsky wrote a letter to his wife, Anna, in which he described the thunderous applause, the tears, and the shouts of "Prophet, prophet!" that were directed toward him.[27]

Much of this had to do, it seemed, with Turgenev's great failure to articulate a contrary position. Instead, the famous author of *Fathers and Sons* had underplayed Pushkin's importance in universal terms and merely identified him as a vital poet in Russia, one who had sought to communicate a cultural enlightenment to his own people. Further ambiguities abounded: Turgenev communicated his deepest hopes in such an equivocal manner that he lost the very audience that had come to hear him. It is no surprise that the assembled turned the next day to Dostoevsky with rapt attention, a feat that Levitt has described as the hijacking of the celebration.[28]

Dostoevsky directed his remarks to the Europeanized Russian elite that he was challenging with increasing passion by the 1870s. He made three strong points in his speech, albeit in a manner that attributed all of them to Pushkin, whom Dostoevsky identified as a prophet of universal significance. Dostoevsky pleaded for Russia's liberal elites to understand that their fascination with Western intellectual trends had been enormously destructive. These Russian liberals had turned their backs on the (Russian and Orthodox) People, the *narod*, who carried within themselves the only true hope of the world. In this way, he used his speech to take on the Eurocentric social Darwinism that had achieved such a strong hold on "the professors."

Timing is everything, it seems, and all the more so with Pushkin in Dostoevsky's telling of it. Early in his speech he reminded those assembled that this greatest of all Russian prophets had appeared on the Russian stage at a time when Russians were coming to terms with the Petrine revolution. Pushkin's genius — and here was Dostoevsky's first major point — was that he had seen how Europeanized Russians (Dostoevsky called them Russia's "wanderers") had lost everything in running after fleeting European trends. They had unwittingly become confused and ridiculous, homeless, detached from the People in their midst, and generally a people without culture who persisted in the delusion that European culture was somehow the world's sole universal culture.[29] Dostoevsky located all of this in Pushkin's careful depictions of key male protagonists, especially Aleko and Onegin.

As bleak as all of this sounded, the good news for Dostoevsky was that Pushkin did not see Russia's wanderers as irretrievably lost. On the contrary (and here was Dostoevsky's second point), Pushkin had deliberately provided a way back for these lost souls. That way hinged on the courage shown by the women in Pushkin's works, especially Tatiana in *Eugene Onegin*. These women's voices called out to the lost Europeanized Russians, having witnessed the truth that Europe did not hold the cultural key to the future. These same women had witnessed the great moral strength that could be found in Russia alone. In some ways, Pushkin had made it so simple: all that these wanderers needed was to be found in Russia itself, and in the Russian People in their faith and truth. "Humble thyself, O haughty man; first curb thy pride. Humble thyself, O idle man; first labor on thy native soil."[30] Unexpectedly, and to the considerable surprise of his listeners, Dostoevsky even seemed to extend an olive branch to Turgenev when he credited one of the characters in his rival's novel *A Nest of Gentle-*

folk with having come to realize Russia's moral richness. It is also in this section of his remarks that Dostoevsky advanced yet again the singular (anti–social Darwinian) virtues of sacrificial love, honor, and selfless living. In sum, Dostoevsky ascribed to Pushkin the prophetic ability to call his own Europeanized peers back to the People, for it was there alone that they would find their spiritual power and—seemingly against all odds— the salvation of the world itself.

Turgenev may have hesitated to describe Pushkin as of universal importance; Dostoevsky did not when making his third point. Quite the contrary: he suggested that Pushkin was actually greater than the greatest of literary types to have emerged in Western culture (here he named Shakespeare, Cervantes, and Schiller). All the others were identified mainly with their national cultures. By contrast, Pushkin was a prophet of universal significance because his vision was of a future world civilization that would be grounded in the faith of the Russian People—those whom Russia's liberals had persisted in bypassing. These wanderers could not be more mistaken, for "the mission of the Russian is unquestionably pan-European and universal. To become a real Russian, to become completely Russian, perhaps, means just (in the final analysis—please bear that in mind) to become a brother to all people, a *panhuman*, if you like."[31]

This was so, Dostoevsky concluded, because the Russian People carried within themselves the Russian heart, which contained the law of Christ's Gospel. Dostoevsky recognized that Pushkin's own references to Christ were scant; even so, there was no question for him that this greatest of all Russian poets was headed there at the time of his untimely death. With that, Dostoevsky ended his assessment of Pushkin's significance for Russia and for the world.

Dostoevsky's address received an immediate, impassioned, and positive response. Testimonies abound of lifelong enemies who pledged that they would henceforth reconcile in response to the moral force of his address. He had brilliantly utilized this great public moment as a platform for his own universalizing agenda, one that historian Wayne Dowler has successfully linked back to Dostoevsky's prison years. For it was in those years of confinement that this exiled Russian writer directly encountered the People and their underlying nobility, whereas it was the nobility of Russia's European elite that he found wanting over time.[32] Though it took years for Dostoevsky to link this Russian universalism back to Russia's Orthodoxy, he had clearly done so by the time he arrived in Moscow in June 1880. This shift came about, Dowler demonstrates, because the previous two decades had witnessed the relentless (and for Dostoevsky, alarming) up-surge in Western notions of "the modern contractual and pluralistic soci-ety."[33] It was a trend to which Dostoevsky felt compelled to respond, es-pecially as he regarded it as only superficially pluralistic.

James Scanlan's account of this shift is somewhat puzzling in one re-spect, for he attributes Dostoevsky's panhuman ideal, as exemplified in his Pushkin speech, to Western and Enlightenment notions of universalism that Dostoevsky had unwittingly incorporated into his own thinking.[34] But surely the evidence that Scanlan himself produces makes the opposite point, in that he cites an occasion when the novelist wrote, "We are by no means such *pochvenniki* that we deny a panhuman ideal. . . . We . . . are Chris-tians, fully Christians. And the first dogma of Christianity is the common-ness of the law for all, the commonness of the ideal, all are brothers."[35] *Pochvenniki* referred to a native-soil conservative movement that Dosto-evsky had strongly supported on his return from exile.[36] The centrality of Orthodoxy to that movement might have reinforced Russian and paro-chial sensitivities, but the claims of faith generated by Orthodoxy were al-ways and necessarily universal in their scope. Dostoevsky acknowledged as much when he declared that all—as in all humankind—were subject to the same law of faith, all shared a common ideal, and all were brothers. It was entirely consistent for him to argue, then, that one could be fully Rus-sian and fully universal at the same time. As he had declared years before, Russia also had an ethic to give to the whole world, one unlike that which had previously so captivated and misled Russia's own elites: it was the uni-versal mission of the Russian and Orthodox Christ, and Dostoevsky did not need an iota of Enlightenment thinking to reach that all-encompassing conclusion; any Orthodox treatise would have worked quite nicely.

Dostoevsky on Dostoevsky:
The Case for a European-Style Ethic of Imposition

Though scholars commonly point to Gradovsky's critique of Dostoevsky's wildly successful speech as the first such to emerge, the truth is that Dos-toevsky himself provided an even earlier commentary on his own speech in the form of an introduction published alongside the speech in *Diary of a Writer*. The tone of Dostoevsky's introduction is decidedly different from the speech itself, in large part because the former contains several warnings not found in the latter. These arise as he considers the force that Europeanized Russians might threaten to utilize in order to impose their worldview on the empire. Again he encapsulates his key point: Pushkin was prophetically important in identifying the alienation of the Russian People from the "Europeanized intelligentsia,"[37] to the considerable detriment of both. Dostoevsky then declares—as he does in the speech itself—that he genuinely hopes that the intelligentsia will yet make its way back to the People, as Pushkin had anticipated. But Dostoevsky adds several ominous warnings in his introduction. Clearly his tone is more combative and far less conciliatory than it was only a few weeks earlier.

It is possible, he now suggests, that this "Europeanized intelligentsia" will not realize that it would be disastrous to continue turning to Europe and its misguided understanding of universalism. It is possible that the wanderers will maintain that European atheism and European science comprise the last word, one that is humanitarian and enlightened and must be followed. What then? What then, especially given their supposed commitment to individual liberty and free will? Will they freely lead the People, who wildly outnumber the Europeanized intelligentsia, into a future in which all will have an equal say?

Hardly, warns Dostoevsky, though he does appreciate that these Europeanized Russians will want the "civic order" that is found in Europe—just not yet, and certainly not now. For this to happen, the People will first need to be transformed, for, in Dostoevsky's words, the Europeanized elites cannot bear the thought of a primitive (Russian) People that is able to lord it over a civilized minority that has already grasped more advanced understandings of state and society. Dostoevsky imagines that these wanderers will account for their actions as follows: "Our People themselves are impoverished and foul, as they always were, and they are incapable of having either personality or ideas." If that is the case, those with a meaningful past and present (the Europeanized elite) will first and necessarily need to transform the People before the People can be entrusted with full participation in the civic order. And how will they know at what point the People can be so entrusted? It will happen, Dostoevsky suggests, when they arrive at the point whereby they too reject their Russian past and all that goes with it. The People must be made to see that past as shameful, or so Dostoevsky further constructs the thinking of this Europeanized Russian:

> He who curses the past is already ours — that's our motto! We shall apply it completely when we set about raising the People to our level. If the People prove incapable of education, then "do away with the People." For then it will already be clear that our People are no more than an unworthy, barbaric mass that must be compelled merely to obey. For what can be done here: truth resides only in the intelligentsia and in Europe, and even though you may have eighty million People (something you boast of, it seems), all these millions must first serve this European truth, since there is not and cannot be any other.[38]

Thus, Dostoevsky's warns in his introduction to the publication of his Pushkin speech that the intelligentsia will — mistakenly, in his view — conclude that European truths are the only valid universal truths in existence. It follows logically that the Russian People must come to accept them, even as they shed their own primitive and barbaric beliefs. We can easily deduce from where Dostoevsky ends his Pushkin speech that this is a reference to anachronistic beliefs in the Russian Christ. And what will compel the Russian People to undertake this transformation if they choose not to? We know it will not be the Europeanized intellectuals on their own, for how can they hope to succeed when there is a population of eighty million delinquents rallied against them? No — Dostoevsky concludes that, under those circumstances, a Europeanized civic order will be needed to do the deed, by means of a thoroughly modern Europeanized state. In making this connection, Dostoevsky has equated the modernizing late-nineteenth-century European state with the ethics of imposition. But how exactly can this come about? Surely the former negates the possibility of the latter in contemporary discourse.

In fact, there seem to be two ways in which Dostoevsky associates a modernity inclusive of liberalism with the suppression of individual freedoms. We will consider the one when we turn shortly to *The Brothers Karamazov*. For now, it is important to note that mainstream Russian liberals in the second half of the nineteenth century consistently argued for a strong, centralized state to safeguard "progressive" reforms and reformers from the peasant — and therefore "backward" — majority. We see this, for example, in the person of Boris Chicherin, regarded as Imperial Russia's most renowned liberal philosopher and historian.[39] In some ways, Chicherin's biography is typical for contemporary Russian liberals. He was born in 1828 into a family of Russian nobles. Historian Gary Hamburg has observed that though Chicherin's mother was devoutly Orthodox, young Boris Nikolaevich was much more influenced by his father, Nikolai:

> Nikolai Vasilievich was a religious man, but his religion was enlightened and undogmatic. He attended Orthodox services on Sundays and Holy Days, and tried to live a morally upright life. Yet he did not regard church attendance as especially meritorious, nor did he assume individual goodness necessarily to be correlated with endorsement of particular religious doctrines or membership in a particular confession. For him religion was an invitation to be mindful of an extramundane reality whose truths could not be captured in any dogma. He often told Boris Nikolaevich that feeling can apprehend much that is beyond the reach of mere reasons. "His [religious] feeling was broad and tolerant," Boris Nikolaevich concluded. "In him there was nothing of prejudice or sectarianism."[40]

The implication was clear for Nikolai, who regarded the works of the German philosopher Schelling to be much more authoritative, progressive, universal, and free of bias than the sectarian prejudices of his wife's Orthodox faith. Later, in his own memoir, Boris reflected extensively on his father's influence, on how he stressed reason over religious prejudice and was devoid of any bias whatsoever, whereas he gave only a few short paragraphs to his mother's influence on his life.[41]

Chicherin's parents wanted only the best for their son, which of course meant an education in Europe. But their finances were limited, so Boris instead was sent off to Moscow, where he studied at Russia's oldest university. Fortunately, the son's liberal appetite was unexpectedly fed there by his encounter with T. N. Granovsky, the leading liberal and Westernizer of his generation (and the person who later served as the basis for Stepan Trofimovich in *Demons*). Granovsky, a Europeanized Russian, had already rejected the Orthodox view of Russia that the peasants alone had preserved. At the same time, he regarded religious devotion as mere prejudice and saw Russia's only hope for the future in the secular and French notion of "liberté, égalité and fraternité."[42] It was Granovsky who persuaded the young Chicherin to adopt the Hegelian view—strongly emergent at that time—that celebrated liberated individuals who were free of the strictures associated with the community. But how exactly would the interests of the modern individual be safeguarded?

The answer was to be found in the expanded role that the contemporary state would need to play for Russia's liberals. The state would need to be strong enough to intervene from time to time in the interests of both the individual and society. At the same time, it could not be expected to represent all interests equally, nor should it. Instead—and this is crucial to an understanding of liberalism in Dostoevsky's time—the state always needed to take a "universal" perspective, by which it would determine its interventions on the basis of an "absolute" or "universal" cohort of citizens who might be described as the leading edge of society. These were the citizens who, working in concert with the state, would advance the bulk of society to a higher cultural and civic plane than they presently enjoyed. All of this necessitated the establishment of a strong government of laws—a *Rechtsstaat*.[43]

Chicherin later recalled the degree to which he adopted these European ideas as universally relevant. Not surprisingly, he spent his entire adult life advocating for a strong Russian state that would safeguard the rights and interests of the modern individual, whom he saw most ideally in the Europeanized Russians of his generation. Like most of his contemporaries, he maintained throughout the 1860s and 1870s that a future liberal Russia could only be achieved through a state that was strong enough to overcome and transform the peasant majority, which he maintained was still suffering from centuries of medieval and Orthodox primitiveness. Indeed, mounting peasant unrest in the 1860s persuaded Chicherin and his intellectual peers that it was necessary to delay the expansion of civil freedoms in Russia until the peasant masses were culturally ready for them. Thus this stalwart of Russian intellectual and political progressivism was able to maintain his staunchly liberal identity[44] alongside the conviction that post-Emancipation Russia was still not ready for a representative government because the bulk of the population was simply not sophisticated enough to handle it; and for *sophisticated* one could easily substitute *Europeanized*.[45]

One sees in Chicherin all of the characteristics that Dostoevsky would later pull together in his introductory comments on his own Pushkin speech in *Diary of a Writer*. Here we have a contemporary liberal who advocated

for a strong state and civic order to help transform a backward peasant society into a thoroughly modern and Europeanized conglomeration of individuals. Dostoevsky had good reason to believe that, at least in Russia,
liberal freedom and liberal imposition went hand in hand. And it did not
take him long to state it in the most extreme manner.

Pro and Contra: Liberal Reaction to the Pushkin Speech, and Dostoevsky's Response

A. D. Gradovsky was a distinguished professor of civil law at the University of Moscow, though that was not to be his primary legacy. That legacy
came instead when he joined the stream of commentators who responded
to Dostoevsky in the immediate aftermath of the Pushkin speech. Scanlan
describes Gradovsky as "one of the many liberal-minded Westernists who
responded to the speech in print."[46] The Russian academic's response appeared in the Russian journal *Voice* (*Golos*) on June 25, 1880.

For some reason, Gradovsky was the only "liberal-minded Western-
ist" Dostoevsky responded to. Frank suggests that Dostoevsky responded
because Gradovsky's critique was "such a cogent and well-reasoned statement of the liberal Westernizer position, free from the acerbities of critics
more influenced by radical ideas."[47] Gradovsky had been respectful of
Dostoevsky's position; he even strongly affirmed the writer's ability to
comprehend Pushkin's greatness. That said, there was much in Dostoevsky's Pushkin speech of which Gradovsky was highly critical, including his
explanation for why Russian Europeans had become so alienated from
Russian society (the People who so captivated Dostoevsky). Gradovsky
believed that the essence of elite alienation from Russian society was
entirely justifiable, given the manner in which the whole society had been
repressed by the twin evils of serfdom and tsarist despotism.[48] Gradovsky implied that Russia's liberals had themselves suffered from these same
scourges. As a legal authority, he also rejected Dostoevsky's conclusion
that Russia's elite wanderers needed a conversion of the heart. The heart
was one thing, Gradovsky wrote, but what was needed above all was a
pragmatically developed social and civil order within society that would
work toward social betterment. As evidence for such a need, Gradovsky
pointed out that there were slaves as well as masters among the earliest

Christians, thanks to the Apostle Paul's earliest missionary activity, but that Christianity alone had proved incapable of challenging the institution of slavery itself.[49] A more progressive movement—the suggestion is clear that it was liberalism emergent—was needed for that evil institution to be overthrown in the nineteenth century. Lastly, Gradovsky criticized Dostoevsky's ahistorical claim that the People carried within themselves an absolute truth. Did the esteemed Russian writer not understand that the People were themselves historically bound and continuously in a "process of *formation* and *development*"?[50] Gradovsky's article offered a clear, compelling, and reasonable critique.

Dostoevsky published his response to Gradovsky in the issue of the *Diary of a Writer* that followed the publication of his speech. It was a withering attack—indeed, it was perhaps the writer's most cogent assault on European intellectual trends in general and on 1870s Russian liberalism in particular. It is certainly his most strident. In the course of that attack, he tried to obliterate the argument that liberalism marked an impartial advance in world civilization, one that all of Russia needed to embrace for its own moral advancement. He structured his critique in what he called "lectures," a four-part series addressed to the broader readership, for it was pointless to address Gradovsky himself. There was, after all, no hope that those committed to Gradovsky's "old toothless liberal skepticism" would ever be persuaded of their intellectual shortcomings.[51]

Dostoevsky's First Lecture: On Europe's Supposed Enlightenment

Dostoevsky begins by quoting Gradovsky directly, and it is worth our while to consider the latter in his own words, given their relevance to this present inquiry. Gradovsky deems Western trends to be unmistakably universal ones in the following way:

> For two centuries now, in one way or another, we have found ourselves under the influence of European enlightenment, an enlightenment that has had an exceptionally strong effect on us, thanks to the Russian's "capacity to respond to the whole world," which Mr. Dostoevsky recognizes as our national characteristic. We have no way to escape this enlightenment, and no reason to try to escape it. It is a fact that we can do nothing

about, for the simple reason that every Russian person who wishes to enlighten himself *necessarily* acquires his enlightenment from a west European source, owing to the complete absence of any Russian sources.[52]

In response, Dostoevsky first asks what Gradovsky means by the word *enlightenment*. Dostoevsky does not deny that the West is a fount of scientific and commercial enlightenment, but he sees no evidence whatsoever to conclude that it is similarly a fount of spiritual enlightenment, the kind that "illuminates the soul." Here the West has nothing to offer, all the more so given that the Russian People became enlightened centuries ago when "they took Christ and His teachings as their essence."[53] This foundation in Christ is profoundly embedded in the People, he contends, and this is so despite the many sinful and otherwise evil acts perpetrated by the People themselves. Here again, Dostoevsky declares that he knows of what he speaks, having lived with the People for years. (He is referring, of course, to his years in a Siberian prison.) In doing so, he pointedly distinguishes himself from more genteel Europeanized Russians, who in his view live luxurious lives made possible by the blood and sweat of the People themselves (whom the so-called enlightened elites have purposely enslaved, and whom they simultaneously have decried for their illiberal beastliness).[54] This is, for Dostoevsky, a grave shortcoming of Europeanized Russians: they speak the language of equality, yet they live on estates or—by virtue of their control of Russia's growing number of factories— in a manner that suppresses untold numbers of menial laborers. These elites may claim to be democrats, but they act in the most authoritarian manner. And now they claim to represent some sort of moral and advanced Enlightenment? Hardly, at least by Dostoevsky's reckoning.

Dostoevsky's Second Lecture:
Moral Indifference and the Russian Liberal

Dostoevsky next addresses Gradovsky's claim that Pushkin's "wanderers" were not hostile to the People. After all, were these wanderers not the ones who cared for the People by working so tirelessly for their moral and social betterment? And in the end, were not these same liberal wanderers the ones who had made possible the recent and much-longed-for emancipation of the serfs?

Again, Dostoevsky will have none of it. He steadfastly maintains that Russia's liberal elite have nothing but disdain for the People themselves. To make the point, he recalls an incident from his youth when, horrified, he watched helplessly as a Russian courier, wearing his "uniform tailcoat and a three-cornered plumed hat," mercilessly beat his peasant driver for failing to move quickly enough. Years later, Dostoevsky believed that in this single incident he could glean the whole of Russia's Europeanized society beating the Russian People. Surely the courier in that moment had acted as one must in attempting to transform a Russian into a European, and surely the son of that courier is now "a professor, perhaps—meaning a patented European."[55]

It follows, of course, that Dostoevsky refuses Gradovsky's contention that the wanderers may have hated serfdom but never the serf. Had that been the case, why was there not a single instance in which a Europeanized Russian estate owner had liberated his own serfs—as was his right—in advance of the actual Emancipation Proclamation? Surely the answer is that, in the French mode, the Russian elites were able to shed great tears in support of the notion of "liberté, égalité, fraternité," all the while despising the People themselves. Dostoevsky claims that in point of fact, Russian liberals depended on servile labor to maintain their extravagant lifestyles, and it was the likes of the Slavophile Samarin who had led the campaign to abolish serfdom. Dostoevsky then asks why, even after that great day of liberation in 1861, there was no evidence that these Europeanized estate owners suddenly treated their former serfs as equals. Did these now-former serf owners henceforth give the People more land and better conditions than was required of them by law, for instance?[56] Of course they had not; instead, they sought to profit as much as possible in the post-Emancipation era by selling off their remaining lands and forests to the highest bidders, even if it worsened the lot of the People they claimed to care so deeply about.

Dostoevsky's Third Lecture: Christian Love, Civil Law, and the Just Society

Dostoevsky next tackles Gradovsky's twofold charge that (a) the People do not possess great Ethical Truths, given that they are in fact still undergoing historical development and formation, and (b) it is unrealistic to imagine that just societies can be founded on anything but civil law. Again, Dostoevsky quotes Gradovsky at length in order to set the stage for his own rebuttal:

> Mr. Dostoevsky urges us to work on ourselves and humble ourselves. Personal betterment in the spirit of Christian love is, of course, the first prerequisite for any activity, large or small. But it does not follow that people *who have personally perfected themselves in a Christian sense* would necessarily form a perfect society. . . .
>
> Personal and social morality are not the same. From this it follows that no *social* betterment can be realized *only* through improvement of the personal qualities of the people who comprise that society. . . .
>
> The betterment of people in a *social* sense cannot be done only through work "on oneself" and through "humbling oneself." One can work on oneself and curb one's passions in a wilderness or on an uninhabited island. But as *social* creatures, people develop and improve in working *alongside one another, for one another, and with one another.* That is why people's social betterment depends in such a large measure on the betterment of *social institutions* that develop, if not their Christian, then their civic virtues.[57]

So, at best, Gradovsky can imagine that religion might play a supporting and personal role in society—it might be able to govern individual moralities. But it is inappropriate to construct a social order on individual religious beliefs, especially given that serfdom lasted as long as it did even though many of the estate owners were Christian. How then, wondered Gradovsky, can Christianity be viewed as the basis of a just and future social order?

Dostoevsky's response is again categorical. He maintains that Christianity can serve as the social foundation of society. Indeed, it *must* do so, for to do otherwise would be to split "a living, homogenous organism" of Christian faith in two, to the utter disfigurement of both. The just society cannot possibly be established once religion is abolished, for only the perfection of religious belief and practice will allow society to reach that glorious endpoint of ethical perfection. For example, serfdom itself would

have disappeared in an instant had Christian faith been perfected generations ago in Russia. Besides, what will the basis of civic order be if it is not
to be found in religious faith? How will we be able to establish and aspire
to any civic goals if we are not grounded in "a fundamental, great, moral
idea," which only the absolute claims of faith can give? Surely individual
striving for personal gain will be all that is left in a post-Christian world,
the common good be damned. Dostoevsky suggests the following as the
sort of moral motto that society will be left with should that ever happen:
"Chacun pour soi et Dieu pour tous" (Everyone for themselves, and God
for all).[58] Surely the reduction of religious faith to personal matters will
only rob society of its moral ideals so that individual flourishing is all that
is left—or so Dostoevsky argues. And that will necessarily result in the
preeminence of a secular state with its own claims of absolute faith and
authority. Such a state may well declare that it is firmly committed to a just
society built on "liberté, égalité, fraternité," though it can be counted on to
add one more ideal to the mixture, a fourth, and it is this: death to those
who do not accept the dominant societal reading of the first three.[59]

So once again we see Dostoevsky's firm conviction that even the most
modern and liberal ethic will necessarily be grounded in an ethic of imposition, regardless of its most deep-seated goals and convictions. Dostoevsky also repeats here his claim that the only civil order worth imagining
is one that will be founded on Christ, and in a way that obliterates the distance between individual pieties and societal moralities. The perfection of
one will necessarily lead to the betterment of the other.

Dostoevsky's Fourth Lecture:
A Russian Ethical Ideal, and a Universal One to Boot

Dostoevsky seems to run out of steam toward the end of his response,
though he still has one point to address: Gradovsky's objection that the Europeanized Russians were being called (by Dostoevsky) to humble themselves, while the People were being told to exalt themselves as the future
not just of Russia but of the whole world. By what logic must the most
obviously progressive be brought low, and the most backward suddenly
elevated? How can any of this be? Gradovsky wonders.

It *can* be, Dostoevsky contends. It *will* be. It *must* be, though he dis-
putes that this call of exaltation is somehow arrogantly prideful. Surely

that cannot be the case, he retorts, when what is being lifted up by the People is nothing less than "Christ Himself, in slavish garb," and "His ultimate word."[60] This is an odd sort of exaltation, if it is one at all. Dostoevsky believes that he has really been calling for a universal reconciliation, one based on Christ's example of sacrificial love. Even if most of Russia's liberals failed to grasp this message from Dostoevsky's speech at the Pushkin Festival, he did take great comfort in knowing that countless others did. How else could he account for the warm reception he subsequently received in Moscow, or for the many acts of reconciliation that were said to have followed it as erstwhile enemies embraced one another?[61]

By this means, then, Dostoevsky sought to dismantle objections to his call for a universal ethic based on the Russian Christ. It must be said that his arguments, as laid out in *Diary of a Writer*, did not win the day in any absolute way, nor did his liberal critics back away quietly. Another prominent Russian liberal historian and jurist, Konstantin Kavelin, published a "Letter to F. M. Dostoevsky" later that same year. Scanlan has called it "a more sophisticated critique" than the one Gradovsky wrote. In it, Kavelin argues that all moralities are relative and socially constructed. He further claims that there is no basis on which one can argue for the absolute truth of any particular ethical system, including one grounded in the Russian Christ. In a way, Kavelin's words were the last in this exchange, for Dostoevsky's rebuttal to it remained unpublished. Notes for it are found in his last notebook, including jottings that he recorded in January 1881, within days of his final illness and death.[62] Yet if Dostoevsky cannot be seen as having won the argument, his insistent critique of European liberalism, and his corresponding belief in the absolute truths of the Russian Christ not only for Russia, but for the salvation of the whole world, cannot be easily dismissed. At the very least, he directly challenged those Europeanized Russians who had long maintained that European culture was exclusively and necessarily universal its grasp. Perhaps European civilization had created an ethic that was universal in its scope, he declared, but if so, it had done it hopelessly, imperfectly, and ultimately unsuccessfully. For in the end, all would see that Russia contained no less than a universal ethic of its own. He had made this same statement emphatically, and with matchlessly more compassion, in his last novel.

Pro and Contra à la Pushkin:
The Brothers Karamazov

Dostoevsky's personal correspondence from May and June 1880 indicates how much his Pushkin speech and his final novel, *The Brothers Karamazov*, had become intertwined. This should not surprise us, for he participated in the monumental June celebrations in Moscow just as his novel was beginning to appear in serial form and at a time when he had not even finished writing it. He had to leave the festivities earlier than he had hoped so as to write its final section. As one might expect, then, many of the same themes appear in both. As Miller notes, Dostoevsky's soaring success with *Diary of a Writer* had by then demonstrated his ability to successfully blend fact with fiction.[63]

But does the novel reinforce the stark either/or, pro/contra ethical worldview that Dostoevsky delineated in his Pushkin speech? At first glance that seems impossible, given the stunning complexity of *The Brothers Karamazov*, which features a father with three or four sons (depending on how one counts the illegitimate Smerdyakov) born to him from two (or three) different women. Dostoevsky traces their respective developments over the course of a novel that has four main parts, twelve sections (along with an epigraph, foreword, and epilogue), and more than one hundred chapters. The sons themselves appear at the outset to be sharply distinguished: we have the incurable romantic (Dmitrii), the hard-nosed realist (Ivan), the innocent Orthodox novice (Alyosha), and the seemingly obsequious manipulator (Smerdyakov). Each develops in ways that cannot be anticipated. Then there is the matter of the novel's countless subplots. As the novel progresses, Dostoevsky continues to introduce new ones, the foremost of which involves "the boys," to whom we are introduced briefly in book 4 and who become a dominant storyline in the final quarter of the novel. Dostoevsky added yet another layer of complexity when he decided to remain one step removed from the novel itself through the creation and utilization of an intermediary, a fictional narrator. And there are the "cameo" characters, including the Grand Inquisitor from medieval Seville, another who is perhaps a devil, and Jesus Christ Himself. We meet the latter in a multilayered manner, reading about Him by way of Dostoevsky the author; by way of the fictional narrator who is said to be telling the story that becomes this novel; and by way of Ivan's own invention of this same Christ. And we "hear" the Legend of the Grand Inquisitor for the first time when Ivan tells it to brother Alyosha in a tavern after their chance encounter. There are also several different genres in the novel itself, including an entire book (book 6) that has often been viewed as more hagiographic than novelistic. Some have questioned its appropriateness within the work as a whole. Lastly, the novel is laced with a sometimes bewildering array of literary and symbolic allusions—to contemporary scientific discoveries, biblical expositions, gruesome murders from the contemporary Russian press, flights of sheer fancy, conversations and recollections gleaned during the author's Siberian exile, assorted childhood memories, and numerous literary references—among which Goethe's *Faust* surely has pride of place. Naturally, the novel remains the subject of intense debate as to the author's ultimate intent.

Yet for all the novel's manifold complexity, many scholars have highlighted two ways in which Dostoevsky created a remarkable simplicity in *The Brothers Karamazov*. The first concerns its relatively straightforward plot, involving the murder of Fyodor, the family patriarch. Officials subsequently investigate, arrest, and prosecute his eldest son, Dmitrii (Mitya), who is charged with the murder. A guilty verdict is eventually rendered, but not before Mitya's youngest brother, Alyosha, has begun to develop a mentoring relationship with a dozen or so boys in the village, including the feeble and deathly ill Ilyusha. The novel ends in the immediate aftermath of Dmitrii's trial and Ilyusha's death. All of these events unfold in the mid-1860s, though the fictional narrator waits some thirteen years to record them. This basic synopsis reveals a certain straightforwardness of plot and player in this drama, even as the intricacies and entanglements on any given page defy distillation.

Second, it is possible to reduce *The Brothers Karamazov* to its thematic core in a manner that corresponds directly to Dostoevsky's Pushkin speech. By this means, the novel can also be viewed as Dostoevsky's presentation to readers of their need to choose between two mutually exclusive scenarios for Russia's moral universe. Although scholars have presented this bifurcation in different ways, there is surprising agreement on what Dostoevsky believed these two absolutely distinct alternatives looked like, even if not all agree on where he stood personally on the matter.

William Leatherbarrow, for instance, describes Dostoevsky as offering readers a choice between a "world harmony," made possible by Christian love, and a harmony that seeks the same endpoint through a social love in the abstract (a love that the novel also links with romantic love) and is at best indifferent to Christ's claim on our lives. Put another way, Dostoevsky would have readers choose between an earthly paradise that can be devised by politics and one dependent on Christian love.[64]

This choice, between a transcendent and immanently available Christian love on the one hand and an earthbound love in the service of an earthbound and just society on the other, calls to mind Diane Oenning Thompson's summary of *The Brothers Karamazov*: "Dostoevsky's last novel is very much about the intense modern struggle between a pregiven, absolute standard of virtue and truth and the shifting, relative values asserted by self-willed individuals, between a divine plan and an endlessly self-creating universe, between piety and romanticism."[65]

Murav has similarly depicted *The Brothers Karamazov* as polarized between sacred and scientific worldviews so as to compel readers to choose between the sacred and the demonic—for the latter is inescapably the endpoint of all scientific groundings.[66] There is good reason to conclude that Dostoevsky was offering the same stark either/or choice in *The Brothers Karamazov* that he simultaneously set out at the unveiling of the Pushkin Monument. We can see how he establishes this binary opposition by examining a few brief extracts from the novel: first, the epigraph, which we considered previously in another context; second, the famous chapter "The Grand Inquisitor"; and third, book 6, "The Russian Monk."

The epigraph for *The Brothers Karamazov*—the window through which we enter this great work—is a single verse from the Bible, John 12:24: "Except a grain of wheat falls into the ground and dies it remains just a single grain. But if it dies it bears much fruit" (NRSV). John has been deemed the most Christological and trinitarian of the four Gospels. As noted earlier, evidence from Dostoevsky's own many markings in the Bible he carried with him throughout his Siberian exile demonstrate how important this particular Gospel was for him.[67] John 12:24 is pivotally situated in that Gospel; Christ speaks these words immediately after He has turned toward Jerusalem, fully aware that His passion and death await Him there. This section marks the end of Christ's public ministry. Recall the verse that immediately precedes the novel's epigraph: "Jesus answered them, 'The hour has come for the Son of Man to be glorified.'" The hour had come indeed. Christ's glorification here refers to the criminal's death that awaits Him on a cross-scarred hill, followed by a different kind of glorification through resurrection. Seen in this light, Christ speaks not only of His own death in John 12:24; in that moment He also calls His followers to embrace their own individual deaths, so that they might thereby enter fully into a resurrection that He has already secured for them through His own.

The early church claimed that Christ's death had somehow conquered all death once and for all. In fact, it is hardly death as such that confronts believers at the end of their lives, even as one cannot truly be said to be alive until after one has "died" with Christ. None of this would have been at all alien to Dostoevsky's own understanding. So it is that he managed to alert readers through a single verse that *The Brothers Karamazov* would be concerned with Christ's death and resurrection, with the reader's own dying, and with the imperishable life that awaits those who embrace the death that precedes it. The force of this epigraph is such that Thompson contends that the entire novel is already set out within it.[68] Readers must choose. They will view death either as an absurd travesty in a materialist universe or as the gateway to eternal life. Correspondingly, Christ either is the means to that immortality or was the grandest of illusionists and the most heartless of all long-dead visionaries. Dostoevsky will brook no middle ground, and not just with regard to the epigraph.

The ethical implications of this bifurcated worldview are spelled out early in the novel, when the patriarch meets with his three sons in a monk's cell at the local monastery. In the course of a wide-ranging conversation, Ivan suggests that a belief in immortality is essential if one is to have an ethical worldview. Without it, all things will be permitted, even cannibalism.[69] It is surely no accident that the name Ivan is the Russified form of John, the source of the novel's epigraph, and thus a double of sorts. This same Ivan will go further when he finally gets a chance to sit down with his younger brother Alyosha. By now it is clear that the middle brother has rejected not only God's existence in any Orthodox sense but also Christ's command to love our neighbor as ourselves. For "Christ's love for people is in its kind a miracle impossible on earth," he confides to a stunned Alyosha. "It's still possible to love one's neighbor abstractly, but hardly ever up close."[70] So saying, Ivan enters into one of the most astonishing passages that Dostoevsky ever composed: "The Grand Inquisitor."

This legend—which has been mentioned at various points in this study—is most commonly viewed as a cautionary tale against totalitarian regimes that brutally shape their populations in their own image, and scholars such as Travis Kroeker and Bruce Ward do not dispute the usefulness of this pedagogical framework. That said, they provocatively suggest that the legend's application to only the most egregious violations of human freedom conceals the fact that Dostoevsky was equally alarmed by Russian liberals in his time and their temptation to seize authoritarian control in the interests of "freedom."[71] Kroeker and Ward favor this broader application. They see in the legend Dostoevsky's "sustained meditation on the modern idea of history as progress."[72] Rowan Williams suggests the same in his reflections on a world that is seemingly divided between the forces of progressive Western secularism and "the nightmare of terrorism and fundamentalism"—a depiction that Williams rejects as superficial. In his view, "One of the things that make Ivan's Inquisitor such a perennially haunting figure is that his voice is clearly audible on both sides of the current global conflict."[73] But how is this broader case to be made?

We know that Dostoevsky had been troubled by modernity's faith in the seemingly inevitable progress of human history since the early 1860s, the days of *Notes from Underground*. He had long rejected the idea that humans were motivated by reason alone. He consequently did not believe they would be able to reason out a just society on their own. Nor had he changed his mind by the end of the 1870s. We see this same attempt to create a just society on our own terms in the musings of Ivan Karamazov, who is the actual author of the legend (at least in Dostoevsky's construction thereof).[74] As the novel opens, Ivan is the voice of a Europeanized secular humanist. We first meet him as he returns to his father's estate from an unnamed university where he has been studying the natural sciences. He confides to Alyosha that he does not intend to stay long. He hopes thereafter to travel somewhere in Europe until the age of thirty or so, at which point he will likely be through with life and walk away from it.[75] The suggestion of suicide is clear. Nor will this early exit surprise the reader, for there is much in this world that threatens to drive Ivan mad. As one ultimately committed to reason, he finds the claims of love to be particularly galling. Ivan has been trained in the hard sciences, and in place of an ethic grounded in love's command, he is determined to transfer insights gleaned from those very sciences to his own construction of the ethical life.

The legend is his handiwork, and it serves as his strongest attempt to establish an earthly paradise without God. Dostoevsky himself regarded this legend as a profound creation, and he knew of what he wrote. After all, he himself had lived through a similar stunning negation of the divine.[76] Ivan seems to have composed the legend in response to the acts of human depravity he sees all around him, above all those that victimize and brutalize children. He goes so far as to conclude that it is irrational to believe in an all-powerful God in an often cruel and heartless world. Put another way, no omnipotent God is worth following if that same divine omnipotence sees such unspeakable cruelties and yet does not intervene. Kroeker and Ward quote philosopher David Hume when capturing Ivan's own summation: "Is God willing to prevent evil but not able? Then he is impotent. Is he able but not willing? Then he is malevolent. Is he both able and willing? Whence then evil?"[77] So it is that Ivan decides to abandon any interest in God's existence at the outset of his telling of the legend. Instead, he famously "returns the ticket." In Leatherbarrow's analysis, "Ivan concentrates his own revolt on his insistence that he would write the narrative of Creation better than God, that is to say, more transparently and humanely."[78]

Ivan cannot let go of his longing for a perfect world, one that will be rid of the senseless suffering that has so shaken his spirit. But how will this perfect world come about if there is no divine presence to shape it? Ivan concludes that humans will need to carry out this task of creating a perfect society themselves. There is no one else to do the deed. Dostoevsky's composition allows Ivan to continue to believe, then, that good will overcome evil in the end. It is just that—contrary to the Christian fallacy—it will henceforth be immoral to wait on some divine being to bring it about. Instead, we will need to do what the belief in God has failed to accomplish.

Seen in this light, "The Grand Inquisitor" is about an individual who is ahead of his time—something that Dostoevsky reinforces by placing him "back" in the sixteenth century, but in such a way as to allow him to predict the period of time between the sixteenth century and Dostoevsky's telling of it in the late nineteenth.[79] The Inquisitor as created by Ivan understands that God is absent or nonexistent and that Christ's call for sacrificial love has become thoroughly discredited in a world cruelly marred by too many child victims. Not to worry, however, as the Inquisitor takes the initiative. He creates the most just society possible, and he does so because he understands that history is on his side. Until its culmination, power will need to reside with the few, those who see the magnitude of the challenge before them and who carry within themselves the germ of the future rational and perfect order. And what if the great masses rebel and reject the authority that the Inquisitor has assumed for himself? What if they do not accept that the Inquisitor is sacrificing all for them, on their behalf? Well, the fires of the auto-da-fé continue to burn and will solve any problem of opposition that he cannot. Nor is he powerless in the attempt, for the Grand Inquisitor lays claim to the triune entities of "miracle, mystery, and authority" as the best means by which he can correct that which Christ failed to accomplish. And he claims each and every one of these for his own.[80]

Kroeker and Ward make a compelling case for seeing Dostoevsky's treatment of the legend as a profound challenge to all attempts to create the just society outside of Christ, including the one offered by moderate nineteenth-century liberals such as Gradovsky. It is to Dostoevsky's credit that he was able to engage both extremes of contemporary secular thought: that world history was a rational unfolding to a rational end on the one hand (as in Ivan's Euclidian mind) and, on the other, that it was not, in which case the most progressive (as embodied by the Grand Inquisitor) were necessarily compelled to seize the moment.

In the attempt, Ivan comes painfully to understand that the core idea of this counter-Christ ethical foundation is not best named socialism, or humanism, or even liberalism, though it may contain aspects of any or all of them. Rather, the alternative to a Christlike ethic will necessarily evolve into demonism and the outright rejection of God, something the Grand Inquisitor confesses to a captive Christ when he declares, "Listen then: we are not with you, but with *him* that is our secret!"[81]

Dostoevsky reveals the inevitable endpoint of this Christ-less ethic in two other distinct ways in *The Brothers Karamazov*. First, toward the end of the novel Ivan actually encounters the devil—at least in his mind—and confronts the existential bleakness of his position and its fundamental irrationality. Second, we see the power of this new Christ-less ethic at work in Ivan's self-proclaimed protégé, his half-brother Smerdyakov, who murdered their father. When pushed to account for his bloody deed, Smerdyakov taunts Ivan with the latter's own words: "You used to be brave once, sir, you used to say 'Everything is permitted,' sir, and now you've got so frightened."[82]

Jacques Catteau argues that Ivan's greatest tragedy may be his awareness, at the start of his legend, that he has already failed and that any attempt to establish either "socialism with a human face, or even liberal societies," simply will not be realized.[83] Instead, in a world where children are brutalized, justice can only be realized if it is imposed from above. And this external imposition will not be shaped by love and forgiveness, both of which are entirely absent in Ivan's telling of the legend, for who has the right to forgive someone who has cruelly tortured a child to the point of death? Ivan asks his brother that very question at the outset: "Is there in the whole world a being who could and would have the right to forgive?"[84] Alyosha's response is immediate. For him it is Christ, the innocent, crucified Lamb of God, who has for all time earned the right to forgive, and Alyosha is surprised that Ivan himself does not know this to be true. Time will tell if he does in the end. Similarly, Robert Jackson concludes that the Grand Inquisitor sees two options for humankind: it will either bow down to him and acknowledge his authority as essential, or bow to Christ and His moral suasion.[85] But by what means will Christ's justice be realized? And if the Grand Inquisitor is ultimately doomed to fail, does not the same bleak endpoint await the latter option? This question haunted Dostoevsky at the time he was writing this novel. Having created such a powerful figure as Ivan's Grand Inquisitor, he feared that all attempts to depict a Christ-centered moral alternative would fall short of the mark. We turn now to Dostoevsky's portrayal of the Russian monk Zosima, whom he deemed the heart of his answer to the Grand Inquisitor.

Father Zosima plays a vital role in *The Brothers Karamazov.* At one level he represents a double for Fyodor Karamazov, in that he plays a fatherlike role with Alyosha. Zosima's rootedness in Christian faith provides an essential mooring for Alyosha when, in the words of the novel's foreword, everyone, including his own birth father, had been tossed about by some sort of overpowering wind.[86] So what does Zosima have to say about the search for justice in our world, and how is it in contradistinction to the Grand Inquisitor's vision?

Here the contrast could not be more dramatic. Recall that the Grand Inquisitor's world is one in which Christ has been robbed of His transcendent power. He is silent throughout His interrogation, then rendered invisible when He is released to wander silently "in the dark squares of the city."[87] Not so with Zosima's Christ, who is literally everywhere. A younger Zosima once declared as much to a young man whom he encountered at a river's edge. The setting is wondrous: a warm July night, the broad river before them, a refreshing breeze, birds flitting about softly. In the course of their conversation, Zosima suddenly bursts out with his conviction that Christ is in every element of creation, even as all of creation strives toward that same Christ, who, according to the first verse of John's Gospel, is the eternal Word of God. In Zosima's recorded words, "How could it be otherwise. . . . For the Word is for all, all creation and all creatures, every little leaf is stirring towards the Word, sings glory to God, weeps to Christ, unbeknownst to itself, doing so through the mystery of its sinless life."[88] None of this, of course, makes any rational sense, nor can it be reasoned out in any manner that satisfies. Yet what is striking about Zosima is his utter disinclination to argue out his faith.

For whatever reason, Zosima does not focus on God's eternal judgment or the corresponding threat of eternal damnation, and there is little here of an apocalyptic tenor. Similarly, we do not hear warnings in book 6 of Christ's imminent return as the fearsome and omnipotent Pantocrator, a notion that was at the heart of contemporary Orthodox theology. Lastly, Zosima does not seem to be drawn to the miraculous, as in the Christ who walks on water, heals the sick, and so on: the only images we get of Christ the miracle worker are provided by Ivan's jaded picture of Christ in the legend. Instead of these we have what Gary Saul Morson has called "the mythic prosaic."[89]

Seemingly mundane and utterly small deeds are the means by which a just world can be created on this earth. Above all is love. Zosima repeatedly nudges those around him to love actively and indiscriminately (see chapter 3). Other attributes heralded by Zosima include joy, obedience, and long-suffering patience. Zosima believes that by this means we can daily enact the sort of just society we long for, even if it comes at great personal cost to us.

And that takes us to the mythic or theological elements of Zosima's ethic. For Dostoevsky believed that his readers were able to do all these seemingly mundane things in his moral universe because they would, through the exercise of active love, come to grasp a deep truth: Christ is.

His image[90] eternally unites all in all, and all for all, and once his readers grasped that, even death would hold no power over them. What is so striking in *The Brothers Karamazov* is how death serves as both the ultimate outrage in Ivan's moral universe and as nothing at all, really, in Zosima's. If anything, death is for the dying Elder but a threshold at which the divine and the earthly encounter each other. Points of contact between heaven and earth are everywhere present and always available, as his riverside reflection above makes clear. He tells those around him as he is dying that even though his earthly life is passing away, a "new, infinite, unknown, but swiftly approaching life" fills him with joy and radiance.[91] Here we see Dostoevsky's epigraph fulfilled as nowhere else in the novel.

All of this confronts Zosima with a different kind of mystery than the one the Grand Inquisitor envisions. Mystery for the Grand Inquisitor is the means by which he can maintain power and authority on this earth alone. By contrast, Zosima had long ago observed that no mystery was greater than, for instance, the ability of a long-suffering and severely maligned Job (a figure from the Hebrew scriptures, but also the Christian Old Testament) still to declare, "Naked came I out of my mother's womb, and naked shall I return to the earth; the Lord gave and the Lord has taken away: blessed be the Name of the Lord henceforth and forevermore."[92] No mystery is greater than Zosima's joy-filled confession that the earthly and the eternal can touch each other, "and over all is God's truth, moving, reconciling, all-forgiving!"[93]

None of this, of course, is reasonable or rational. It is as if Dostoevsky's either/or compelled his Europeanized readers in *The Brothers Karamazov* to choose between a faith in earthly justice that was intellectually indefensible (the Grand Inquisitor) or a faith rooted in a miracle-working Christ who dwelt at great remove from the world. Clearly, Dostoevsky will have neither of these. Stewart Sutherland concludes his own thoughtful exposition of the legend by suggesting that Dostoevsky actually redefines miracles in *The Brothers Karamazov*, as they are relegated to the purview of the Grand Inquisitor in their more electrifying variations. In their place, Zosima redefines the miraculous as the human capacity to love and to experience a change of heart.[94] In the end this ethic may not be any more sustainable than one grounded in disenchanted human reason, but in

Dostoevsky's world it is the only alternative available. And as we will see, everyone has equal access to it.

A Parting of Ways: Gradovsky, Ivan, and the Subtleties of The Brothers Karamazov

In no place is the distinction between Dostoevsky the publicist and Dostoevsky the novelist more dramatic than in their respective treatments of contrary views. Recall the way Dostoevsky eviscerated the polite and entirely respectful critique offered to his Pushkin speech by the Russian liberal Gradovsky. Perhaps no image is more graphic than Dostoevsky's charge that Gradovsky is akin to one of many liberal corpses that should have been buried long ago. "You and I," he writes, "will never come to an agreement; and so I have no intention whatsoever of trying to persuade or dissuade you."[95]

If *The Brothers Karamazov* has any continuity in this line, it is to be found in Dostoevsky's categorical refusal to attempt, in so many words, to change Gradovsky's thinking. It is here that we get a sense of Williams's strong emphasis on Dostoevsky as a writer who eschewed literary argumentation. In its stead, Dostoevsky chooses in *The Brothers Karamazov* to remain consistently and "theoretically helpless," in Williams's apt terms.[96] Thus Dostoevsky the publicist may wish to be rid of Gradovsky once and for all, but Dostoevsky the novelist is always open to dialogue and the possibility of conversion. The latter approach always runs the risk of not providing Zosima with enough traction to make his case against the forceful logic of the Grand Inquisitor. Zosima is never permitted to argue it out once and for all, as Leatherbarrow has pointed out in his own summation.[97] Yet such an approach allows for unanticipated outcomes. Those who have chosen a Christ-less ethic are always on the edge of finding their way back in *The Brothers Karamazov*, largely because they are never written off. Nowhere is this more dramatic than with Ivan and his half-brother Smerdyakov.

In Zosima's world, as in Ivan's, the ability to love and the language of faith seem to go hand in hand. Ivan expresses something of this in his initial conversation with Alyosha, during which he acknowledges both his inability to comprehend God with his Euclidian mind and the impossibility of loving his neighbor. He does not even believe that the great saints of the church were able to love the poor with their whole hearts. Surely each such act of "love"—toward hungry and frozen passersby, for instance—was undertaken dishonestly, "by strain of a lie."[98]

It will not surprise readers, then, that toward the end of *The Brothers Karamazov*, Ivan, as he is bound for Smerdyakov, reacts violently to a drunken, disoriented, and impoverished peasant whom he encounters in the midst of a nighttime blizzard. "He'll freeze," Ivan thinks dismissively.[99] But he does nothing about it—that is, not until after his meeting with Smerdyakov. During this third and final conversation with Ivan, Smerdyakov finally confesses that he murdered Fyodor Karamazov. Ivan, now more aware of his own personal responsibility for this murder at numerous levels, is determined to set the record straight the next day, if not before. So he leaves Smerdyakov's room and heads back out into the blinding snowstorm, whereupon he again stumbles across something. It is the peasant, still alive, though barely, with snow almost completely covering his face. We are told that Ivan in that moment experiences true happiness and that joy has entered his soul. It is no surprise that Ivan responds to that soul-filled joy with an act of love for the peasant, whom he pulls out of the snow and carries on his back to get help, and at Ivan's own cost. He may not have been his brother's keeper for much of this novel, but in that moment he becomes a brother of sorts to the kind of person who had repulsed him only days before. Could this be the start of Ivan's lasting conversion? It seems as if it is—that is, until he decides a moment later not to go to the prosecutor right then in order to turn in Smerdyakov (and himself, potentially). But even as he turns instead for home (and a waiting devil), Ivan's longing for a just wholeness is never far from him, even if the outcome is very much in question.[100] Miller has rightly called this "Ivan's uncompleted journey of conversion."[101] Thompson has concluded, unsurprisingly, that Ivan's atheism is by no means absolute in the novel, even after he turns toward home.[102] And with that hope for faith lies the prospect of true brotherly love as well, at least in Dostoevsky's understanding of it.

No less astonishing is Lee Johnson's suggestion that Smerdyakov himself yearns for what Johnson calls "theosis," or the "divine capacity within."[103] This seems absurd, given that this self-confessed murderer tortured cats as a twelve-year-old and later instructed village boys on the dark arts of assorted cruelties to dogs. It is he who taunts Ivan, his erstwhile mentor, with the assurance that all is permitted, including the murder of Fyodor Karamazov. Yet Johnson believes that Dostoevsky's own identification with Smerdyakov is at least partly reflected in the fact that in the novel the unacknowledged son is stricken with epilepsy like the author. At a more profound level, Johnson links the Orthodox belief in apotheosis—by which humans in Christ are elevated into divine beings—to Smerdyakov's own deep longing for wholeness. Sadly, this illegitimate son comes under Ivan's rationalist and Euclidian spell for much of the novel. But that in itself does not take away Smerdyakov's desire for wholeness.

There are other hints that Smerdyakov longs for conversion even as he enters his final hours of life. Ivan, having just arrived for his final conversation with Smerdyakov, confesses that he is no longer certain whether his half-brother is real or a dream or some dread spirit. But Smerdyakov assures Ivan that the latter is not the case, for he is real, and no ghost is present, even though a third being is indeed present. "Who is he?" a suddenly alarmed Ivan asks, and Smerdyakov replies, "That third one is God, sir."[104] Is this enough to suggest that Smerdyakov is searching for wholeness while on the verge of his own suicide? If not, what of the fact that the only book lying on Smerdyakov's table when Ivan enters his room is the well-worn *Homilies of Our Father among the Saints, Isaac the Syrian*? This book was treasured by Dostoevsky himself and appears to have played a vital role in Elder Zosima's spiritual formation. We also know that this book was present to Smerdyakov for his entire life: the servant Grigorii had painstakingly read from it at a time when he and his wife were rearing the motherless child.[105]

In summarizing his own reflections on Smerdyakov, Johnson reminds the reader that, at the outset, the fictional narrator of *The Brothers Karamazov* likened the bastard son to Ivan Kramskoi's painting *The Contemplator*. In that painting, a peasant stands in the forest in winter. He is clearly contemplating something, some great task he wants to undertake. But *what* exactly? wonders the narrator. We know he will store these various contemplations over the course of a lifetime and then suddenly put them to some great act of good, or evil, or perhaps both.[106] The tragedy of Smerdyakov's suicide is that we will never know, nor will he, where his earthly journey would have taken him, had he but turned from Ivan's mentorship to the likes of St. Isaac the Syrian. But what of the novel as a whole?

Alyosha's Speech from the Stone:
Facing the Future with Hope

Remember that Dostoevsky delivered his speech at the Pushkin Memorial in June 1880. Although he did not compose the ending for *The Brothers Karamazov* until that July, he had certainly begun to sketch it out several months earlier. No wonder, then, that these two great works flow into and through each other. Murav, who has carefully considered this connection, suggests that Dostoevsky was moved by the rapturous response he received in Moscow following his Pushkin speech. If his oration created a spontaneous community in which lifelong enemies embraced and pledged to love one another unconditionally, then why not evoke that same sense of shared community of love at the end of *The Brothers Karamazov*?[107]

The speech that almost ends the novel itself is delivered by Alyosha Karamazov immediately following the youngster Ilyusha's funeral, which according to the narrator takes place in an old church, "and rather poor, many of the icons were without settings, but one somehow prays better in such churches."[108] Almost no one had attended that solemn occasion, save for Ilyusha's distraught father, Alyosha himself, and about twelve boys from the village who had befriended the frail nine-year-old during the final weeks of his life. Following the liturgy, the boys carry the coffin out to a grave within the churchyard. Ilyusha's earthly remains are lowered into the earth after a final heart-wrenching scene involving the boy's father, Captain Snegirov. Then all return to the captain's modest home, where Ilyusha's sisters and infirm mother await them. A scene of deep and aching pathos unfolds as the funeral cortege arrives. Alyosha and his youthful companions feel compelled to step outside for a few minutes. They find themselves wandering, seeking their own solace, until they arrive at a large stone. Alyosha gazes upon the stone, and we are told that he immediately sees the big picture of what Ilyusha's father had once told him.

That previous conversation between Alyosha and the captain took place near the start of the novel, when they themselves had walked to this very place. It was close to the captain's heart even then, for he often came there with Ilyusha to share an evening walkabout. This large stone represented something so important to Ilyusha that he had asked to be buried underneath it (though this did not happen, for the landlady and others urged the father to choose the church cemetery instead, where the deceased would continue to hear when sacred texts were read and sung). The stone was near a wattle fence that marked the border of the town's common lands, and it served as a public square and as a crossroads of sorts.[109] During that early conversation Captain Snegirov told Alyosha he had come to that spot just recently with his dear son, who had railed against Alyosha's oldest brother, Dmitrii, for having assaulted Snegirov on this very spot. The captain had suffered terribly when the younger and stronger Dmitrii dragged him about by the beard, in plain view. Ilyusha happened upon this pathetic scene while walking home after school with his friends and vainly tried to intervene on behalf of his father, pleading that Dmitrii kindly forgive his father, as mad as it sounds.

Captain Snegirov recounts all of this to Alyosha, including how much this assault had devastated his beloved Ilyusha. "Papa," Ilyusha had burst out as he again stood at the scene of that humiliation. "Papa! . . . Papa, the way he treated you papa! . . . Don't make peace with him, papa, don't make peace."[110] Ilyusha's great fear was that his father would settle for peace without justice, whereas the son above all preferred justice to peace. Justice in this instance required that Dmitrii be humiliated or killed. Nothing less would settle the score for Ilyusha. His father would have none of it, so on their return to the stone he pleaded with his son to set thoughts of revenge aside. Snegirov told Ilyusha it was a sin to kill. Ilyusha could find no solace in half-measures and instead begged his father at least to move the family to a town that was good in a way that theirs had clearly proven not to be. In the end, Ilyusha sought to impose his own justice against a Karamazov with a stone-tossing fight of his own initiation, this time with his classmates, who had taunted him with his father's weakness. In this exchange Ilyusha suffered wounds that contributed greatly to his death. All of this comes back to Alyosha—so we are told—who finds himself staring at the large stone and hears Ilyusha again saying to his father, "Papa, papa, how he humiliated you!"[111]

Is Alyosha now able to make sense of all that lies in fragments before him? Perhaps. He did see that Ilyusha had unwittingly proposed the Grand Inquisitor's solution to the problem of injustice in the world, which was to impose justice on those deemed unjust, by violence if necessary, and by whatever means, including the sword. (Ilyusha had in fact imagined using the latter against Dmitrii when he was older and better able to settle matters on his father's behalf.) We are told that something shook in Alyosha's soul as he recalled all of this in the aftermath of the funeral, and as he gazed out at the twelve dear bright faces—and this mention of Alyosha and the twelve can only be a barely concealed allusion to Christ and His twelve disciples. Some of these same "dear, bright faces" had only a short time ago jeered Ilyusha after Dmitrii's assault on the captain. Many had also wounded Ilyusha with stones when he lashed out at them in anger. Yet somehow, in time, and with Alyosha's gentle encouragement, they had come to make their peace with him. More than that, they had come to love him.

"Gentlemen," Alyosha now announces, "I should like to have a word with you, here on this very spot." We see how Alyosha gathers together the nucleus of a new family, a new (churchly) community, and all this on the public square, the crossroads. Though this particular gathering happens in the immediate aftermath of Ilyusha's pathetic death and funeral, Alyosha's words are full of past assurances cast forward with certainty. He suggests, in the language of every Orthodox funeral service of Dostoevsky's time and after, that Ilyusha will never be forgotten: "Let us never forget him, and may his memory be eternal and good in our hearts now and unto ages of ages!"[112] The boys respond enthusiastically, lovingly, with "Yes, yes, eternal, eternal," followed by "Memory eternal for the dead boy" from Alyosha. Again the boys respond with "Memory eternal."[113] In every way Dostoevsky ends his last and greatest novel with the firmly expressed conviction that we already know the future, for we can already effectively remember it as rooted in a past crucifixion and resurrection. In no way does it henceforth need to be feared.

Scholars have commented on the "Speech from the Stone" to powerful effect. Alyosha is viewed as Christlike as he gathers the twelve together, and this is reinforced when he announces he will depart soon and possibly for a long time—a clear reference to Christ's ascension in the Book of Acts. Miller reminds us how much the big stone around which they gather hearkens back to the Apostle Simon, whom Christ calls and henceforth names Peter (translated as "rock").[114] Jackson contrasts Ivan's repeated use of the first-person singular "I" in his "Rebellion" and the legend of the Grand Inquisitor with Alyosha's intensely interactive appeal to the collective in his own speech. Ivan rejects all talk of unity as personal affront, whereas Alyosha looks to a present and future unity that is already imperishable. Jackson stresses how the suffering and death of a child mysteriously makes possible this future harmony for Alyosha, something that Ivan rejected out of hand, along with any talk of future reconciliation.[115] And Thompson links Alyosha's closing speech back to the novel's beginning, noting how Dostoevsky is thereby able to affirm the deep truths of the novel's epigraph. Life has come to the very place where death appeared cruelly victorious only moments before.[116]

Though these observations are powerful, I want to comment briefly on what follows the speech before making my concluding observations on this chapter. Dostoevsky allows Alyosha to do what he himself had done after the Pushkin speech in *Diary of a Writer*, which is to comment on and thereby summarize and reshape his own recently delivered oration. In this manner Alyosha is able to deliver three linked assurances.

He makes the first of these after the boys—in a manner that points back to the emotional outpouring that immediately followed Dostoevsky's Pushkin speech—respond to his words with "deep feeling in their faces," with shouts of "Eternal, eternal," and with their own expressions of love. To all of this Alyosha responds, "Ah, children, ah, dear friends, do not be afraid of life! How good life is when you do something good and rightful."[117] The Russian word for "rightful" is *pravdivoe*, which also suggests truthfulness and uprightness. The implication is clear: a good life is measured by something that is truthful, upright, and rightful, or *pravdivoe*.

Alyosha delivers his second assurance in response to a question he is asked after he declares once again, "Memory eternal for the dead boy!" Kolya, the one who will lead the twelve in Alyosha's absence, is still unconvinced. He wants to know if these words actually have content, if anything is truly eternal, so he asks Alyosha, "Karamazov! . . . Can it really be true as religion says, that we shall all rise from the dead, and come to life, and see one another again, and everyone, and Ilyushechka?" Alyosha's reply is immediate and categorical: "Certainly we shall rise, certainly we shall see and gladly, joyfully tell one another all that has been." In this manner, Alyosha (and perhaps the fictional narrator alongside him, or even Dostoevsky himself) is able to declare his faith in the general resurrection of the dead, which is linked directly to Christ's return, the time when the Orthodox believe all will rise from the dead and the final summation of history will transpire.

Kolya responds, "Ah, how good that will be," suggesting that Alyosha's words are more than sufficient for him. This last interaction opens the door for Alyosha to deliver his third and final assurance. Earlier, Kolya had ques-

tioned how it could be that all of them would be invited back to the captain's home—and in the midst of such raw grief—for a funeral feast of
pancakes. How could one justify laughter in the place where Ilyusha had
suffered and died only days earlier, and within minutes of the funeral service and burial? Kolya finds it all unnatural, even if it is accepted in their religion.[118] Alyosha did not comment on any of this at the time, but he does
so immediately after he has affirmed both the resurrection of the dead
and Christ's lordship over history. Alyosha gently urges the twelve not to
be troubled by the funeral feast that will soon follow, for it is "an ancient,
eternal thing, and there's good in it too." Here the word for "good"—
khoroshee—is the same used in his first assurance, concerning the joy we feel
when we live lives defined by that which is good and truthful. In this way all
three assurances are woven together to form a single and indivisible whole.
So saying, Alyosha and the boys head for the feast with shouts of "Eternally
so!" In this way, Dostoevsky brings this great novel to a close.

Conclusion

Whither Russia morally? It is clear that Dostoevsky was troubled by this
question for much of his life. It is equally clear that he had a preferred answer to this question, one he was increasingly determined to give voice to
as he entered the final years of his life. He did not dispute that all civilizations developed their own global mission. He championed this perspective in *Diary of a Writer* as early as 1877. What *did* alarm him was the per-
ception that Europe had created a civilization that was somehow morally
advanced. Quite the contrary, he regarded it as severely flawed in its Catholic, Protestant, socialist, and liberal variants. In truth, he regarded any moral
system as flawed if it was not grounded in "the Russian Christ." So he was
distressed to see Russia's own leading intellectuals, "the professors" included, unwittingly chasing after European visions of civilization with increasing vigor. He likened this to a boar consuming acorns that were needed
to grow into oak trees. And he did not fear just for Russia's Europeanized
elites in this time of moral confusion; it troubled him that this fissuring of
Russian society had long ago wounded all sectors.

But all was not lost: he remained convinced to the end of his days
that the great Russian People—the *narod*—had kept alive the moral vision

that not only Russia but the entire world needed so desperately. And the People had managed to do so in spite of both their own manifest brutality and the brutality visited upon them over many generations. Great truths had endured. Father Zosima summarized it this way: "Whoever does not believe in God will not believe in the people of God. But he who believes in the people of God will also see their holiness, even if he did not believe in it at all before. Only the people and their future spiritual power will convert our atheists, who have severed themselves from their own land."[119]

This talk of God, and of the people of God and their holiness, may have been a fool's hope, but if so, a fool he would be. Dostoevsky genuinely believed it was the only way forward, and he devoted almost all of his energies toward that end in the last years of his life. This chapter has considered the two distinct ways in which he made the case that one needed to choose either salvation in an extravagant love rooted in Christ or a salvation in politics by humankind alone. He firmly believed it was one or the other, or at least he believed in a politics necessarily rooted in a salvation that was Christ's alone to offer and forever thereafter embodied in the church. Dostoevsky the publicist argued this out directly, and in that arena he was dismissive of his foes, blindly pursuant of his own ends, and rigorously argumentative in his prose. He understood the risks involved in speaking so forthrightly, for his most cherished ideals often defied easy explanation. Yet he could not resist the opportunity to speak on the platform that he himself had created in *Diary of a Writer*. In doing so, he risked so alienating those with contrary opinions that they might not stay and hear him out. It seems likely that his legacy would have faded over time had it depended largely on the legacy of Dostoevsky the publicist.

Not so with Dostoevsky the novelist. I hope this brief examination of *The Brothers Karamazov* has demonstrated as much. It was here that Dostoevsky entered fully into a wide range of positions, sometimes so deeply— as with the Grand Inquisitor—that he feared for his ability to provide a viable alternative to the views that troubled him most. Here also he found the time he needed to allow characters to develop and change over time. Over that time they were able to make terrible decisions, but also to make terribly good ones. Here he could show compassion for all, even the most seemingly abhorrent, because all had the opportunity in one instant to place themselves at the threshold where heaven and earth touched each other. Such a threshold was less an idea for Dostoevsky than it was a person—the person of "the Russian Christ." Yet even those hostile to this Christ-centered endpoint could find a portion of their voice by reading *The Brothers Karamazov*—sometimes a large enough portion to dispute that such a Christ-centered endpoint even existed in the author's mind. One can easily see how Dostoevsky the publicist could have been dismissed as the creator of cardboard caricatures and assorted straw men. But Dostoevsky the novelist? Never!

Dostoevsky the novelist was also and always the creator of beauty, and nowhere is this more evident than in the novel's final pages, where we encounter Alyosha's "Speech from the Stone" and the dialogue that follows it. In a way, this brief section at the novel's end puts paid to Ilyushka's earlier longing for justice by means of violence. Such a longing might have made sense to the Grand Inquisitor. It would undoubtedly have made sense occasionally to Dostoevsky the publicist, but it could never win the day for Dostoevsky the novelist.

In her reflections on the mass violence that scarred the twentieth century, Hannah Arendt concluded that violence cannot be counted on to bring an end to violence. It can only be counted on to breed more violence. So she questioned those who believed that their acts of violence were ever truly independent, because in truth those acts were always reactions to a perceived injustice and undertaken in response to something else. It is so with Ivan in the tavern and the demand that victimized children be vindicated. It is so with Ilyushka at the big stone when he pleads with his father that Dmitrii be either killed or humiliated. It is so with the Grand Inquisitor's supreme confidence that Christ got it so utterly wrong during the period of His earthly ministry. Arendt frames it this way:

In contrast to revenge, which is the natural, automatic reaction to transgression and which because of the irreversibility of the action process can be expected and even calculated, the act of forgiving can never be predicted; it is the only reaction that acts in an unexpected way and thus retains, though being a reaction, something of the original character of action. Forgiving, in other words, is the only reaction which does not merely re-act but acts anew and unexpectedly, unconditioned by the act which provoked it and therefore freeing from its consequences both the one who forgives and the one who is forgiven.[120]

It is precisely this sort of radical new departure, this refusal to merely re-act, that makes the last page of *The Brothers Karamazov* as much a beginning as an ending. In Dostoevsky's either/or world of ethical grounding, Alyosha and the twelve set out in the only direction that will actually lead somewhere. Alyosha assures us that all who set out on this path will still err mightily at times, even a thousand times more if not ten thousand times. Henceforth and forever more, each will carry within him a memory of a time when love won over hatred, when death gave way to life and funerary sorrow erupted in festive joy. Each will have within himself the memory of a time when the boundaries of heaven intersected for even a single moment with earth, when the universe was suddenly deemed meaning-filled and not meaningless. Taken together, that path remains the only true way to achieve a universal moral reconciliation, even as it had been preserved all along by the Russian People themselves.

Conclusion

Dostoevsky's "Ridiculous" Ethic,
for His Time and Ours

Much depends on the conclusion, it seems, and no one believed this more than Dostoevsky. Looking back, his plea for a love-based ethical world-view grounded in willful and joy-filled suffering, one that assumes a reckless responsibility for all, seems to have lost the day in Russia as everywhere else. By contrast, the erstwhile western European ethic that celebrates autonomous individuals in possession of individual rights—an ethic that troubled Dostoevsky so greatly—has become a global phenomenon in our time, with no sign of abating. But we do well to ask: will that seemingly irreversible global ethic stand the test of time?

Of course, the answer to that question depends greatly on our ability to know what time it is in the first place. On this matter Dostoevsky was unabashedly optimistic, and he expressed that optimism in various ways over the years, though never more directly than in a series of notes titled simply "Socialism and Christianity." In those notes, composed in 1864 on the eve of his greatest literary outpouring, he articulated a three-stage history of the world that included literally all of time. For him, the first stage of world history had ended long ago. It had comprised primitive patriarchal communalism—a time when humans had lived in immediate relation to one another and their surroundings with a directness that suggested a complete absence of contrived thought. In the best sense, this was an age when people were able to live thoughtlessly unselfconscious lives.[1]

171

Dostoevsky called the second stage of world history simply "civilization," and he viewed it with woe. This was the stage of world history he was living in, as are we by his reckoning. It is characterized by people who deem themselves superior to those who have gone before. In this second stage, individuals have abandoned their faith in the divine. They do not recognize that this abandonment is, as historian James Scanlan puts it in his own reflections on this text, a "'diseased' condition," for it has robbed people of access to the source of life itself.[2]

What did ethics look like during this second stage, at least for those who believed that no other stage would follow it? I have argued throughout this study that Dostoevsky understood the ethical life in the era known as "civilization" to be tragically groundless, an orphan's lament. This second stage is ultimately about nothing at all, even if full of promise at the outset. We see this encapsulated in one of the last short stories Dostoevsky ever wrote, "The Dream of a Ridiculous Man," about a self-proclaimed "ridiculous" (*smeshnii*) person who has for years lived the life of a modern, joyless, and vile Russian progressive.[3] Why so? Because he long ago came to realize that nothing in the world matters. At the start of this story, his awareness of that makes him ridiculous. This text is peppered with the phrase *"vse ravno"*: "it makes no difference" or "it's all the same to me." In one incident, our ridiculous protagonist chances upon three friends who are engaged in a heated discussion about something seemingly provocative and vital. Our ridiculous man scorns the lot of them. He tells them their arguments are absurd because all three are, in fact, profoundly indifferent to any and all of it, just as he is. Indeed, the phrase "it makes no difference" is repeated four times in five consecutive sentences: "They talked about something provocative and suddenly even grew excited. *But it made no difference to them*, I could see that, and they got excited just so. I suddenly told them that: 'Gentlemen,' I said, *'it makes no difference to you.'* They weren't offended, but they all started laughing at me. It was because I said it without reproach and simply *because it made no difference to me*. And they could see that *it made no difference to me*, and found that amusing."[4]

What is it exactly that makes no difference to him? The universe, for starters. As a modern progressive well versed in science and philosophy, he has long ago abandoned belief in a divine presence; for him, the world is what it is and nothing more. It is simply and coldly governed by inertia. It is as if the universe itself will cease to exist on his death: "There would indeed be nothing after me, and as soon as my consciousness was extinguished, the whole world would be extinguished at once, like a phantom, like a mere accessory of my consciousness."[5]

This thoroughly modern Russian firmly declares that he has reasoned this out and as a result has found himself morally indifferent in a finite world that is entirely explainable by the immutable laws of physics. It all seems absurd to him, and as with so many of Dostoevsky's characters, he has had enough of it. One evening, on his way home, he looks up into the dark skies that seem like so many meaningless and "bottomless black spots."[6] He then puts two and two together: if everything he does makes no difference, if the universe itself is governed by nothing more than mindless inertia, why not cut to the chase and end it all now? As he is reasoning this out, he suddenly feels a tug. Beside him in the dark is a young girl who is clearly in desperate straits. He casts her off, however, and she runs across the street to another man for whatever assistance he might offer, her future unknown. Why should the ridiculous man even care about her in a meaningless world that will one day end in nothing but nothing, and all the more so as he intends shortly to blow his brains out? As he puts it, "If I was going to kill myself in two hours, for instance, then what was the girl to me and what did I care then about the same or anything in the world? I turned into a zero, an absolute zero."[7]

So he goes up to his rented fifth-floor flat (a small irony for me here, for I began to write this final chapter in the heart of St. Petersburg, where we were staying in a rented fifth-floor flat). He is haunted by his abrupt rejection of that girl. Nevertheless, he pulls out his loaded revolver, for tonight will be his last night of existence. But he falls asleep in his chair before he ends it all, and in that sleep he has a dream.

In some ways, the ridiculous man's callous disregard for the desperately vulnerable young girl is all Dostoevsky has to say about the endpoint of ethics in a universe of our own making. But this fictional account also demonstrates how Dostoevsky will always link the grandest philosophical ruminations (on ethics, justice, the meaning of life) with concrete and discrete situations in daily life. (Will the ridiculous man respond to the desperate girl's plea for help?) Robert L. Jackson observes that the ordering here is vital, for the ridiculous man's ethical indifference does not lead him to his moral and spiritual apathy in a seemingly godless universe; it is the other way around. For Dostoevsky, we are always in danger of ethical indifference once we have deemed ourselves to exist in a disenchanted universe.

Thus, the turn from transcendent (in this instance, Orthodox Christian) faith has its ethical dangers, starting with the crisis of values that results from the devaluation of all that was once deemed sacrosanct.[8] We see much the same in "Bobok," the short story examined earlier in this study, composed by Dostoevsky in 1873 about the desperate search for any diversion at all in the face of a world from which God seems absent. It is for the sake of a diversion that the story's protagonist, Ivan Ivanych, takes in a funeral service. He literally just wanders in. What he encounters there, however, is not the transcendent love of a God who can conquer death, but odor, and lots of it, from the fifteen or so corpses that arrive at about the same time for burial.[9] During the liturgy (by which the Orthodox proclaim God's ultimate victory over death), Ivan Ivanych steps out of the church for some air—a clear suggestion that the Orthodox liturgy and faith have begun to suffocate him.

One assumes that it is the need for air and more diversion that brings Ivan Ivanych to the cemetery, where he overhears the pathetically trivial conversations of the recently departed coming up to him from beneath the earth. That is what he gets in this macabre world of the hopelessly dead, for in this scenario the dead are able to do little more for the weeks immediately following their death than live out their assorted ethical and spiritual perversions. In chapter 2 I referred to Mochulsky's conclusion that "Bobok" was the most terrible of Dostoevsky's metaphysical visions, because the moral putrefaction of the interred souls has preceded and overwhelmed their physical decay, and all the more so for the Russian elite who have fallen prey to a Europeanized worldview (they comprise the vast majority of the babblers in the story). For Joseph Frank,[10] Dostoevsky's meaning in this story is again unequivocal: a godless world is always in danger of becoming a world ruled in the end by moral decay, arbitrary power, endless diversions, and the walking dead, who eventually are heard to mumble little more than the meaningless "bobok."

In the words of one recently departed, "I suggest that we all spend these two months as pleasurably as possible, and for that we should all set things up on a different basis. Gentlemen! I propose that we not be ashamed of anything!"[11] Two months here is the period for which the participants in this macabre charade will still possess consciousness. This promise of life without shame sweeps through the cemetery and is re-peated four times in the next few sentences. And what will replace mo-rality's burden of shame? The answer, it seems, will be in the eager willing-ness of the recently interred to fashion their ethical lives on "new and now reasonable principles."[12]

I have argued throughout that Dostoevsky deemed an ethical world-view based on a godless universe to be irredeemably bleak and existen-tially hopeless, even if many who held that perspective were profoundly good, ethical, and hope-filled. But surely the point for Dostoevsky was that they need not have been good, ethical, or hope-filled if they had indi-vidually chosen otherwise. And by whose measure was any of this to be determined anyway? Bruce Ward has provocatively called this "the crisis of liberal humanism," which is marked by the inability to answer the fol-lowing questions raised first by George Grant: "What is it, if anything, about human beings that makes the rights of equal justice their due? What is it about human beings that makes it good that they should have such rights? What is it about any of us that makes our just due fuller than that of stones or flies or chickens or bears?"[13] Not much, as Ward sees it, and in that moral confusion and indeterminacy lay the gravest of Dostoevsky's moral concerns.

Fortunately, that second stage of world history, which Dostoevsky called the era of "civilization," would not have the final word. Indeed, in "Socialism and Christianity" he identified it as merely a transitional (*pere-khodnoe*) phase along the way to something else, however long that transi-tion might take. Perhaps most surprising was his claim that this third and final period of world history had already been inaugurated and assured by Christ, whom Dostoevsky considered the eternally living image of the di-vine, the one who had already signaled the final triumph of Christianity. Dostoevsky stressed how even those who rejected the divinity of Christ continued to see an ideal image of all humankind in His person. Yet there was nothing to suggest that Dostoevsky's Christ was ever merely human. He was always necessarily transcendent. It was this very Christ who had once and for all modeled a moral life whereby the "I" could be freely and joyfully sacrificed for all.[14] To settle for anything less, in Liza Knapp's retelling of it, would have meant settling for a material world ruled by the mechanics of death—a perpetual death sentence.[15] In his examination of Dostoevsky, faith, and fiction, Rowan Williams concludes along similar lines, arguing that Dostoevsky "in effect challenges the reader to explain exactly *what* the truth outside or without Christ would be, and stakes the claim that truth about the human world is not going to [be] possible if faith is removed from the equation."[16]

This problem of how one might find a trustworthy ethical foundation in a godless world was deemed a real one and vigorously debated in Imperial Russia before 1900. An important voice in that debate was Dostoevsky's protégé of sorts, the young philosopher Vladimir Sergeyevich Soloviev, who distinguished between two kinds of absolutes in the second of his sensational public lectures "On the Divine Humanity," begun in St. Petersburg in January 1878. The first, "negative absoluteness," was most pronounced in what Soloviev called "western civilization," which had successfully liberated the modern individual from every external limitation. "Human beings today," he wrote with some measure of concurrence, "are conscious of themselves as inwardly free, as higher than any independent external principle. They assert themselves as the center of everything."[17] This was the measure of their negative absoluteness, in that they did not regard themselves as bound or restrained by anything. Though there was something admirable about this, Soloviev suggested that it came at a terrible price because it denied those same Westernized individuals the opportunity to possess their "positive absoluteness." By this, we long to be more than profoundly meaningless physical entities. Quite the contrary, Soloviev maintained that we individually long for lives lived in a "fullness of being."[18] We long for *something*, to think on *something*, to feel *something* that is objectively beyond us. We long to believe that our existence as moral beings is oriented to some notion of "absolute goodness, truth, and beauty" that is—by definition—beyond ourselves. This is what he meant by "positive absoluteness."[19] And for Soloviev, the great and heretofore unresolved tension within Western civilization was that it could not achieve the latter while absolutely embracing the "negative absoluteness" of the former. For their part, according to Soloviev, Russian intellectuals could come up with nothing better than the following strange syllogism: "Man is descended from the apes. Therefore we ought to love one another."[20] But where was the logic in that, wondered the noted Russian philosopher Nikolas Berdyaev?

Soloviev later declared that Dostoevsky's greatness lay in his dynamic ability to portray Russian society both where it was then and where it might yet go if it but chose to do so.[21] Dostoevsky himself was confident in the attempt because he believed that, in the end, the universe had to be meaning-filled. It had to make sense, and it surely would. And if that was already true, it followed that absolute goodness, absolute beauty, and absolute truth were certain to persevere in the end. He declared this to be so countless times and in countless ways over the years. It was there, he decreed in his reflections on "Christianity and Socialism," wherein the third and final period of earthly time would necessarily result in the full flowering of Christ's reign.

But it was no less evident in his ponderings on Holy Thursday, April 16, 1864, as he kept silent vigil over the earthly remains of his first wife, Marya Dmitrievna. As I noted in chapter 3, it was then that Dostoevsky reasoned out the necessity of a life beyond this one, for otherwise we, here, would have no assurance that our own earthly strivings for wholeness would ever be realized. Those strivings would be utterly senseless if everything ended here. Yet Dostoevsky could not countenance such an ending; instead he chose to reaffirm the centrality of Christ as the eternal sign of God's sovereignty. Christ was, for Dostoevsky, the assurance that the positive absoluteness of the divine had taken human form while remaining absolutely true and objectively beautiful.

What did those assurances change? Everything, as Dostoevsky saw it, for the certain future victory of Christ's reign meant that even small deeds now were never wasted. For every one of them—and every sacrifice made—would end in a victory, a portion of which could already be joyfully realized. Thus, suffering could be embraced, and even death itself, because in the end both suffering and death would be vanquished, even as they already had been vanquished by means of an abandoned cross and an empty tomb. This ageless assurance of the final victory of truth, beauty, and love is what made the ethical life possible for him.

None of this great hopefulness was evident in "Bobok," but we get a hint of it in Dostoevsky's conclusion to "The Dream of a Ridiculous Man." We left off with that man falling asleep on the verge of shooting himself and bringing his senseless world to an end. He dreams that he in fact does shoot himself, but in the heart, not the head. (Is Dostoevsky suggesting here that the man's fatal flaw has been his inability to love? In this instance, to love the girl who had approached him in desperate circumstances?) He dreams that he is then placed in a closed coffin, and that he is unexpectedly conscious of this in a way that conjures up the ghoulish circumstances of "Bobok." The ridiculous man is buried, and then— what an indignity!—he becomes aware that his coffin is slowly filling up with water from the damp earth. In anger, he shouts into the vast nothingness, for this waterlogged indignity has gone too far. Yet at that instant he is met by a companion (I did indicate that this was the dream of a ridiculous man, did I not?), who transports him through the galaxy to some land he could never have imagined, somewhere up where the stars are. It is a land of utter peace and tranquility, and the people he meets there take this heart-wounded person and fully embrace him. He is stunned by their disinterest in science, by their limitless expressions of love, by their serenely calm personae and utter lack of deceit. Perhaps most amazing of all is that the place he has arrived at is a seeming double to the earth he has just left. He observes the outline of the European continent as he nears it, and the Atlantic Ocean beyond it.[22]

The ridiculous man finds himself deposited in an idyllic part of the world, something similar to the Greek islands of the Aegean that appear elsewhere in Dostoevsky's major works. He calls the people he encounters there the children of the sun and notes their beauty and their childlike joy. He describes the place overall as undefiled by the so-called fall, the moment when Adam and Eve defied God's clear instruction in the Garden of Eden. The ridiculous man comes to love the people of this strange new land—almost immediately, it seems. They have an understanding of life that is loftier than science. They live in communion with every living thing, from trees to flowers, and all animals live at peace with them. Indeed, they have already won the animals over with love (it undoubtedly helps that they are vegetarians).[23] Love seems to be everywhere. It even seems to transcend death itself, which is entered into joyfully because the barriers between the living and the dead are almost nonexistent. And they have no religion in this world, as we see from a section that is perhaps best quoted in full:

> They barely understood me when I asked them about eternal life, but they were apparently so convinced of it unconsciously that it did not constitute a question for them. They had no temples, but they had some essential, living, and constant union with the Entirety of the universe; they had no faith, but instead had a firm knowledge that when their earthly joy was fulfilled to the limits of earthly nature, there would then come

for them, both for the living and for the dead, a still greater expansion of their contract with the Entirety of the universe. They waited for this moment with joy, but without haste, without suffering over it, but as if already having it in the presages of their hearts, which they conveyed to one other.[24]

It is, in short, a world that our recently deceased protagonist cannot help but love. And that is when things really became strange. For instead of "happily ever after," we are told that the ridiculous man begins to corrupt this entire newfound land. He starts innocently enough when he tells a joke at someone's expense, but soon it spreads widely as others follow his unkind example. Rather quickly they all lose their concept of honor. In his own reflection, "They began to abuse the animals, and the animals fled from them into the forests and became their enemies. There began a struggle for separation, for dissociation, for individuality, for 'mine' and 'thine.'"[25] All the warring parties come to believe in science and its ability to help them defeat the other. There are now either weak or strong, and none of them have any sense of shame. And when the ridiculous man tries to persuade them that they need to return to their previous state, all of them declare that they like it better in this now defiled and broken world.

The ridiculous man knows what he has done but can hardly believe he has had such a monstrous impact. Even more amazingly, he realizes that he has come to love this now-tortured land, with its now-tortured people, almost as much as when it was in a state of perfection. He suddenly realizes that he himself wants to suffer for them all, to have his own blood spilled on their behalf. He asks to be crucified to that end, on a cross, and teaches them how to make crosses, but they instead come to see him as the odd one, the dangerous one who needs to be locked up for everyone's sake.

Then our ridiculous man awakens.

He is back in his rented apartment after a night of sleep in the chair where he had once intended to shoot himself. But he knows he is not the same person as he was before this dream. He pushes the loaded revolver away from his person, for more than anything he wants life. Raising his arms, he "called out to the eternal truth; did not call out, but rather wept; rapture, boundless rapture, elevated [his] whole being."[26] Why? He feels he has seen pure truth with his own eyes. He has beheld its glory.

What is this truth that has so captivated him? Is it a Christian truth? This seems to follow from the suggestion that all of this reflected life "before the fall" and from the reference to crosses, and given the fact that Orthodox Christians routinely refer to the divine as eternal truth and beauty and to Christ as the living truth and transcendent image of the divine. Or does this revelation leave the ridiculous man only on the edge of such a Christian faith, as others have suggested? Is the idyllic world he encounters a harbinger of the world that preceded the era called "civilization," or is it a foreshadowing of the world that awaits us once this civilization has passed? So many questions!

None of them seem to matter for our ridiculous man, for since the time of his dream he has begun to preach endlessly. He now loves without restraint. He even loves those who think him absurd, for he is now deemed ridiculous in a different manner than before. He now believes he has beheld a living truth that is infinitely more than a state of mind, one that is ineffably beautiful. He now believes that "the main thing" is for us to love others as ourselves. It is an old truth, yet he dares to suggest that this truth marks our way to a paradise that will surely come and already is. And no act of love is ever wasted, for each one portends a time when love will be everywhere and in all. When will that time be? The ridiculous man believes with all his heart that it could be realized today, even in a single hour, if we but began to love without reservation or limit.

Dostoevsky and the Search for a Global Ethic for Our Time

But that was then. It is fair to ask, as we reach our final destination, what relevance does Dostoevsky still hold in our time? Put another way, is there a firm and fixed proposal by which his nineteenth-century voice might offer something of value to a twenty-first-century reader in search of an ethical worldview, and all the more so in an age where no firm and fixed ethical coherence can be supposed? In some ways, these questions have been the backdrop for all I have written so far. I want to conclude by suggesting four important challenges that a careful engagement with Dostoevsky's moral thought raises for those who seek to be ethically engaged in our time.

First, Dostoevsky challenges his readers to reconsider the ethical land-scape, and most especially the notion that a global ethic must necessarily emerge from the Western philosophical tradition, one that considers itself to be uniquely universal, impartial, and somehow above the global ethical fray. So, in chapters 1 and 4, I have investigated Western ethical construc-tions that reject Orthodoxy's claim to absolute truth, though their critique might as easily have been applied to ethical claims made by any of the world's religions. After all, how is it possible for any one of these to be ab-solutely true? It is by this logic that most contemporary ethical surveys maintain that Western moral thought is sufficient for those seeking to cre-ate their own individual ethical worldviews.

The problem arises when readers push this perspective to the Dosto-evskian extreme, for at some point they will either conclude that one of the absolute ethical claims out there may in fact be absolutely true or, alter-natively, that absolutely no particular truth claim (from Islam, say, or from Orthodox Christianity) can possibly be true. But what claim can be more absolute than one that absolutely dismisses all other absolute claims as flawed? If Dostoevsky's stinging rebuke to "the professors" in chapter 4 must be taken seriously, why should it be any different now?

Dostoevsky challenges his readers to see the Western ethical tradition as one among many, each of which inescapably makes absolute claims. This is not to say that Western moral discourse is not somehow unique among all others. In that regard, Cardinal Joseph Ratzinger—who in April 2005 became Pope Benedict XVI—once undertook a noted exchange with the German neo-Marxist philosopher Jürgen Habermas. The two met at the invitation of the Catholic Academy of Bavaria on January 19, 2004, to de-bate the "dialectics of secularization." Their comments, which were pub-lished later as a dialogue, make it clear they held each other in high regard.[27] Early in their exchange, Habermas comments on a discussion he had had not long before regarding the West's Enlightenment and its subsequent secularization. It occurred in Tehran, when a colleague at an academic con-ference informed the German philosopher "that the comparative study of cultures and religious sociology surely suggested that *European seculariza-tion* was the odd one out among the various developments—and that it ought to be corrected."[28] Habermas's response to this frontal attack on an intellectual development that was obviously dear to him is in many ways fascinating. He links such thinking to ideas swirling in the German intellectual community during the Weimar years; he then cautions that it is "better not to push too far" the questions raised by the critique offered in Tehran. In short, he does not engage the observation at all—a fact not lost on Ratzinger. The theologian gently returns to this comment later when he suggests that "the question put by Jürgen Habermas' colleague in Teheran [*sic*] seems [to Ratzinger] not devoid of significance—namely, the question of whether a comparative study of cultures and the sociology of religion suggest that European secularization is an exceptional development and one that needs to be corrected."[29] One may, of course, agree with Habermas, though even then the challenge posed by Ratzinger and the unnamed colleague cannot be glibly dismissed.

Thus readers will meet one of Dostoevsky's great challenges when they begin to see themselves as alive in a world of competing and absolute ethical claims. For that reason alone, there is no obvious reason why Western moral thought—or any other moral order, including the one based on "the Russian Christ"—should be given pride of place. Stanley Hauerwas has argued over a long and distinguished career that there is no exception to this, however much we may wish there to be.[30]

Second, Dostoevsky challenges his readers to see a world of competing ethical claims as one of more promise than peril. It will be so if readers fearlessly engage the moral task before them, for they will suddenly have some ethical choices to make, and there is work to be done. The good news is that this realization of manifold ethical possibilities will not require readers to abandon their belief in what Dostoevsky called "the great binding idea" of an all-encompassing moral order, one that every great society requires. Nor should it trouble readers if they are initially unsure as to which particular binding idea is absolutely the best of the ethical options available to them. Dostoevsky reflects on this in the July–August 1877 edition of *Diary of a Writer*. He begins by stating how he wished once more to see the former Dostoevsky family estate near Moscow, and the peasant village located there, so that he could once again experience the setting of so many happy childhood years. He tells this to a friend, and they reflect on the importance of sacred memories; from here, they reflect on the youth of their day and finally on their mutual wonderment that people try to live today without any "binding ideas." To live that way seems impossible. Dostoevsky accepts that a particular binding idea may have been false in the past, but at least it bound and therefore always allowed for the possibility of choosing a binding idea in the end that was sound: "Please note as well that this idea, this faith, might even be a mistaken one, so that the best children would themselves later renounce it, or at least improve upon it, for their own children, but still, the very existence of this common idea that binds society and the family is already the beginning of an order—a moral order, I mean—which, of course, is subject to change, progress, and modification, I grant you, but which is still a moral order. Whereas in our day there is no such order, for there is nothing common and binding."[31]

Thus readers who follow Dostoevsky's lead will worry less at the outset as to which of the absolute ethical worldviews before them is correct and instead simply move the whole lot of them into the public square. Once they do so, readers will need to reinvigorate their understanding of debate, out of which will undoubtedly emerge a reinvigorated society, one comprised of globally engaged citizens. It should not surprise that Dostoevsky, the master of the polyphonic novel—to borrow Bakhtin's famed ascription one last time—desired a truly polyphonic public square. In a probing study, Alasdair MacIntyre has even suggested that we will need to reinvent the modern university if this reinvigorated moral debate is ever to occur within its confines.[32] Zygmunt Bauman has issued similar warnings. We seem to have arrived at a place where we prize bystanders and pleasure-seeking consumers over critically engaged citizens.[33] If Bauman's diagnosis is correct, we will need to work hard to re-create a spirit of critical democratic engagement in our society. We will need to redevelop the art of debate and remaster the art of nonviolent suasion. And we will need to retrieve a notion of "complex space," in John Milbank's telling of it, whereby institutions such as the mosque, the First Nation band council, the church, and the synagogue will again be seen to play a vital role in the public square. Otherwise, the risk remains for Milbank that a "controlling centre" will pit itself over and against "controlled individuals" within a liberalized modernity.[34]

Readers will have to get involved, in other words, at multiple levels and for the long haul. I have attempted, with this study, to suggest that Dostoevsky's voice must be one of those heard in a revitalized public square as we interrogate the current dominant ethic of procedural impartiality coupled with absolute ethical indifference and seemingly endless distraction.

Dostoevsky presents a third challenge to his readers, one concerned with the actual content of what a truly transformed global ethic might comprise. To understate, the Russian writer had strong opinions on this matter. Perhaps most surprisingly, several components of such a trans- formed Dostoevskian ethic may already provoke a deep resonance with diverse peoples and faiths around the world. For example, there is already substantial common ground for an ethic based on corporate responsibility for all and everything, as opposed to the narrow definition of individual guilt and responsibility embraced by Western law and reinforced daily in popular culture.

Similarly, it may be time to follow Dostoevsky's lead and ponder the elevation of love over law and of compassion over reason. Love's hege- mony over law is hardly an idea associated with the great Western tradi- tions, within which reason, law, and science have long held trump. Carol Gilligan has suggested that philosophical considerations of "love" and "care" have rarely appeared in the West for hundreds of years.[35] Bruce Ward has effectively demonstrated how Dostoevsky's understanding of love as "an independent reality" contrasts sharply with a dominant Western discourse that understands love to be a primal "drive" or "psychic force" within us.[36] Yet eruptions of love-based compassion have appeared over time, as in the person and thought of Simone Weil. Richard Bell, in an aptly titled study, has underscored Weil's belief that compassion is the way of justice.[37] Weil viewed compassion as "the madness of love." She believed that those committed to works of justice had no choice but to love, even though it might come at great personal cost to them. She also character- ized compassion as a refusal to use force, an attention to suffering, and hu- mility before others.[38]

Dostoevsky himself was fascinated by the role of law, especially as legal reforms introduced in the 1860s brought the question of judicial pro- cesses to the fore. It is not by accident that reflections on legal understand- ings of justice pervade his novels, most especially in *Crime and Punishment*, where Raskolnikov himself is studying to become a lawyer. In almost every instance, Dostoevsky distinguishes sharply between true justice and legal certitude. In one of his first post-exilic novellas, *Winter Notes on Summer Impressions*, Dostoevsky observed that legal codes in the West afforded only a limited kind of equality. What they really meant was that the wealthy were free to do as they pleased because they were under the protection of the law.[39] Thus, both the great splendor and the deep squalor of mid- nineteenth-century London might have been legally constituted, but this hardly made for a just society. No wonder Dostoevsky soon transformed this real world of gross inequality into the dramatically imagined ethos of Shigalevism (see chapter 2) with its vast and legally buttressed disparities. In a real way, then, Dostoevsky was challenging his readers to reconsider the relationship between law and justice.

In the same way, Dostoevsky challenges his readers to reconsider the primacy of law over love, the inversion of which would correspond to countless moral orders that prize a seemingly reckless love for all— especially for the most vulnerable. A global ethic premised on love over law might also lead directly to that Dostoevskian worldview that privileges obligations over rights. To give but one corresponding example, the opening of Simone Weil's *The Need for Roots* is so striking that it needs to be quoted at some length: "The notion of obligations comes before that of rights, which is subordinate and relative to the former. A right is not effectual by itself, but only in relation to the obligation to which it corresponds, the effective exercise of a right springing not from the individual who possesses it, but from other men who consider themselves as being under a certain obligation towards him. Recognition of an obligation makes it effectual. An obligation which goes unrecognized by anybody loses none of the full force of its existence. A right which goes unrecognized by anybody is not worth very much."[40]

Rights for Weil meant nothing unless preceded by obligations motivated by compassion and love for the Other, even at the expense of one's own rights. This language of obligations before rights remains strikingly at odds with much of the contemporary discourse on ethics. So in the end, a new, great, binding ethical idea may emerge in a rejuvenated public square, one that will follow Dostoevsky's lead—and those of countless other moral traditions—and radically challenge our understanding of love, law, individual rights, and societal obligations and of how we are to prioritize these.

The fourth and final challenge that Dostoevsky's nineteenth-century voice still brings to twenty-first-century readers is this: even now, almost a century and a half after his passing, Dostoevsky continues to challenge readers to reconsider the merits of an ethic that is grounded in a metaphysically transcendent love, hope, joy, and beauty. We strive for no less than these, which is why millions of advertising dollars can generate billions of revenue dollars by persuading us that their products will provide peace of mind, joy, lasting relationships, and all the rest. It is perhaps a fit-ting irony that, in March 2008, the Paradise Beauty Salon occupied the ground floor of Dostoevsky's apartment building on St. Petersburg's Kuz-nechnyi Street—the very building where he lived for the four years prior to his death in 1881. Dostoevsky might have appreciated the irony that moderns associated paradise with a beauty salon; that on the sign, the word *Paradise* was written in English, with the Latin script; and that beauty itself was being associated with what transpires in a beauty salon. Dostoevsky might have been flattered to have a street named after him near his final home, as well as a hotel around the corner on Vladimirskaya. That said, the shine might have been diminished, given his addiction to gambling, had he seen the "Golden Land [*Zolotaya Strana*] Casino" on the same prem-ises. Put it all together and we might conclude that he would barely have recognized his old neighborhood.

But in many ways he would have recognized this place, our world, for then as now we seek love, beauty, and a taste of paradise. Some would say that the longing for them is what makes us human, that we remain restless until we have found what we are looking for—that which we hope will make us whole. Surely Dostoevsky's own writings repeatedly and passion-ately cause his readers to reflect on this profound longing and the ways we seek to assuage it. Similarly, Orthodox theologian David Bentley Hart has recently equated ethics with "social love" more than with some sort of "infinite pitiless obligation." We do not engage the good because we must, he writes, but out of our own deepest need, for "once love has been roused, sympathy stirred, or joy evoked, the self begins to be able to bear and struggle against any suffering or evil with a real moral passion." For Hart, this is true love, a love that begins in love of self, and it is the founda-tion of the ethical life.[41]

What has happened, however, is that our world's dominant ethical dis-course has led to a place where the fulfillment of these essentially existen-tial aspirations has taken us to means and ends that are primarily material. How else can one summarize a perspective that suggests we come from nowhere and will end up there again in the end? It seems that the ghosts of "Bobok" still haunt us. In a sense, we are living out Dostoevsky's greatest fears. And he was not alone in this forewarning, though in truth, this search for fulfillment in the physicality of our lives—a search that verges on the existentially hopeless—remains an overwhelmingly minority perspective within the world's great civilizations.

Surely a reinvigorated public square will put that particular position alongside all other traditions, the vast majority of which join Dostoevsky in the belief that we come from somewhere and are part of something much greater than our quotidian material existence. Perhaps a new global ethic might emerge from scattered moral traditions that understand life itself to be a gift, and in a way that inescapably links the ethical with the Giver. Here, of course, a profound disagreement is certain to arise: Is the Giver's name Allah? Is it Manitou? Are the Givers in fact legion? Or is it the God who is eternally three-in-one and who took human form in the Russian Christ who so captivated Fyodor Mikhailovich Dostoevsky?

Surely what will matter most in the reinvigorated public square is the realization that our lives and our world exist in the very place and time where nothing at all had to exist. Surely our moral understanding of ourselves, our neighbors, and our world will be profoundly and joyfully transformed in the process. It is hard to imagine that our world will be worse off for the attempt.

CHAPTER I. *Why Dostoevsky? Why Now? Why Here?*

1. These numbers come from the 2006 Human Development Report, pages 33–34, available at http://hdr.undp.org/sites/default/files/reports/267 /hdr06-complete.pdf. See also Brahma Chellaney, *Water, Peace, and War: Confronting the Global Water Crisis*, updated edition (Lanham, MD: Rowman & Littlefield, 2015), chapter 1.

2. Torbjörn Tännsjö, *Understanding Ethics: An Introduction to Moral Theory* (Edinburgh: Edinburgh University Press, 2002). For an approach that is similar in key respects see, more recently, Kimberly Hutchings, *Global Ethics: An Introduction* (Cambridge: Polity Press, 2010).

3. Tännsjö, *Understanding Ethics*, 11–12.

4. Hutchings, *Global Ethics*, 19.

5. Ibid., chapters 2 and 3.

6. Tännsjö, *Understanding Ethics*, 15.

7. See ibid., 7, 9, 11, as well as chapter 9.

8. Ibid., 13.

9. Hutchings, *Global Ethics*, 19; emphasis in the original.

10. Tännsjö, *Understanding Ethics*, 136–37.

11. Ibid.

12. Zygmunt Bauman, *Life in Fragments: Essays in Postmodern Morality* (Oxford: Blackwell, 1995); Michael Allen Gillespie, *Nihilism before Nietzsche* (Chicago: University of Chicago Press, 1995); and Charles Taylor, *Sources of the Self: The Making of the Modern Identity* (Cambridge, MA: Harvard University Press, 1989).

13. Alasdair MacIntyre, *A Short History of Ethics* (New York: Macmillan, 1966), 268. See also his signature work, *After Virtue: A Study in Moral Theory*, 2d ed. (Notre Dame, IN: University of Notre Dame Press, 1984).

14. Marina Kostalevsky, *Dostoevsky and Soloviev: The Art of Integral Vision* (New Haven, CT: Yale University Press, 1997), 174–76.

15. Dipesh Chakrabarty, *Provincializing Europe: Postcolonial Thought and Historical Difference* (Princeton, NJ: Princeton University Press, 2000), 4.

16. Immanuel Wallerstein, *European Universalism: The Rhetoric of Power* (New York: New Press, 2006), 70, 84.

17. Jonathan Lear, *Radical Hope: Ethics in the Face of Cultural Devastation* (Cambridge, MA: Harvard University Press, 2007).

18. For the succinct version, see Michael Cook, *Forbidding Wrong in Islam: An Introduction* (Cambridge: Cambridge University Press, 2003), 19, and chapter 3.

19. Richard H. Bell, *Simone Weil: The Way of Justice as Compassion* (Lanham, MD: Rowman & Littlefield, 1998), 42 (quote), 52, 54.

20. Catherine Chalier, *What Ought I to Do? Morality in Kant and Levinas* (Ithaca, NY: Cornell University Press, 2002), 34–35, 40, 53, and 74. See also Jeffrey Bloechl, *Liturgy of the Neighbor: Emmanuel Levinas and the Religion of Responsibility* (Pittsburgh: Duquesne University Press, 2000), 32, 69. It is this same search for alterity that leads both Weil and Levinas to see a link between physical and metaphysical reality, in the form of a divine and transcendent being.

21. Jill Robbins, ed., *Is It Righteous to Be? Interviews with Emmanuel Levinas* (Stanford, CA: Stanford University Press, 2001), 24, 28.

22. Joseph Frank, *Dostoevsky: The Years of Ordeal, 1850–1859* (Princeton, NJ: Princeton University Press, 1990), 58.

23. The Decembrist revolution, famously referred to as "the first Russian revolution," occurred in 1825 as Nicholas I was coming to the throne following the death of his brother Alexander. Anatole Mazour, *The First Russian Revolution, 1825: The Decembrist Movement, Its Origins, Development, and Significance* (Berkeley: University of California Press, 1937).

24. David Denby, "Can Dostoevsky Still Kick You in the Gut?" *The New Yorker*, June 11, 2012, available at http://www.newyorker.com/books/page-turner /can-dostoevsky-still-kick-you-in-the-gut.

25. *ADT*, viii.

26. Ibid., x.

27. Joseph Frank, *Dostoevsky: The Mantle of the Prophet, 1871–1881* (Princeton, NJ: Princeton University Press, 2002), chapter 21.

28. Frank, *Mantle of the Prophet*, 755.

29. For the English translation, see Nicholas Berdyaev, *Dostoevsky* (New York: New American Library, 1934), 227.

30. Berdyaev, *Dostoevsky*, 16.

31. Kostalevsky, *Dostoevsky and Soloviev*, 174.

32. Rowan Williams, *Dostoevsky: Language, Faith, and Fiction* (Waco, TX: Baylor University Press, 2009); and Bruce K. Ward, *Redeeming the Enlightenment: Christianity and Liberal Values* (Grand Rapids, MI: Eerdmans, 2010).

33. Derek Offord, "The People," in *A History of Russian Thought*, ed. William Leatherbarrow and Derek Offord (Cambridge: Cambridge University Press, 2010), 242–43; and Elise Kimerling Wirtschafter, *Social Identity in Imperial Russia* (DeKalb: Northern Illinois University Press, 1997).

34. Peter C. Erb, *Murder, Manners, Mystery: Reflections on Faith in Contemporary Detective Fiction* (London: SCM Press, 2007), 6. The reference to Weil, noted by Erb, is Simone Weil, "Reflections on the Right Use of School Studies with a View to the Love of God," in *Waiting on God*, trans. Emma Crawford (London: Routledge & Kegan Paul, 1951).

35. Williams, *Dostoevsky*, 47.

36. Alice Crary, "J. M. Coetzee, Moral Thinker," in *J. M. Coetzee and Ethics: Philosophical Perspectives on Literature*, ed. Anton Leist and Peter Singer (New York: Columbia University Press, 2010), 254.

37. Anton Leist and Peter Singer, "Introduction: Coetzee and Philosophy," in *J. M. Coetzee and Ethics*, ed. Leist and Singer, 13.

38. For an excellent introduction into the changing historiography on Dostoevsky, see George Pattison and Diane Oenning Thompson, "Introduction: Reading Dostoevsky Religiously," in *Dostoevsky and the Christian Tradition*, ed. George Pattison and Diane Oenning Thompson (Cambridge: Cambridge University Press, 2001), 1–30.

39. For the English version, see Mikhail Bakhtin, *Problems of Dostoevsky's Poetics*, ed. and trans. Caryl Emerson (Minneapolis: University of Minnesota Press, 1984).

40. For an example of the more recent scholarship on Bakhtin, see Alexander Mihailovic, *Corporeal Words: Mikhail Bakhtin's Theology of Discourse* (Evanston, IL: Northwestern University Press, 1997).

41. Bakhtin, *Problems of Dostoevsky's Poetics*, 31–32, 50. The quotation is from p. 59, and the emphasis is in the original.

42. Edith W. Clowes, *Fiction's Overcoat: Russian Literary Culture and the Question of Philosophy* (Ithaca, NY: Cornell University Press, 2004), part 1.

43. *UND*, 13.

44. Ibid., 34.

45. *WD*, 215–16.

46. *IDT*, 217 ff; and again on 407 ff.

47. For a perceptive article on icons, see Sophie Ollivier, "Icons in Dostoevsky's Works," in *Dostoevsky and the Christian Tradition*, ed. Pattison and Thompson, 51–68.

48. *BK*, 18–19.

49. For a classic introduction to Orthodox icons, see Leonid Ouspensky and Vladimir Lossky, *The Meaning of Icons* (Boston: Boston Book & Art Shop, 1969).

50. Gary Saul Morson, "Introductory Study," in *WD* 1, for example, p. 47.

51. Jacques Catteau, *Dostoyevsky and the Process of Literary Creation* (Cambridge: Cambridge University Press, 1989), 192.

52. Geoffrey C. Kabat, *Ideology and Imagination: The Image of Society in Dostoevsky* (New York: Columbia University Press, 1978), 163–64; and Laura Engelstein, *Slavophile Empire: Imperial Russia's Illiberal Path* (Ithaca, NY: Cornell University Press, 2009), 119.

53. Robert Louis Jackson, *The Art of Dostoevsky: Deliriums and Nocturnes* (Princeton, NJ: Princeton University Press, 1981), 114.

54. James Scanlan, *Dostoevsky the Thinker* (Ithaca, NY: Cornell University Press, 2002), 4.

55. A. Boyce Gibson, *The Religion of Dostoevsky* (London: SCM Press, 1973), 1; emphasis in original.

56. Williams, *Dostoevsky*, 8.

57. Wayne Dowler, *Dostoevsky, Grigor'ev, and Native Soil Conservatism* (Toronto: University of Toronto Press, 1982).

58. Victor Terras, *Reading Dostoevsky* (Madison: University of Wisconsin Press, 1998), 89.

59. Irina Kirillova, "Dostoevsky's Markings in the Gospel According to St. John," in *Dostoevsky and the Christian Tradition*, ed. Pattison and Thompson, esp. 42.

60. Nor am I alone in this perspective among Dostoevskian scholars. See Mikhail Fyrnin, "Mir spaset krasota!" in *Sobranie myslei Dostoevskogo* (Moscow: Zvonnitsa - MG, 2003), 8–20, where a similar view is advanced.

61. Nikolai Nasedkin, *Samoubiistvo Dostoevskogo* (Moskva: Algoritm, 2002), 250.

62. This is found in part 1, book 2, chapter 3 of *BK.*

63. Joseph Frank, *Dostoevsky: The Miraculous Years, 1865–1871* (Princeton, NJ: Princeton University Press, 1995), 202; and *ID*, notes, p. 619.

64. *WD*, 513.

65. P. Travis Kroeker and Bruce K. Ward, *Remembering the End: Dostoevsky as Prophet of Modernity* (Boulder, CO: Westview Press, 2001), 247–48.

66. *IDT*, viii.

67. Ibid., ix.

68. Ibid., 217 ff and 407 ff.

69. Ibid., 218.

70. *CP*, 171, 471, and 482.

71. See the incident with "the bump" in *UND*, 55.

72. *BK*, 69. The words are those of the purported writer of *The Brothers Kara-mazov* and refer in this instance to statements made by Ivan Karamazov.

73. Frank, *Mantle of the Prophet*, 526.

CHAPTER 2. *Orphans' Lament*

1. The story is found in *WD*, November 1876; as found in Fyodor Dosto-evsky, *A Writer's Diary*, vol. 1, *1873–1876* (Evanston, IL: Northwestern University Press, 1994), 677–717; or separately in Fyodor Dostoevsky, *The Eternal Husband and Other Stories*, trans. Richard Pevear and Larissa Volokhonsky (New York: Bantam Classics, 1997), 248–95.

2. *WD*; the first quote is at 679, the second at 681.

3. Ibid., 683; italics in the original.

4. Ibid., 693; italics in the original.

5. Ibid., 653.

6. *BK*, 174, for example.

7. Ibid., 97.

8. One of Dostoevsky's earliest novels, *The Double*, played explicitly with the idea of dual images and mirrored personalities. He continued to employ this technique throughout his career, and to much more literary acclaim than received in the first attempt.

9. *BK*, 287 (for Zosima) and 515 (for Kolya).

10. *ADT*, 9. Her father has been dead for several years.

11. References to this loveless arrangement are everywhere at the start of the novel. See *ADT*, 110, 116, 123, and 206 for the contrast between what Arkady longs for and what his natural father is willing (able?) to deliver.

12. See *DEM*, 92, 259, and 306, for but a small sampling of three main figures found in the novel.

13. W. J. Leatherbarrow, *The Devil's Vaudeville: The Demonic in Dostoevsky's Fiction* (Evanston, IL: Northwestern University Press, 2005), 58.

14. Liza Knapp, *The Annihilation of Inertia: Dostoevsky and Metaphysics* (Evanston, IL: Northwestern University Press, 1996), 40.

15. For example, see Gillespie, *Nihilism before Nietzsche*, 197.

16. Friedrich Nietzsche, *The Gay Science*, trans. Walter Kaufmann (New York: Vintage, 1974), section 25.

17. *BK*, 171.

18. *DEM*, 29.

19. Ibid., 37.

20. Ibid., 53.

21. *IDT*, 219–21.

22. *DEM*, 213.

23. Ibid., 397.

24. Ibid., 427.

25. *BK,* part 2, book 5, chapter 3.

26. Ibid., 235.

27. Ibid., part 2, book 5, chapter 5.

28. Ibid., 249.

29. Ibid., 262.

30. Ibid., 259.

31. *ADT,* 466–67.

32. Ibid., 470; emphasis in original.

33. Knapp, *Annihilation of Inertia,* 133–35, 147–51.

34. *BK,* 131 and 135.

35. *ADT,* especially 84 ff.

36. Ibid., 451.

37. *IDT,* 132–33, 304, 335, 336, and 339.

38. *WIN,* 36–37.

39. Joseph Frank, *Dostoevsky: The Stir of Liberation, 1860–1865* (Princeton, NJ: Princeton University Press, 1986), 238–39.

40. *WD,* 415.

41. Knapp, *Annihilation of Inertia,* 41.

42. *CP,* 301 (Svidrigailov), 307 (Luzhin), and 232 (Dunya).

43. Ibid., 149.

44. Williams, *Dostoevsky,* 219.

45. *CP,* 50, 62, 273, and 313.

46. Vyacheslav Ivanov, *Freedom and the Tragic Life: A Study in Dostoevsky* (London: Harvill Press, 1952), 78.

47. Jackson, *Art of Dostoevsky,* 238, 243.

48. *DEM,* 319 and 540.

49. *ADT,* 167.

50. Ibid., 20.

51. *WD,* 394–95.

52. There are many translations of "Bobok." See *WD,* 170–85.

53. *BK,* 3.

54. *DEM,* 45–51.

55. Ibid., 240, 267.

56. Ibid., 248.

57. Ibid., 251–54.

58. Ibid., 254.

59. Ibid., 399.

60. Ibid., 236–37 and 556–58.

61. *UND,* 92.

62. Knapp, *Annihilation of Inertia,* 32–33.

63. *UND*, 22, 55, 122; and Jackson, *Art of Dostoevsky*, 163.

64. *CP*, 368–71, 133.

65. *ADT*, 291, 447.

66. Ibid., 63.

67. *BK*, 69.

68. Ibid., 82.

69. Ibid., 225.

70. Ibid., 589.

71. Ibid., 625 and 632.

72. Ibid., 648.

73. Harvie Ferguson, *Melancholy and the Critique of Modernity: Søren Kierkegaard's Religious Psychology* (London: Routledge, 1995).

74. Ibid., 4.

75. Ibid., 19.

76. Ibid., 23.

77. *UND*, 25. See also 18.

78. *WIN*, 10, 25–26.

79. *IDT*, 544–45.

80. *BK*, 574, 581–85; the quote is from 581.

81. John Horton, "The Glamour of Evil: Dostoyevsky and the Politics of Transgression," in *Evil in Contemporary Political Theory*, ed. Bruce Haddock, Peri Roberts, and Peter Sutch (Edinburgh: Edinburgh University Press, 2011), 156–76.

82. *BK*, 173 and 738.

83. Ibid., 127.

84. *WD*, 415 and 737–38.

85. Ibid., 175–85.

86. Konstantin Mochulsky, *Dostoevsky: His Life and Work* (Princeton, NJ: Princeton University Press, 1967), 479.

87. Leatherbarrow, *Devil's Vaudeville*, 44. See also Jackson's insightful comments in Jackson, *Art of Dostoevsky*, 294–99.

88. *ADT*, 63 and 207.

89. *DEM*, 9–10.

90. Ibid., 33.

91. *CP*, 470–71.

92. Ibid., 470–83.

93. *DEM*, 694.

94. *DEM*. The censored chapter was called "At Tikhon's." It was the original part 2, chapter 9, of *Demons*.

95. *BK*, 585.

96. *DEM*, 326–27.

196 Notes to Pages 59–67

97. *ADT*, 32–33.

98. Ibid., 93.

99. *BK*, 383.

100. *DEM*, 31.

101. *CP*, 482.

102. Ibid., 259–60, 263.

103. Ibid., 148–49 (Luzhin) and 484 (Svidrigailov).

104. *BK*, 258–59.

105. Ibid., 259.

106. Stewart R. Sutherland, *Atheism and the Rejection of God: Contemporary Philosophy and* The Brothers Karamazov (Oxford: Basil Blackwell, 1977), 36; emphasis is in the original.

107. J. Michael Holquist, *Dostoevsky and the Novel* (Princeton, NJ: Princeton University Press, 1977), 72.

108. *UND*, 49.

109. Ibid., 55.

110. *IDT*, 293.

111. Ibid., 118.

112. *DEM*, 251.

113. *IDT*, 293.

114. Cf. Zygmunt Bauman, *Modernity and the Holocaust* (Ithaca, NY: Cornell University Press, 1989).

115. *DEM*, 575.

116. *BK*, 243.

117. Ibid., 616.

118. See *CP*, 274 and 415.

119. *CP*, 259–60.

120. *DEM*, 402.

121. Ibid., 403–4.

122. *BK*, 255.

123. Nicholas Berdyaev, *Dostoevsky* (New York: New American Library, 1957), 76.

124. See especially Erich Fromm, *Escape from Freedom* (New York: Farrar & Reinhardt, 1960; first published 1941).

125. *CP*, 490–91.

126. As an indication of how pointed he could be, Dostoevsky begins his response as follows: "The March issue of *The Russian Messenger* of this year contains a 'criticism' of me by Mr. A., i.e., Mr. Avseenko. There's no use in my answering Mr. Avseenko; it's difficult to conceive of a writer who has a poorer grasp of the

subject." Somewhat later he continues, "Mr. Avseenko has been writing criticism for a long time, for some years now, and I confess that I still had some hopes for him: 'If he writes long enough,' I thought, 'he'll finally say something.' But I did not know him very well." *WD*, 427 and 429.

127. *WD*, 427–28.

128. Ibid., 432.

129. Ibid., 442–43.

130. *IDT*, 415.

131. *DEM*, 115.

132. Ibid., 617.

133. N. N. Shneidman, *Dostoevsky and Suicide* (Oakville: Mosaic Press 1984), 98.

134. Irina Paperno, *Suicide as a Cultural Institution in Dostoevsky's Russia* (Ithaca, NY: Cornell University Press, 1997), chapter 6.

135. *WD*, 733.

136. Paperno, *Suicide as a Cultural Institution*, 45–73; and Susan K. Morrissey, *Suicide and the Body Politic in Imperial Russia* (Cambridge: Cambridge University Press, 2006), 177–79, 183.

137. Morrissey, *Suicide and the Body Politic*, 224.

138. *BK*, 303 and 313.

139. *DEM*, 618.

140. *BK*, 366, 405, and 611.

141. *CP*, 499–500.

142. *CP*, 544.

143. *BK*, part 3, book 7, chapter 3.

144. For a good introduction to George Sand, see Robert Godwin-Jones, *Romantic Vision: The Novels of George Sand* (Birmingham, AL: Summa, 1995).

145. *WD*, 129.

146. Bruce Ward, *Dostoyevsky's Critique of the West* (Waterloo, ON: Wilfrid Laurier University Press, 1976), 92.

147. *WD*, June 1876, 508.

148. Ibid., 509.

149. *WIN*, 48.

150. *WD*, June 1876, 513.

151. Ibid.

152. Ward, *Dostoyevsky's Critique of the West*, chapter 2.

153. *DEM*, 236. "Man-God" refers to the belief that man on his own can become godlike. It is an inversion of Christianity's claim that such perfection was only possible in Christ, the "God-man," because he alone was God-incarnate.

154. *DEM*, 232.

155. There are many such passages throughout Dostoevsky's writings, fictional and not. See *WD*, March 1876, section 5: "An Expired Force and the Forces of the Future."

156. Williams, *Dostoevsky*, 212, quotation from 218; Dowler, *Dostoevsky, Grigor'ev, and Native Soil Conservatism*, 168–75; and Malcolm Jones, *Dostoevsky and the Dynamics of Religious Experience* (London: Anthem Press, 2005).

CHAPTER 3. *To Bow at the Crossroads*

1. *CP*, part 6, chapter 7.
2. Ibid., 420.
3. Ibid., 522.
4. Ibid., 526.
5. Ivanov, *Freedom and the Tragic Life*, 5.
6. Ibid., 15, 23 ff.
7. Ibid., 24.
8. Ibid., 24.
9. *UND*, part 1, chapter 2.
10. Ivanov, *Freedom and the Tragic Life*, 75–76. Cf. Jackson, *Art of Dostoevsky*, chapter 7, in which Jackson repeatedly alludes to Raskolnikov's utter fragmentation in the first half of the novel.
11. Bakhtin, *Problems of Dostoevsky's Poetics*, 97.
12. Ibid., 96–97.
13. Vigen Guroian, *Incarnate Love: Essays in Orthodox Ethics*, 2d ed. (Notre Dame, IN: University of Notre Dame Press, 2002), 16. See also Stanley S. Harakas, *Toward Transfigured Life: The Theoria of Eastern Orthodox Ethics* (Minneapolis: Light & Life, 1983).
14. Joseph Woodill, *The Fellowship of Life: Virtue, Ethics, and Orthodox Christianity* (Washington, DC: Georgetown University Press, 1998), 36–38, 73 (from the writings for John Climacus).
15. Avril Pyman, "Dostoevsky in the Prism of the Orthodox Semiosphere," in *Dostoevsky and the Christian Tradition*, ed. Pattison and Thompson (Cambridge: Cambridge University Press, 2001), 108.
16. Cited in Williams, *Dostoevsky*, 204. On Isaac the Syrian, see Hilarion Alfeyev and Kallistos Ware, *The Ascetical Homilies of Saint Isaac the Syrian*, trans. Holy Transfiguration Monastery (Boston: Holy Transfiguration Monastery, 1984).
17. *WD*, 349.
18. Ibid., 351–55.
19. Ibid., 354.

20. Diane Oenning Thompson presents a strong case for the role of memory in Dostoevsky's writings in The Brothers Karamazov *and the Poetics of Memory* (Cambridge: Cambridge University Press, 1991).

21. Both the offense with his servant and the recollections of his eldest brother, Markel, are found in *BK*, part 2, book 6, chapter 2.

22. *BK*, 305.

23. Thompson, The Brothers Karamazov *and the Poetics of Memory*, 98–99.

24. *CP*, 324–25.

25. Ibid., 327.

26. *BK*, 405.

27. *ADT*, 330.

28. Ibid., 331.

29. Ibid., 109.

30. Ibid., 359.

31. Ibid., 350–51.

32. Gibson, *Religion of Dostoevsky*, 144–45.

33. *DEM*, 639, 652–53.

34. Ibid., 654.

35. Ibid., 655.

36. Bakhtin, *Problems of Dostoevsky's Poetics*, 58–59.

37. Sophie Ollivier, "Icons in Dostoevsky's Works," in *Dostoevsky and the Christian Tradition*, ed. Pattison and Thompson, 51.

38. Woodill, *Fellowship of Life*, 82; and Pavel Florensky, *Iconostasis*, trans. Donald Sheehan and Olga Andrejev (Crestwood, NY: St. Vladimir's Seminary Press, 1996), 51–52.

39. Florensky, *Iconostasis*, 60.

40. Paul Evdokimov, *The Art of the Icon: A Theology of Beauty*, trans. Father Steven Bigham (Redondo Beach, CA: Oakwood, 1990), 12–13.

41. Antony Johae, "Towards an Iconography of Dostoevsky's 'Crime and Punishment,'" in *Dostoevsky and the Christian Tradition*, ed. Pattison and Thompson, 175.

42. *WD*, 354.

43. *ADT*, 178 and 334–35; *CP*, 522 and 523; and *DEM*, 592 and 652–56.

44. *DEAD*, 179.

45. Jackson, *Art of Dostoevsky*, 75.

46. *DEAD*, 180.

47. *IDT*, 219–20.

48. Ibid., 222.

49. Johae, "Towards an Iconography," in Pattison and Thompson, 176.

50. *DEM*, 615.

51. Frank, *The Stir of Liberation*, 308–9.

52. I know of no adequate and complete English translation of this vital reflection. The original is found in *PSS*, 20:172 ff. The translation here is mine; the emphasis in the text is in the original.

53. *PSS*, 20:173, translation mine.

54. Ibid.

55. Kroeker and Ward, *Remembering the End*, 253–54.

56. For an excellent introduction to Eastern Orthodox Theology, see Vladimir Lossky, *The Mystical Theology of the Eastern Church* (Crestwood, NY: St. Vladimir's Seminary Press, 1976), esp. chapters 1 and 2.

57. *BK*, 674–75.

58. *WD*, 434.

59. Knapp, *Annihilation of Inertia*, 128–29.

60. *WD*, 128.

61. Berdyaev, *Dostoevsky*, 67.

62. Ibid., 68–69.

63. Ibid., 71.

64. *ADT*, 563.

65. Ibid., 350.

66. Ibid., 481, italics in the original.

67. *DEAD*, 96. Cf. 79 and 221.

68. Ibid., 17.

69. *UND*, 31.

70. Ibid., 26.

71. Ibid., 128.

72. *DEM*, 338–39.

73. Ibid., 580, 592–93.

74. See especially *IDT*, part 1, chapter 16, for a remarkable episode involving a choice of suitors by Nastasya Filippovna, a roaring fire, and a hundred thousand roubles in paper currency.

75. *WD*, 241.

76. Ibid., 244.

77. Ibid., 245.

78. *BK*, 56. The original Russian suggests more of this profound indifference on the part of others, I think, than even Pevear and Volokhonsky's excellent overall translation allows.

79. Ibid., 252.

80. Ibid., 251.

81. Henri de Lubac, *The Drama of Atheist Humanism* (New York: Meridian, 1950), 198.

82. Ibid., 199.

83. *BK*, 264.

84. Ibid., 257.

85. For de Lubac on the new birth that comes out of Christ's resurrection in a manner that does not require Dostoevsky to have been the most devout of Orthodox Christians, see *Drama of Atheist Humanism*, 237.

86. *CP*, 537.

87. Ibid., 548–49.

88. De Lubac, *Drama of Atheist Humanism*, 239–41; the quote is from 239.

89. *BK*, 171.

90. Ibid., 230.

91. *DEAD*, 153.

92. Jackson, *Art of Dostoevsky*, 105–6.

93. *IDT*, 221.

94. *WD*, 289.

95. Ibid., 192–93. Cf. 631.

96. *IDT*, 376.

97. Ibid., 374.

98. Ibid., 379, though the translation here is mine, from the original, F. M. Dostoevskii, *Idiot* (Moscow: Lenizdat, 1987), 380.

99. *DEM*, 664.

100. Knapp, *Annihilation of Inertia*, 128.

101. *ADT*, 133.

102. Ibid., 144; cf. 145 and 157.

103. Ibid., 217.

104. Ibid., 218, where Arkady asks Versilov what his great thought is. Versilov responds, "I really don't know how to answer you on that, my dear prince. . . . If I confess to you that I'm unable to answer it myself, that would be more accurate."

105. *IDT*, 65.

106. Ibid., 225–26.

107. Ibid., 227; emphasis in the original.

108. Ibid., 61.

109. *DEM*, 486.

110. Ward, *Dostoevsky's Critique of the West*, chapter 2.

111. *DEM*, 590.

112. Evdokimov, *Art of the Icon*, 1.

113. *ADT*, 373.

114. *BK*, part 3, book 7, chapter 4.

115. Ibid., 361.

116. Ibid., 363.

117. Frank, *Mantle of the Prophet*, 645.

118. Many of Soloviev's writings have been translated into English. The quotation here comes from V. S. Soloviev, *The Heart of Reality: Essays on Beauty, Love, and Ethics*, ed. and trans. Vladimir Wozniuk (Notre Dame, IN: University of Notre Dame Press, 2003), 7.

119. Vladimir Solovyov, *The Justification of the Good: An Essay on Moral Philosophy*, trans. Nathalie A. Duddington (Grand Rapids, MI: Eerdmans, 2005), 27; emphasis in the original.

120. The reader will observe two different transliterations for the Russian philosopher in question. Though "Solovyov" seems closer to the mark for me, I have opted for the more commonly used "Soloviev."

121. Deborah A. Martinsen, *Surprised by Shame: Dostoevsky's Liars and Narrative Exposure* (Columbus: Ohio State University Press, 2003), 1, 10, 37, 217, 224.

122. *BK*, 353.

123. Ibid., 438.

124. Ibid., 484.

125. Ibid., 492–95.

126. Ibid., 495.

127. *IDT*, 116.

128. *CP*, 543, and Martinsen, *Surprised by Shame*, 19.

129. *DEM*, 711.

130. *BK*, part 3, book 7, chapter 3.

131. Ibid., 297.

132. *WD*, 160.

133. Martinsen, *Surprised by Shame*, 218; emphasis in the original.

134. *BK*, 56.

135. Ibid., 56–57.

136. Ibid., 57.

137. Ibid., 58.

138. See the discussion of "loving-kindness" (Russian: *Umileniye*) in Ouspensky and Lossky, *Meaning of Icons*, 92–93. See also Ollivier, "Icons in Dostoevsky's Works," in Pattison and Thompson.

139. *ADT*, 359.

140. *DEM*, 663.

141. *WD*, 631.

142. *PSS*, 20:174–75.

143. *UND*, 92.

144. *IDT*, 349–50. For another example in this novel of compassionate love, see the prince's account of the schoolchildren and Marie in *IDT*, 67–76.

145. Kirillova, "Dostoevsky's Markings," in Pattison and Thompson, 49–50.

146. *BK*, 319–20.

147. Hilarion Alfeyev, *The Spiritual World of Isaac the Syrian* (Kalamazoo, MI: Cistercian, 2000), 36.

148. Solovyov, *Justification of the Good*, 55–56.

149. *WD*, 598–99.

150. *CP*, 422 and 539. See also how Raskolnikov's sister looks on him with great suffering (518), and how the official, Porfiry, encourages Raskolnikov to embrace his own suffering (461).

151. Scanlan, *Dostoevsky the Thinker*, 110–17.

152. *BK*, 509, 591–92.

153. The story begins in *ADT*, part 3, chapter 4.

154. *ADT*, 398.

155. Ibid., 553.

156. John D. Zizioulas, *Being as Communion: Studies in Personhood and the Church* (Crestwood, NY: St. Vladimir's Seminary Press, 1985).

157. Ibid., 57–58.

158. *DEM*, 584.

159. Ibid., 645.

160. Ibid., 708.

161. *BK*, 591.

162. *ADT*, 263.

163. Williams, *Dostoevsky*, 110.

164. *BK*, 52.

165. *IDT*, 552.

166. *BK*, 292.

167. Ibid., 324.

168. Lossky, *Mystical Theology of the Eastern Church*, 145 and chapter 7 generally.

169. Kroeker and Ward, *Remembering the End*, 115.

170. Margaret Ziolkowski, "Dostoevsky and the Kenotic Tradition," in *Dostoevsky and the Christian Tradition*, ed. Pattison and Thompson, esp. 33–37.

171. Scanlan, *Dostoevsky the Thinker*, 117.

CHAPTER 4. *In Search of a Universal Reconciliation*

1. *WD*, 826.

2. Ibid., 826.

3. Ibid., 813.

4. Ibid., 826.

5. Ibid., 828; emphasis in the original.

6. Ibid., 829–31.

7. Ibid., 831–33.

8. Ibid., 818, 829.

9. Ibid., January 1876, 325; and Harriet Murav, *Holy Foolishness: Dostoevsky's Novels and the Poetics of Cultural Critique* (Stanford, CA: Stanford University Press, 1992), 130–32.

10. *WD*, 812; italics in original.

11. Robert L. Belknap, *The Genesis of* The Brothers Karamazov*: The Aesthetics, Ideology, and Psychology of Text Making* (Evanston, IL: Northwestern University Press, 1990), 53–54.

12. Gary Saul Morson, introductory essay in *WD*, 104.

13. Robin Feuer Miller, *Dostoevsky's Unfinished Journey* (New Haven, CT: Yale University Press, 2007), 16nn42–43.

14. Bakhtin, *Problems of Dostoevsky's Poetics*, 32.

15. Ibid., 128.

16. Marcus C. Levitt, *Russian Literary Politics and the Pushkin Celebration of 1880* (Ithaca, NY: Cornell University Press, 1989), 68.

17. Ibid., 10–11.

18. Frank, *Mantle of the Prophet*, 498–99; emphasis in the original.

19. Cited in Alexander Vucinich, *Darwin in Russian Thought* (Berkeley: University of California Press, 1988), 8n2.

20. Ibid., 8–9.

21. Ibid., 16–17.

22. Ibid., 34.

23. *DEM*, 648.

24. Vucinich, *Darwin in Russian Thought*, 22.

25. Frank, *Stir of Liberation*, 209–10.

26. Mochulsky, *Dostoevsky*, 639.

27. Levitt, *Russian Literary Politics*, 125n8.

28. Ibid., 114, and chapter 4, "Dostoevsky 'Hijacks' the Celebration."

29. *WD*, 1,282–84.

30. Ibid., 1,284.

31. Ibid., 1,295; emphasis in the original.

32. Dowler, *Dostoevsky, Grigor'ev, and Native Soil Conservatism*, 66–67.

33. Ibid., 175.

34. Scanlan, *Dostoevsky the Thinker*, 160.

35. Ibid., 160.

36. For an excellent introduction to the *pochvenniki*, see Dowler, *Dostoevsky, Grigor'ev, and Native Soil Conservatism*, chapter 5.

37. *WD*, 1,274.

38. Ibid., 1,278–79.

39. The classic English-language study of Chicherin remains Gary M. Hamburg, *Boris Chicherin and Early Russian Liberalism 1828–1866* (Stanford, CA: Stanford University Press, 1992).

40. Hamburg, *Boris Chicherin*, 25.

41. Ibid., 26–27.

42. See ibid., chapter 2, "University Years." For a more rounded picture of Granovsky, see Derek Offord, *Portraits of Early Russian Liberals: A Study of the Thought of T. N. Granovsky, V. P. Botkin, P. V. Annenkov, A. V. Druzhinin, and K. D. Kavelin* (Cambridge: Cambridge University Press, 1985), 44–78.

43. Hamburg, *Boris Chicherin*, 56–57.

44. Ibid., 255.

45. Ibid., 287.

46. Scanlan, *Dostoevsky the Thinker*, 95.

47. Frank, *Mantle of the Prophet*, 538.

48. I rely heavily on Frank's nuanced reading of Gradovsky's critique. See Frank, *Mantle of the Prophet*, 538–40.

49. Scanlan, *Dostoevsky the Thinker*, 170.

50. Frank, *Mantle of the Prophet*, 540; emphasis is in the original.

51. *WD*, 1,297.

52. Ibid.; emphasis is in the original.

53. Ibid., 1,298.

54. Ibid., 1,300.

55. Ibid., 1,305.

56. Ibid., 1,311. In truth, some estate owners did liberate their serfs in advance of the 1861 degree, and Dostoevsky may have known of the most publicized instances. The vast majority of serf owners did nothing, however, until compelled to do so.

57. *WD*, 1,312–13; emphasis in the original.

58. Ibid., 1,315. The text can be translated as "Every man for himself, and God for all."

59. Ibid., 1,319.

60. Ibid., 1,325.

61. Ibid., 1,325–26.

62. Scanlan, *Dostoevsky the Thinker*, 95–98.

63. Robin Feuer Miller, The Brothers Karamazov: *Worlds of the Novel* (New York: Twayne, 1992), 14.

64. W. J. Leatherbarrow, *Fyodor Dostoevsky:* The Brothers Karamazov (Cambridge: Cambridge University Press, 1992), 70–71.

65. Thompson, The Brothers Karamazov *and the Poetics of Memory*, 302.

66. Murav, *Holy Foolishness*, 146.

67. Kirillova, "Dostoevsky's Markings in the Gospel According to St. John," in *Dostoevsky and the Christian Tradition*, ed. Pattison and Thompson, 42.

68. Thompson, The Brothers Karamazov *and the Poetics of Memory*, 324.

69. *BK*, 69.

70. Ibid., 237.

71. Kroeker and Ward, *Remembering the End*, 59–77.

72. Ibid., 66.

73. Williams, *Dostoevsky*, 237.

74. Kroeker and Ward, *Remembering the End*, 68–69.

75. *BK*, 230.

76. *PSS*, 27:48.

77. Kroeker and Ward, *Remembering the End*, 68.

78. Leatherbarrow, *Devil's Vaudeville*, 154; emphasis in the original.

79. Kroeker and Ward, *Remembering the End*, 63.

80. Murav, *Holy Foolishness*, 148.

81. *BK*, 257. See comment by Leatherbarrow in *Devil's Vaudeville*, 156–57.

82. *BK*, 625.

83. Jacques Catteau, "The Paradox of the Legend of the Grand Inquisitor" in *Dostoevsky: New Perspectives*, edited by Robert L. Jackson (Englewood Cliffs, NJ: Prentice Hall, 1984), 251.

84. *BK*, 245.

85. Jackson, *Art of Dostoevsky*, 344.

86. *BK*, 3.

87. Ibid., 262.

88. Ibid., 295.

89. See Gary Saul Morson's interesting discussion in "The God of Onions: *The Brothers Karamazov* and the Mythic Prosaic," in *A New Word on* The Brothers Karamazov, ed. Robert L. Jackson (Evanston, IL: Northwestern University Press, 2004), 109.

90. *BK*, 316. The Russian word for "image" here, to be clear, is *obraz*, as in *obrazit*.

91. Ibid., 292.

92. Ibid., 291.

93. Ibid., 292.

94. Sutherland, *Atheism and the Rejection of God*, 119.

95. *WD*, 1,296–97.

96. Williams, *Dostoevsky*, 234–35.

97. Leatherbarrow, *Devil's Vaudeville*, 176.

98. *BK*, 236–37. The reference to Ivan's inability to grasp God with his "Euclidian mind" comes from 235.

99. Ibid., 621.

100. Ibid., 633–34.

101. Miller, *Dostoevsky's Unfinished Journey*, 162.

102. Thompson, The Brothers Karamazov *and the Poetics of Memory*, 312.

103. Lee D. Johnson, "Struggle for Theosis: Smerdykov as Would-Be Saint," in *A New Word on* The Brothers Karamazov, ed. Robert L. Jackson (Evanston, IL: Northwestern University Press, 2004), 74, 82.

104. *BK*, 622.

105. Ibid., 96 and 625. On St. Isaac of Nineveh, see Victor Terras, *A Karamazov Companion: Commentary on the Genesis, Language, and Style of Dostoevsky's Novel* (Madison: University of Wisconsin Press, 1981), 22–23.

106. *BK*, 126–27; and Johnson, "Struggle for Theosis," 85–86.

107. Murav, *Holy Foolishness*, 165.

108. *BK*, 771.

109. Ibid., 206.

110. Ibid.

111. Ibid., 774.

112. Ibid., 775.

113. Ibid., 776.

114. Miller, *Dostoevsky's Unfinished Journey*, 182.

115. Robert L. Jackson, "Alyosha's Speech from the Stone: 'The Whole Picture,'" in *A New Word on* The Brothers Karamazov, ed. Robert L. Jackson, 237–38.

116. Thompson, The Brothers Karamazov *and the Poetics of Memory*, 324–25.

117. *BK*, 775–76.

118. Ibid., 773.

119. Ibid., 294.

120. Hannah Arendt, *The Human Condition* (Chicago, IL: University of Chicago Press, 1958), 241.

Conclusion

1. Dostoevsky, "Socialism and Christianity," *PSS*, 20:190.

2. Ibid., 192. See also comments by James Scanlan in *Dostoevsky the Thinker*, 192.

3. Fyodor Dostoevsky, "The Dream of a Ridiculous Man," in *The Eternal Husband and Other Stories*, trans. Pevear and Volokhonsky, 310.

4. Ibid., 298–99, my emphasis.

5. Ibid., 302.

6. Ibid., 299.

7. Ibid., 302.

8. Jackson, *Art of Dostoevsky*, 273.

9. Dostoevsky, "Bobok," in *The Eternal Husband*, trans. Pevear and Volokhonsky, 230.

10. Frank, *Mantle of the Prophet*, 116–18.

11. Dostoevsky, "Bobok," in *The Eternal Husband*, trans. Pevear and Volokhonsky, 243.

12. Ibid., 244.

13. Ward, *Redeeming the Enlightenment*, 17.

14. *PSS*, 20:192–93.

15. Knapp, *Annihilation of Inertia*, 8–9.

16. Williams, *Dostoevsky*, 229.

17. Vladimir Solovyov [*sic*], *Lectures on Divine Humanity*, rev. and ed. Boris Jakim (London: Lindisfarne Press, 1995), 18.

18. Ibid., 23.

19. Ibid., 30; emphasis on "something" is in the original.

20. Nicholas Berdaiev, "Philosophical Verity and Intelligentsia Truth," in *Vekhi*, ed. and trans. Marshall S. Shatz and Judith E. Zimmerman (Armonk, NY: M. E. Sharpe, 1994), 9.

21. Soloviev, *Heart of Reality*, 7.

22. Dostoevsky, "Dream," in *The Eternal Husband*, trans. Pevear and Volokhonsky, 308.

23. Ibid., 311. The entire section on this idyllic world is found on 309–14.

24. Ibid., 311–12.

25. *WD*, 957.

26. Dostoevsky, "Dream," in *The Eternal Husband*, trans. Pevear and Volokhonsky, 317.

27. Joseph Ratzinger and Jürgen Habermas, *The Dialectics of Secularization: On Reason and Religion* (San Francisco, CA: Ignatius Press, 2006).

28. Ratzinger and Habermas, *Dialectics of Secularization*, 37–38; the words here are those of Habermas; emphasis in the original.

29. Ibid., 75; the words here are those of Ratzinger.

30. An illuminating discussion of Hauerwas's critique of liberal society's exclusive claims to ethical impartiality is found in Arne Rasmusson, *The Church as Polis: From Political Theology to Theological Politics as Exemplified by Jürgen Moltmann and Stanley Hauerwas* (Notre Dame, IN: University of Notre Dame Press, 1995), chapter 12.

31. *WD*, 1,041.

32. Alasdair MacIntyre, *Three Rival Versions of Moral Enquiry: Encyclopaedia, Genealogy, and Tradition* (Notre Dame: University of Notre Dame Press, 1990), chapter 10.

33. Zygmunt Bauman, *Does Ethics Have a Chance in a World of Consumers?* (Cambridge MA: Harvard University Press, 2008), chapter 1, esp. 50–51.

34. John Milbank, *The Word Made Strange: Theology, Language, Culture* (Oxford: Blackwell Publishers, 1997), 272.

35. Carol Gilligan, *In a Different Voice: Psychological Theory and Women's Development* (Cambridge, MA: Harvard University Press, 1982).

36. Ward, *Redeeming the Enlightenment,* 192.

37. Bell, *Simone Weil: The Way of Justice as Compassion.*

38. Ibid., 90–96.

39. *WIN,* 47–48.

40. Simone Weil, *The Need for Roots: Prelude to a Declaration of Duties towards Mankind* (London: Routledge, 2001), 3.

41. David Bentley Hart, *The Beauty of the Infinite: The Aesthetics of Christian Truth* (Grand Rapids, MI: Eerdmans, 2003), 84–85.

BIBLIOGRAPHY

Primary Sources

The Adolescent. Translated by Richard Pevear and Larissa Volokhonsky. New York: Alfred A. Knopf, 2003.

The Brothers Karamazov. Translated by Richard Pevear and Larissa Volokhonsky. New York, Alfred A. Knopf, 1992.

Crime and Punishment. Translated by Richard Pevear and Larissa Volokhonsky. New York, Alfred A. Knopf, 1992.

Demons. Translated by Richard Pevear and Larissa Volokhonsky. New York: Alfred A. Knopf, 1994.

The Double; and, The Gambler. Translated by Richard Pevear and Larissa Volokhonsky. New York: Alfred A. Knopf, 2005.

The Eternal Husband and Other Stories. Translated by Richard Pevear and Larissa Volokhonsky. New York: Random House, 1997.

The Idiot. Translated by Richard Pevear and Larissa Volokhonsky. New York: Alfred A. Knopf, 2002.

Idiot. Moscow: Lenizdat, 1987.

Notes from a Dead House. Translated by Richard Pevear and Larissa Volokhonsky. New York: Alfred A. Knopf, 2015.

Notes from Underground. Translated by Richard Pevear and Larissa Volokhonsky. New York: Alfred A. Knopf, 2004.

Pol'noe sobranie sochineniĭ v tridtsati tomakh F.M. Dostoevskagŏ (The Complete Works of F. M. Dostoevsky). 30 vols. Leningrad: Nauka, 1972–1990.

Winter Notes on Summer Impressions. Translated by David Patterson. Evanston, IL: Northwestern University Press, 1988.

A Writer's Diary. (Vol. 1, *1873–1876,* and vol. 2, *1877–1881,* continuous pagination.) Translated and annotated by Kenneth Lantz. Evanston, IL: Northwestern University Press, 1993.

Secondary Sources

Alfeyev, Hilarion. *The Spiritual World of Isaac the Syrian.* Kalamazoo, MI: Cistercian Publications, 2000.

Alfeyev, Hilarion, and Kallistos Ware. *The Ascetical Homilies of Saint Isaac the Syrian.* Translated by the Holy Transfiguration Monastery. Boston: Holy Transfiguration Monastery, 1984.

Arendt, Hannah. *The Human Condition.* Chicago: University of Chicago Press, 1958.

Bakhtin, Mikhail. *Problems of Dostoevsky's Poetics.* Edited and translated by Caryl Emerson. Minneapolis: University of Minnesota Press, 1984.

Bauman, Zygmunt. *Does Ethics Have a Chance in a World of Consumers?* Cambridge, MA: Harvard University Press, 2008.

———. *Life in Fragments: Essays in Postmodern Morality.* Oxford: Blackwell, 1995.

———. *Modernity and the Holocaust.* Ithaca, NY: Cornell University Press, 1989.

Belknap, Robert L. *The Genesis of* The Brothers Karamazov*: The Aesthetics, Ideology, and Psychology of Text Making.* Evanston, IL: Northwestern University Press, 1990.

Bell, Richard H. *Simone Weil: The Way of Justice as Compassion.* Lanham, MD: Rowman & Littlefield, 1998.

Berdyaev (Berdaiev), Nicholas. *Dostoevsky.* New York: New American Library, 1957.

———. "Philosophical Verity and Intelligentsia Truth." In *Vekhi,* edited and translated by Marshall S. Shatz and Judith E. Zimmerman, 1–16. Armonk, NY: M. E. Sharpe, 1994.

Bloechl, Jeffrey. *Liturgy of the Neighbor: Emmanuel Levinas and the Religion of Responsibility.* Pittsburgh, PA: Duquesne University Press, 2000.

Catteau, Jacques. *Dostoyevsky and the Process of Literary Creation.* Cambridge: Cambridge University Press, 1989.

———. "The Paradox of the Legend of the Grand Inquisitor." In *Dostoevsky: New Perspectives,* edited by Robert L. Jackson, 243–54. Englewood Cliffs, NJ: Prentice Hall, 1984.

Chakrabarty, Dipesh. *Provincializing Europe: Postcolonial Thought and Historical Difference.* Princeton, NJ: Princeton University Press, 2000.

Chalier, Catherine. *What Ought I to Do? Morality in Kant and Levinas.* Ithaca, NY: Cornell University Press, 2002.

Clowes, Edith W. *Fiction's Overcoat: Russian Literary Culture and the Question of Philosophy.* Ithaca, NY: Cornell University Press, 2004.

Cook, Michael. *Forbidding Wrong in Islam: An Introduction.* Cambridge: Cambridge University Press, 2003.

de Lubac, Henri. *The Drama of Atheist Humanism.* New York: Meridian, 1950.

Denby, David. "Can Dostoevsky Still Kick You in the Gut?" *The New Yorker*, June 11, 2012. Available at http://www.newyorker.com/books/page-turner/can -dostoevsky-still-kick-you-in-the-gut.

Dowler, Wayne. *Dostoevsky, Grigor'ev, and Native Soil Conservatism.* Toronto: University of Toronto Press, 1982.

Engelstein, Laura. *Slavophile Empire: Imperial Russia's Illiberal Path.* Ithaca, NY: Cornell University Press, 2009.

Erb, Peter C. *Murder, Manners, Mystery: Reflections on Faith in Contemporary Detective Fiction.* London: SCM Press, 2007.

Evdokimov, Paul. *The Art of the Icon: A Theology of Beauty.* Translated by Father Steven Bigham. Redondo Beach, CA: Oakwood, 1990.

Ferguson, Harvie. *Melancholy and the Critique of Modernity: Søren Kierkegaard's Religious Psychology.* London: Routledge, 1995.

Florensky, Pavel. *Iconostasis.* Translated by Donald Sheehan and Olga Andrejev. Crestwood, NY: St. Vladimir's Seminary Press, 1996.

Frank, Joseph. *Dostoevsky: The Mantle of the Prophet, 1871–1881.* Princeton, NJ: Princeton University Press, 2002.

————. *Dostoevsky: The Miraculous Years, 1865–1871.* Princeton, NJ: Princeton University Press, 1995.

————. *Dostoevsky: The Seeds of Revolt, 1821–1849.* Princeton, NJ: Princeton University Press, 1976.

————. *Dostoevsky: The Stir of Liberation, 1860–1865.* Princeton, NJ: Princeton University Press, 1986.

————. *Dostoevsky: The Years of Ordeal, 1850–1859.* Princeton, NJ: Princeton University Press, 1983.

Fromm, Erich. *Escape from Freedom.* New York: Farrar & Reinhardt, 1960; first published 1941.

Fyrnin, Mikhail. "Mir spaset krasota!" In *Sobranie myslei Dostoevskogo*, 8–20. Moscow: Zvonnitsa - MG, 2003.

Gibson, A. Boyce. *The Religion of Dostoevsky.* London: SCM Press, 1973.

Gillespie, Michael Allen. *Nihilism before Nietzsche.* Chicago: University of Chicago Press, 1995.

Gilligan, Carol. *In a Different Voice: Psychological Theory and Women's Development.* Cambridge, MA: Harvard University Press, 1982.

Godwin-Jones, Robert. *Romantic Vision: The Novels of George Sand.* Birmingham, AL: Summa, 1995.

Guroian, Vigen. *Incarnate Love: Essays in Orthodox Ethics.* 2d ed. Notre Dame, IN: University of Notre Dame Press, 2002.

Hamburg, Gary M. *Boris Chicherin and Early Russian Liberalism 1828–1866.* Stanford, CA: Stanford University Press, 1992.

Harakas, Stanley S. *Toward Transfigured Life: The Theoria of Eastern Orthodox Ethics.* Minneapolis: Light & Life, 1983.

Hart, David Bentley. *The Beauty of the Infinite: The Aesthetics of Christian Truth.* Grand Rapids, MI: Eerdmans, 2003.

Holquist, J. Michael. *Dostoevsky and the Novel.* Princeton, NJ: Princeton University Press, 1977.

Horton, John. "The Glamour of Evil: Dostoyevsky and the Politics of Transgression." In *Evil in Contemporary Political Theory,* edited by Bruce Haddock, Peri Roberts, and Peter Sutch, 156–76. Edinburgh: Edinburgh University Press, 2011.

Hutchings, Kimberly. *Global Ethics: An Introduction.* Cambridge, UK: Polity, 2010.

Ivanov, Vyacheslav. *Freedom and the Tragic Life: A Study in Dostoevsky.* London: Harvill, 1952.

Jackson, Robert Louis. *The Art of Dostoevsky: Deliriums and Nocturnes.* Princeton, NJ: Princeton University Press, 1981.

———, ed. *A New Word on* The Brothers Karamazov. Evanston, IL: Northwestern University Press, 2004.

Jones, Malcolm. *Dostoevsky and the Dynamics of Religious Experience.* London: Anthem, 2005.

Kabat, Geoffrey C. *Ideology and Imagination: The Image of Society in Dostoevsky.* New York: Columbia University Press, 1978.

Knapp, Liza. *The Annihilation of Inertia: Dostoevsky and Metaphysics.* Evanston, IL: Northwestern University Press, 1996.

Kostalevsky, Marina. *Dostoevsky and Soloviev: The Art of Integral Vision.* New Haven, CT: Yale University Press, 1997.

Kroeker, P. Travis, and Bruce K. Ward. *Remembering the End: Dostoevsky as Prophet of Modernity.* Boulder, CO: Westview, 2001.

Lear, Jonathan. *Radical Hope: Ethics in the Face of Cultural Devastation.* Cambridge, MA: Harvard University Press, 2007.

Leatherbarrow, W. J. *The Devil's Vaudeville: The Demonic in Dostoevsky's Fiction.* Evanston, IL: Northwestern University Press, 2005.

———. *Fyodor Dostoevsky:* The Brothers Karamazov. Cambridge: Cambridge University Press, 1992.

Leist, Anton, and Peter Singer, eds. *J. M. Coetzee and Ethics: Philosophical Perspectives on Literature.* New York: Columbia University Press, 2010.

Levitt, Marcus C. *Russian Literary Politics and the Pushkin Celebration of 1880.* Ithaca, NY: Cornell University Press, 1989.

Lossky, Vladimir. *The Mystical Theology of the Eastern Church.* Crestwood, NY: St. Vladimir's Seminary Press, 1976.

MacIntyre, Alasdair. *After Virtue: A Study in Moral Theory.* 2d ed. Notre Dame, IN: University of Notre Dame Press, 1984.

———. *A Short History of Ethics.* New York: Macmillan, 1966.

———. *Three Rival Versions of Moral Enquiry: Encyclopaedia, Genealogy, and Tradition.* Notre Dame, IN: University of Notre Dame Press, 1990.

Martinsen, Deborah A. *Surprised by Shame: Dostoevsky's Liars and Narrative Exposure.* Columbus: Ohio State University Press, 2003.

Mazour, Anatole. *The First Russian Revolution, 1825: The Decembrist Movement, Its Origins, Development, and Significance.* Berkeley: University of California Press, 1937.

Mihailovic, Alexander. *Corporeal Words: Mikhail Bakhtin's Theology of Discourse.* Evanston, IL: Northwestern University Press, 1997.

Milbank, John. *The Word Made Strange: Theology, Language, Culture.* Oxford: Blackwell, 1997.

Miller, Robin Feuer. The Brothers Karamazov: *Worlds of the Novel.* New York: Twayne, 1992.

———. *Dostoevsky's Unfinished Journey.* New Haven, CT: Yale University Press, 2007.

Mochulsky, Konstantin. *Dostoevsky: His Life and Work.* Princeton, NJ: Princeton University Press, 1967.

Morrissey, Susan K. *Suicide and the Body Politic in Imperial Russia.* Cambridge: Cambridge University Press, 2006.

Murav, Harriet. *Holy Foolishness: Dostoevsky's Novels and the Poetics of Cultural Critique.* Stanford, CA: Stanford University Press, 1992.

Nasedkin, Nikolai. *Samoubiistvo Dostoevskogo.* Moskva: Algoritm, 2002.

Nietzsche, Friedrich. *The Gay Science.* Translated by Walter Kaufmann. New York: Vintage, 1974.

Offord, Derek. "The People." In *A History of Russian Thought,* ed. William Leatherbarrow and Derek Offord, 241–62. Cambridge: Cambridge University Press, 2010.

———. *Portraits of Early Russian Liberals: A Study of the Thought of T. N. Granovsky, V. P. Botkin, P. V. Annenkov, A. V. Druzhinin, and K. D. Kavelin.* Cambridge: Cambridge University Press, 1985.

Ouspensky, Leonid, and Vladimir Lossky. *The Meaning of Icons.* Boston: Boston Book & Art Shop, 1969.

Paperno, Irene. *Suicide as a Cultural Institution in Dostoevsky's Russia.* Ithaca, NY: Cornell University Press, 1997.

Pattison, George, and Diane Oenning Thompson, eds. *Dostoevsky and the Christian Tradition.* Cambridge: Cambridge University Press, 2001.

Rasmusson, Arne. *The Church as Polis: From Political Theology to Theological Politics as Exemplified by Jürgen Moltmann and Stanley Hauerwas.* Notre Dame, IN: University of Notre Dame Press, 1995.

Ratzinger, Joseph, and Jürgen Habermas. *The Dialectics of Secularization: On Reason and Religion.* San Francisco, CA: Ignatius Press, 2006.

Robbins, Jill, ed. *Is It Righteous to Be? Interviews with Emmanuel Levinas.* Stanford, CA: Stanford University Press, 2001.

Scanlan, James. *Dostoevsky the Thinker.* Ithaca, NY: Cornell University Press, 2002.

Shneidman, N. N. *Dostoevsky and Suicide.* Oakville, ON: Mosaic, 1984.

Solovyov (Soloviev), V. S. *The Heart of Reality: Essays on Beauty, Love, and Ethics.* Edited and translated by Vladimir Wozniuk. Notre Dame, IN: University of Notre Dame Press, 2003.

———. *The Justification of the Good: An Essay on Moral Philosophy.* Translated by Nathalie A. Duddington. Grand Rapids, MI: Eerdmans, 2005.

———. *Lectures on Divine Humanity.* Revised and edited by Boris Jakim. London: Lindisfarne, 1995.

Sutherland, Stewart R. *Atheism and the Rejection of God: Contemporary Philosophy and* The Brothers Karamazov. Oxford: Basil Blackwell, 1977.

Tännsjö, Torbjörn. *Understanding Ethics: An Introduction to Moral Theory.* Edinburgh: Edinburgh University Press, 2002.

Taylor, Charles. *Sources of the Self: The Making of the Modern Identity.* Cambridge, MA: Harvard University Press, 1989.

Terras, Victor. *A Karamazov Companion: Commentary on the Genesis, Language, and Style of Dostoevsky's Novel.* Madison: University of Wisconsin Press, 1981.

———. *Reading Dostoevsky.* Madison: University of Wisconsin Press, 1998.

Thompson, Diane Oenning. The Brothers Karamazov *and the Poetics of Memory.* Cambridge: Cambridge University Press, 1991.

Vucinich, Alexander. *Darwin in Russian Thought.* Berkeley: University of California Press, 1988.

Wallerstein, Immanuel. *European Universalism: The Rhetoric of Power.* New York: New Press, 2006.

Ward, Bruce K. *Dostoyevsky's Critique of the West.* Waterloo, ON: Wilfrid Laurier University Press, 1976.

———. *Redeeming the Enlightenment: Christianity and Liberal Values.* Grand Rapids, MI: Eerdmans, 2010.

Weil, Simone. *The Need for Roots: Prelude to a Declaration of Duties towards Mankind.* London: Routledge, 2001.

———. *Waiting on God.* Translated by Emma Crawford. London: Routledge & Kegan Paul, 1951.

Williams, Rowan. *Dostoevsky: Language, Faith, and Fiction*. Waco, TX: Baylor University Press, 2008.

Wirtschafter, Elise Kimerling. *Social Identity in Imperial Russia*. DeKalb: Northern Illinois University Press, 1997.

Woodill, Joseph. *The Fellowship of Life: Virtue, Ethics, and Orthodox Christianity*. Washington, DC: Georgetown University Press, 1998.

Zizioulas, John D. *Being as Communion: Studies in Personhood and the Church*. Crestwood, NY: St. Vladimir's Seminary Press, 1985.

INDEX

Adolescent, The
  Arkady, 12, 38, 39, 52, 89, 95, 115, 119
  —and Lambert, 45, 59
  —and Makar, 107, 118
  —and Sofia Andreevna (his mother), 83, 84, 87
  —and Versilov, 16, 43–45, 49, 56, 63, 104
  Kraft, 52
  Makar, 16, 38, 84, 115, 121, 124
  Maxim Ivanovich, 118
  Sofia Andreevna, 38, 121
  Versilov, 31, 38, 39, 52, 73, 84, 119, 121
apocalypse, 45
Arendt, Hannah, 169
atheism, 29, 41, 43, 55, 60, 70, 73, 101, 131, 139, 161
atheists, 13, 40, 50, 71, 73, 168

Baal, 46
Bakhtin, Mikhail, 20–23, 78, 86, 132, 183
Bauman, Zygmunt, 7, 66, 183
beauty, 15, 16, 35, 51, 77, 86, 87, 93, 100, 105–7, 116, 125, 131, 169, 176–78, 180, 185, 186
Belinsky, Vissarion, 13, 71
Belknap, Robert, 131

Berdyaev, Nikolas, 17, 24, 66, 94, 176
Bible, 82, 85, 88, 107, 152
  Apostle Paul, 144
  Job, 159
  John, 25, 82, 108, 122, 152, 153, 158
  Lazarus, 82, 122
  Luke, 24, 25, 85
  Matthew, 93
  New Testament, 14, 82, 105, 116
  Philippians, 123–24
  Revelation (Apocalypse), 46, 85, 105
  Sermon on the Mount, 93, 112, 118
"Bobok," 14, 49, 56, 174, 177, 178, 186
boredom, 54, 55–58
Brothers Karamazov, The
  Alyosha, 12, 26, 41, 109, 112, 115, 120, 124, 150
  —and Fyodor, 38
  —and Grushenka, 70, 108, 110
  —and icons, 22, 105
  —and Ivan, 42, 64, 151, 153–54, 157, 160
  —and Lise, 58
  —and Paissy, 101, 108
  —and Rakitin, 53
  —and Snegirov, 163–67
  —and the twelve boys, 163–67, 169–71
  —and Zosima, 40, 71, 82, 98, 107, 108, 116, 123

Brothers Karamazov, The (cont.)
  Fyodor, 2, 3, 16, 38, 44, 55, 59, 61, 97, 99, 120, 122, 151, 157, 161, 162
  Grigorii, 2, 162
  Grushenka, 3, 38, 70, 71, 99, 108, 110, 111, 112
  Ilyushechka (Ilyusha), 123, 151, 163–67, 169
  Ivan, 26, 38, 43, 53, 69, 70, 89, 99, 101, 153, 158, 161, 162, 165, 166
  —Grand Inquisitor, 16, 41, 42, 52, 60, 61, 64, 66, 68, 97, 98, 150–52, 154–57, 159, 160, 164, 168, 169
  Kolya, 38, 166, 167
  Lise, 55, 58, 102
  Madame Khokhlakov, 55, 97, 102, 113, 114
  Markel, 81, 99, 121
  Mitya (Dmitrii), 2–4, 7, 13, 16, 22, 38, 41, 53, 59, 70, 82, 93, 97, 99, 110–12, 118, 120, 124, 150, 151, 164, 165, 169
  Paissy, 40, 101, 108
  Rakitin, 53
  Smerdyakov, 12, 26, 38, 53, 56, 64, 68, 97, 150, 156, 160–62
  Snegirov, 163, 164
  Stinking Lizaveta, 38
  Zosima, 16, 26, 99, 124, 162
  —as Alyosha's mentor, 40, 98, 101–2, 112, 116, 157
  —conversion, 81
  —death and decomposition, 70, 71, 107, 108, 110
  —as Elder, 28, 82, 97, 113–15, 121, 122
  —as orphan, 38
  —teachings, 70, 123, 158, 159, 160, 168

Catholicism, 9, 11, 42, 71, 73, 74, 127, 181
Catteau, Jacques, 23, 157
Chicherin, Boris, 141, 142
civilization, 9, 43, 51, 65, 134, 137, 144, 149, 167, 172, 175, 176, 180, 187
Clowes, Edith, 21
compassion, 9, 10, 28, 42, 70, 73, 113, 116, 117, 149, 168, 184, 185
Crime and Punishment
  Dunya, 47, 60
  Luzhin, 47, 52, 60, 61
  Marmeladov, 47
  Raskolnikov, 15, 46–48, 52, 57, 60, 65, 66, 70, 75–78, 82, 87, 89, 97, 99, 111, 112, 117, 120, 123, 184
  Razumikhin, 70
  Sonya, 57, 67, 76, 77, 78, 82, 87, 89, 101, 111, 112, 117, 120, 123
  Svidrigailov, 47, 57, 59, 60, 61, 65, 67, 68, 70, 82, 97, 125
crosses, religious, 28, 29, 77, 78, 81, 86–89, 113, 123, 124, 153, 177, 179, 180
crossroads, 75, 76, 82, 89, 112, 122, 123, 164, 165

Darwin, Charles (and Darwinism), 51, 134–37
deists, 20, 44, 73
de Lubac, Henri, 98, 100
Demons
  Erkel, 64
  Fedka, 122
  Kirillov, 51, 69, 70, 73, 89, 97, 99, 106, 125
  Liputin, 40
  Lyamshin, 65

Nikolai Vsevolodovich Stavrogin, 50, 51, 57, 58, 60, 64, 68, 82, 89, 99, 112, 120, 125

Pyotr Stepanovich, 58, 84, 96

Shatov, 63, 64, 87, 88, 96, 106, 120, 122

Shigalev, 65, 68

Shigalevism, 65, 98, 185

Sofya Matveevna, 85, 88, 93

Stepan Trofimovich, 32, 41, 56–58, 73, 84–86, 88, 93, 96, 99, 101, 103, 104, 106, 112, 115, 120, 124, 134, 141

Tikhon, 57, 112, 120, 124

Varvara Petrovna, 96

devil, 53, 96, 150, 156, 161

Diary of a Writer, 14, 22, 23, 28, 37, 49, 64, 67, 71–73, 80, 96, 113, 128–31, 139, 142, 144, 149, 150, 166–68, 182. *See also* "Bobok"; "Dream of a Ridiculous Man, The"; "Meek One, The"; "Peasant Marey, The"

diversions, 55, 57, 58, 61, 68, 91, 104, 108, 174

Dowler, Wayne, 24, 74, 137, 138

"Dream of a Ridiculous Man, The," 172, 177, 178

Easter, 80

egoism, 104, 116, 119, 128

Enlightenment, 42, 56, 131, 135, 138, 144, 145, 181

epilepsy, 12, 15, 26

Evdokimov, Paul, 87, 107

evil, 17, 42, 50, 52, 53, 55, 57, 61, 63, 64, 67, 94, 96, 98, 117, 143–45, 150, 155, 156, 161, 162, 186

Ferguson, Harvie, 54

Florence, 26, 27

forgiveness, 32, 36, 73, 119, 120, 121, 157

fragmentation, 8, 16, 48, 49, 78, 89, 103

Frank, Joseph, 13, 32, 46, 90, 109, 133, 143, 174

freedom, 17, 36, 60, 65, 66, 94–100, 104, 128, 133, 142, 143, 154

French Revolution, 53, 72

Fromm, Erich, 66

Gibson, A. Boyce, 24, 85

gift of tears, 118, 119

God-man, 32, 73, 79, 197n.153

Gradovsky, A. D., 32, 130, 138, 143–49, 156, 160

Grigorievna, Anna (Dostoevsky), 27, 80, 135

Guroian, Vigen, 79

Habermas, Jürgen, 5, 181, 182

Hart, David Bentley, 186

Hauerwas, Stanley, 182

Holbein's *Dead Christ*, 22, 23, 28, 29, 41, 43, 88, 101, 105

Holquist, Peter, 61

Holy Spirit, 84, 92, 93, 119

Holy Week, 83, 85

humanism, 91, 156, 175

Hutchings, Kimberly, 5, 6, 9

icons, 22, 23, 35, 36, 37, 41, 70, 86, 87, 89, 105, 107, 109, 115, 125, 163

idea, binding, 103, 104, 182, 183

Idiot, The
    Evgeny Pavlovich, 63, 64
    Ganya, 111
    General Ivolgin, 104
    Ippolit Terentyev, 29, 63, 68

Idiot, The (cont.)
  Lebedev, 45, 103, 104
  Nastasya Filippovna, 99, 116,
    200n.74
  Prince Myshkin, 12, 15, 29, 45, 55,
    88, 89, 96, 101, 103–5, 111, 116
  Rogozhin, 29, 88, 89, 101, 105
immortality, 31, 42, 52, 53, 69, 70, 89,
    90, 92, 93, 97, 114, 115, 125, 153
inertia, 44, 46, 172, 173
Ivanov, Vyacheslav, 48, 77, 78, 125

Jackson, Robert, 23, 24, 48, 52, 88,
    101, 157, 165, 173
Johae, Antony, 87, 89
Johnson, Lee, 161, 162
Jones, Malcolm, 74

Kierkegaard, Søren, 54
Kirillova, Irina, 116
Knapp, Liza, 40, 44, 46, 51, 93, 103, 175
Kostalevsky, Marina, 8, 17
Kroeker, Travis, 28, 92, 123, 124,
    154–56

Leatherbarrow, William, 39, 56, 152,
    155, 160
Levinas, Emmanuel, 1, 10
Levitt, Marcus, 133, 135
liberalism
  and *The Brothers Karamazov*, 52, 156
  contemporary trends, 129, 131,
    140, 142, 144, 149
  and *Demons*, 48, 56, 57, 84, 93
London, 26, 31, 45, 46, 55, 66
Lorrain's *Acis and Galatea*, 43, 44
Lossky, Vladimir, 123

MacIntyre, Alasdair, 7, 8, 183
man-God, 73, 197n.153

Martinsen, Deborah, 110, 111, 113
Mary, Mother of God, 23, 35, 84, 86,
    105, 115
Marya (Masha) Dostoevsky, 26, 90,
    92, 99, 115, 123, 177
"Meek One, The," 37, 39, 40, 46, 47,
    48, 61, 64, 68, 69, 90, 115
Milbank, John, 183
Miller, Robin Feuer, 132, 150, 161, 165
Mochulsky, Konstantin, 56, 135, 174
modernity
  contemporary trends, 2, 8, 40, 47,
    54, 61, 140, 154, 183
  Crime and Punishment, 57
  and *Diary of a Writer*, 49, 67, 102
  The Idiot, 64, 103
  and Nietzsche, 44
  Notes from Underground, 55
  Winter Notes on Summer Impressions, 46
moderns, 43, 54, 60, 61, 62, 63, 67,
    68, 70, 71
morality, 6, 31, 48, 50, 53, 61, 79, 134,
    147
Morrissey, Susan K., 70
Morson, Gary, 18, 23, 131, 158
mortality, 15
Moscow, 2, 12, 30, 39, 83, 130, 133,
    135, 138, 141, 143, 149, 150, 163,
    182
Murav, Harriet, 129, 130, 152, 163
mystery, 32, 66, 92, 96, 98, 107, 123,
    158, 159

Napoleon, 30, 46, 47, 53, 60, 65, 100
Napoleonic Wars, 11
narod (People), 18, 24, 80, 101, 102,
    112, 117, 128, 131, 136, 137, 139,
    140, 143–46, 148, 149, 167, 170
Newton, Isaac, 40, 44, 60
Nietzsche, Friedrich, 15, 40, 44

nihilism, 15, 16, 40, 41, 73, 84, 85, 134

Notes from a Dead House, 14, 15, 88, 95, 101

Notes from Underground, 14, 16, 21, 27, 51, 61, 154
   Liza, 51, 116
   Underground Man, 15, 31, 39, 52, 55, 61, 62, 68, 95, 96, 116

obligations, 4, 5, 9, 10, 15, 32, 77, 185
Offord, Derek, 18
Ollivier, Sophie, 86
orphans, 2, 12, 31, 35–39, 40, 43, 47, 59, 60–62, 68, 172

Paperno, Irina, 69, 70
Paris, 8, 26, 27, 66
peace, 52, 78, 99, 105, 164, 165, 178
"Peasant Marey, The," 12, 81, 83, 87, 102
Peter the Great, 11
Pevear, Richard, 16, 28
pity, 93, 111, 116, 117
progress, 44–47, 53, 64, 65, 100, 102, 134, 154, 183
public square, 75, 78, 132, 164, 165, 183, 185, 187
Pushkin, Alexander, 25, 32, 130–33, 135, 137, 139, 140, 142, 143, 149, 150–52, 163, 166
Pyman, Avril, 80

railroad, 27, 28, 45, 103
repentance, 112, 113, 116
rights, human, 4, 5, 8–10, 32, 46, 61, 63, 64, 67, 77, 131, 142, 171, 175, 185
Russian Christ, 25, 33, 78, 93, 125, 140, 149, 167, 169, 182, 187

Salvestroni, Simonetta, 80
Sand, George, 28, 32, 71, 72
Scanlan, James, 24, 117, 124, 138, 143, 172
science, 40, 44, 47, 50, 63, 72, 103, 106, 128, 131, 134, 135, 139, 154, 155, 172, 178, 179, 184
shame, 32, 77, 109–11, 113, 124, 130, 175, 179
Shneidman, Norman, 69
Siberia, 2, 13, 14, 17, 26, 30, 77, 80, 81, 87, 100, 101, 111, 129, 130, 145, 151, 152
sin, 61, 117, 118
Slavophile, 24, 146
socialism, 52, 106, 127, 129, 156, 157, 171, 177
socialists, 71, 72, 90, 106, 120, 127, 128, 167
Soloviev, Vladimir, 24, 109, 110, 117, 176
St. Petersburg, 3, 13, 15, 26, 27, 29–31, 35, 45, 52, 58, 59, 60, 70, 75, 78, 122
suicide, 31, 39, 58, 68, 69, 70, 83, 90, 112, 115, 122, 125, 154, 162
Sutherland, Stewart, 61, 159

Tännsjö, Torbjörn, 5–9, 32
Taylor, Charles, 7
theism, 41
Thompson, Diane Oenning, 82, 152, 153, 161, 166
tragedy, 37, 52, 58, 77, 99, 104, 108, 125, 128, 157, 162
Turgenev, Ivan, 109, 133, 135, 136, 137

"Vlas," 14, 113
Voltaire, 42

Ward, Bruce, 17, 28, 72, 92,
    123, 124, 154–56, 175,
    184
Weil, Simone, 1, 9, 19, 184, 185
Williams, Rowan, 17, 19, 24, 47,
    74, 121, 154, 160, 175

Winter Notes on Summer Impressions,
    27, 45, 55, 72, 184
Woodill, Joseph, 79, 86

Ziolkowski, Margaret, 124
Zizioulas, John, 119

LEONARD G. FRIESEN

is associate professor of history at Wilfrid Laurier University.

He is the author of *Rural Revolutions in Southern Ukraine:*

Peasants, Nobles, and Colonists, 1774–1905.

CPSIA information can be obtained
at www.ICGtesting.com
Printed in the USA
LVHW041540260721
693702LV00001B/24